NAME _____

LESSON MASTER 1–1
QUESTIONS ON SPUR OBJECTIVES

■**SKILLS**   *Objective A* *(See pages 74–78 for objectives.)*
1. Is the following statement universal, existential, or neither?

The sum of two integers is also an integer.   _____

■**SKILLS**   *Objective B*
2. Consider the following statement.

All countries have national anthems.

Rewrite this statement by filling in the blanks.

∀ _____ ∃ _____ such that

_____

■**SKILLS**   *Objective D*
In 3–5, tell if the statement is true or false.

3. ∀ *real numbers x, sin x ≤ 1.*   _____

4. ∃ *a real number r such that r = -r.*   _____

5. ∀ *real numbers y, log (y²) = (log y)².*   _____

■**PROPERTIES**   *Objective E*
6. *Multiple choice.* If the statement ∃ *x in S such that p(x) is true, then*   _____

    (a) $p(x)$ is true for all x in S.
    (b) $p(x)$ is true for more than one x in S.
    (c) $p(x)$ is true for at least one x in S.
    (d) $p(x)$ is never true.

■**PROPERTIES**   *Objective F*
7. Use universal instantiation and the true statement

∀ *nonnegative integers x,* $\sqrt{4x} = 2\sqrt{x}$

to simplify $\sqrt{28}$.   _____

■**PROPERTIES**   *Objective H*

8. Consider the following statement.

   The result of doubling a number is always less than the result of squaring it.

   a. Write this sentence in the form $\forall\, x$ in S, $p(x)$.

   _____

   b. Give a counterexample to show that the statement is false.

   _____

In 9 and 10, prove or disprove.

9. $\exists\, n$ such that $\frac{8}{n}$ is an integer.   10. $\forall\, n$, $\frac{8}{n}$ is an integer.

■**USES**   *Objective I*

In 11 and 12, tell if the sentence is a statement. If it is, determine whether it is *true* or *false*.

11. *All guitars are powered by electricity.*   _____

12. *He is wearing a blue shirt today.*   _____

LESSON **MASTER** **1-2**
QUESTIONS ON **SPUR** OBJECTIVES

■**SKILLS** *Objective C* (See pages 74–78 for objectives.)
In 1–4, write the negation of the statement.

1. *All diamonds are made of carbon.*

_____

2. ∀ *real numbers x, -3 < x.*

_____

3. *Some equations have no solutions.*

_____

4. ∃ *a real number x such that* ∀ *real numbers y, x is a factor of y.*

_____

■**SKILLS** *Objective D*
5. *Let p: No parallelograms have more than two lines of symmetry.*

a. Write *p.* _____

_____

b. Which is true, *p* or *~p?* _____

■**PROPERTIES** *Objective E*
6. *True* or *false?* The negation of a statement
For all x in S, p(x) is the statement *For no x
in S, p(x).*   _____

7. Let *p:* ∃ *y in R such that q(y).* Write *~p.* _____

8. If a statement is false, what can
be said about its negation?   _____

9. The negation of an existential statement is an _____ statement.

■**USES** *Objective I*
In 10 and 11, tell which is true, the statement or its negation.

10. ∀ *months m, the name for m begins with a
consonant.*   _____

11. ∀ *states s,* ∃ *a city c such that c is the capital
of s.*   _____

LESSON **MASTER** **1-3**
QUESTIONS ON **SPUR** OBJECTIVES

■**SKILLS**   *Objective B (See pages 74–78 for objectives.)*
In 1 and 2, express the inequality by writing out each implied *and, or,* and *not*.

1. $20 \leq a < 52$ 2. $n \not> 6.2$

_____   _____

■**SKILLS**   *Objective C*
In 3–5, use De Morgan's Laws to write the negation of the statement.

3. *35 is divisible by 5 and 6.*

_____

4. *I will come Thursday or Friday.*

_____

5. *x > -2 or x < -16*

_____

■**SKILLS**   *Objective D*
6. Let *p(x): x ≤ 12* and *q(x): x is even.* Is the
following statement true?

   not (p(9) or q(9))   _____

■**PROPERTIES**   *Objective E*
7. According to De Morgan's Laws, what is the negation of *p and q*?

                                                _____

8. *True* or *false?* The negation of an *or*
statement is an *and* statement.   _____

■**PROPERTIES**   *Objective H*
9. Find a counterexample to show the following statement is false.

   ∀ *positive real numbers x, log x > 0 and log x³ = 3 log x.*

_____

■ **USES** *Objective I*

10. According to the United States Constitution, those persons "who
shall not have attained to the age of thirty-five years, and been
fourteen years a resident within the United States" are ineligible to
be President. Let *t: A person is at least thirty-five years old,* and *f: A
person has been a resident of the United States for fourteen years.*

    a. Use the symbols *t*, *f*, and ∼ to describe an
ineligible person, as given in the above
quote.   _____

    b. Use De Morgan's Law to rewrite your
answer to part **a**.   _____

■ **USES** *Objective K*

11. Rewrite the following line of a program using De Morgan's Laws.

   100   IF NOT (A=B AND C<>0) THEN PRINT "ERROR"

_____

■ **REPRESENTATIONS** *Objective M*

12. Complete the truth table below.

p	*q*	*∼q*	*p or ∼q*	*q and (p or ∼q)*
T	T			
T	F			
F	T			
F	F			

13. Write the truth table for ∼(∼*p and q*).

LESSON **MASTER** **1–4**
QUESTIONS ON **SPUR** OBJECTIVES

■**REPRESENTATIONS**   *Objective L* *(See pages 74–78 for objectives.)*
1. Consider the following network.

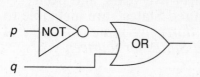

a. Write the logical expression that
corresponds to the network.   _____

b. Write an input-output table for the network.

2. Fill in the input-output table below for this network.

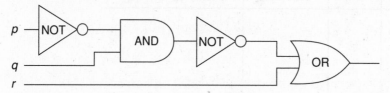

p	q	r				
1	1	1				
1	1	0				
1	0	1				
1	0	0				
0	1	1				
0	1	0				
0	0	1				
0	0	0				

Precalculus and Discrete Mathematics © Scott, Foresman and Company

3. Suppose an AND gate costs 3¢, an OR gate 2¢, and a NOT gate 1¢.

a. What is the cost of the network in Question 2? _____

b. Draw a network that has the same output signals as those in Question 2, but has a lower cost.

4. What is the output signal produced by the network below if *p* carries a signal of 1, *q* a signal of 0, and *r* a signal of 0? _____

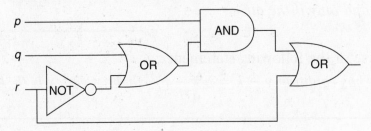

5. Use input-output tables to show that the two networks are functionally equivalent.

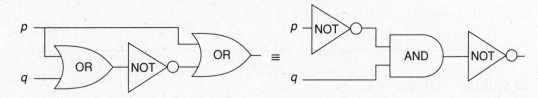

NAME _____

LESSON **MASTER** 1–5
QUESTIONS ON **SPUR** OBJECTIVES

■**SKILLS** *Objective A* *(See pages 74–78 for objectives.)*
1. Consider these four statements.

   (1) *If the air conditioning is on, then Ed is cold.*
   (2) *If Ed is cold, then the air conditioning is on.*
   (3) *If the air conditioning is not on, then Ed is not cold.*
   (4) *If Ed is not cold, then the air conditioning is not on.*

   a. Name a pair of statements that are contrapositives of each other.

   _____

   b. Which statement is the converse of (3)?   _____

■**SKILLS** *Objective B*
2. The union of which two statements from Question 1 is equivalent to the following statement?

   Ed is cold if and only if the air
   conditioning is on.   _____

3. Write the inverse of the following statement.

   If a parabola has equation $y - k = a(x - h)^2$, then its vertex is (h, k).

   _____

   _____

4. Write the following statement in if-then form, using the symbol ∀.

   All numbers divisible by 12 are even.

   _____

■**SKILLS** *Objective C*
5. Write the negation of the following statement.

   If an object is on the moon, then its
   weight is about $\frac{1}{6}$ its weight on Earth.   _____

   _____

6. Let *p:* ∀ *real numbers x, if $x^2 = 20$, then $x \neq \sqrt{20}$.*

   a. Write ~*p.* _____

   _____

   b. Which is true, *p* or ~*p*? Justify your answer. _____

   _____

8 *Continued*   *Precalculus and Discrete Mathematics* © Scott, Foresman and Company

■ **SKILLS**   *Objective D*
7. Let *p(x):* $|x + 2| < 5$ and *q(x):* $x + 2 < 5$. Is
the statement ∀ *x, if p(x), then q(x)* true?   _____

■ **PROPERTIES**   *Objective E*
8. Under what conditions is the following statement false?

If the team plays at home, then it wins.

_____

9. *Multiple choice.* A conditional statement is
logically equivalent to its

(a) converse.   (b) inverse.   (c) contrapositive.   _____

■ **USES**   *Objective I*
10. Find a counterexample to the following statement.

If a food is nutritious, then it tastes good.

_____

_____

■ **USES**   *Objective K*
11. Consider the computer program below.

```
10   INPUT A
20   IF (A > -10) AND (A < -5) THEN PRINT "TRUE"
30   END
```

a. What is the output if the input is *A* = -2?   _____

b. Write line 25 so that the program will print FALSE for all cases in
which *A* is not in the interval -10 < *A* < -5.

_____

■ **REPRESENTATIONS**   *Objective M*
12. Write a truth table for the expression $p \Rightarrow \sim q$.

LESSON **MASTER** **1–6**
QUESTIONS ON **SPUR** OBJECTIVES

■**PROPERTIES**   *Objective G* *(See pages 74–78 for objectives.)*
In 1–4, each match symbolic statement with one of the terms below.
   (a) Law of Detachment   (b) Law of Indirect Reasoning
   (c) transitivity   (d) invalid argument

1. $a \Rightarrow b$	2. $g \Rightarrow k$	3. $n \Rightarrow p$	4. $d \Rightarrow e$
$\sim b$	k	$p \Rightarrow r$	d
$\therefore \sim a$	$\therefore g$	$\therefore n \Rightarrow r$	$\therefore e$

_____ _____ _____ _____

■**PROPERTIES**   *Objective H*
In 5 and 6, draw a valid conclusion from the given premises.

5. *If an instrument is in the percussion section, then it is placed in the back of the orchestra.*
   If an instrument is played with a stick, then it is in the percussion section.

   _____

6. *If a figure is a square, then it has four sides.*
   A pentagon does not have four sides.

   _____

7. Below are two statements from a Lewis Carroll puzzle. Put each statement into if-then form, then draw a valid conclusion. (You may need to use the Contrapositive Theorem.)

   No bald person needs a hairbrush.   *No lizards have hair.*

   _____

   _____

   _____

■**USES**   *Objective J*
In 8 and 9, tell if the argument is valid   (a) Law of Detachment
or invalid. If it is valid, tell which of   (b) Law of Indirect Reasoning
the laws at the right it follows.   (c) Law of Transitivity

8. *If a state was one of the thirteen original colonies,*
      then it was settled by Europeans prior to 1776.
   California was settled by the Spanish in 1769.
   ∴ California was one of the thirteen original colonies. _____

9. *What goes up must come down.*
   A rocket goes up.
   ∴ The rocket must come down. _____

Precalculus and Discrete Mathematics © Scott, Foresman and Company

LESSON MASTER 1-7
QUESTIONS ON SPUR OBJECTIVES

■**PROPERTIES** *Objective H (See pages 74–78 for objectives.)*

1. Show that $14x + 6y$ is even if x and y are integers.

2. Show that $\forall$ integers a, $20a + 7$ is odd.

3. Supply the missing steps in the proof of the following theorem.

   If m is an even integer and n is any integer that is a multiple of 3, then m · n is a multiple of 6.

   Suppose _____.

   Then there exists an integer r such that $m = $ _____

   according to _____. According to

   the definition of multiple, there exists an integer s such that $n = 3s$.

   By substituting, $m \cdot n = $ _____ $= 6 \cdot$ _____.

   Because _____ is an integer, $m \cdot n$ is a multiple of 6.

In 4 and 5, give a direct proof of the statement.

4. If m and n are odd integers, then $m - n$ is even.

5. If m is even, m^3 is a multiple of 8.

LESSON **MASTER** 1-8
QUESTIONS ON **SPUR** OBJECTIVES

■ PROPERTIES *Objective G (See pages 74–78 for objectives.)*
In 1 and 2, a. is the argument valid? b. is the conclusion true?

1. *If $a < 5$, then $a^2 < 25$.*
   $-8 < 5$
   $\therefore 64 < 25$

   a. _____ b. _____

2. *If the freezing point of water is 212°F, then the moon is made of green cheese.*
   The moon is not made of green cheese.
   $\therefore$ The freezing point of water is 212°F.

   a. _____ b. _____

3. Under what conditions is an argument guaranteed to produce a true conclusion?

   _____
   _____

4. Joe noticed the following facts:
   3, 4, and 5 form a Pythagorean triple, and $3 \cdot 4 \cdot 5$ is divisible by 60.
   5, 12, and 13 form a Pythagorean triple, and $5 \cdot 12 \cdot 13$ is divisible by 60.
   7, 24, and 25 form a Pythagorean triple, and $7 \cdot 24 \cdot 25$ is divisible by 60.
   Joe concluded that if a, b, and c form a Pythagorean triple, then abc is divisible by 60. Is Joe's conclusion valid? Why or why not?

   _____
   _____

5. Give an example of a valid argument that has a false conclusion.

   _____
   _____
   _____
   _____

6. Give an example of an invalid argument that has a true conclusion.

   _____
   _____
   _____
   _____

■USES *Objective J*

7. a. Write a symbolic form for the
argument below.

   *If a year is divisible by 10, then the U.S.
   census is taken that year.
   The census was taken last year.
   ∴ Last year was divisible by 10.*   _____

b. Is the argument valid?   _____

8. Consider the following statement.

   All math teachers can balance a checkbook.

a. Illustrate this situation with a diagram.

b. Write the converse of the given statement.

_____

_____

c. Write the inverse of the given statement.

_____

_____

d. Suppose Mr. Smith is not a math teacher.
Name the type of argument that would
lead to the conclusion that Mr. Smith
cannot balance a checkbook.   _____

e. Is the type of argument named in part **d**
valid?   _____

LESSON MASTER 2-1
QUESTIONS ON SPUR OBJECTIVES

■ **PROPERTIES**   *Objective C (See pages 146–150 for objectives.)*

1. The table below shows how hurricanes are classified according to their strength. Let c = category, w = wind speed, f: category → wind speed, and g: wind speed → category.

Category	Sustained Winds	Damage
1	74–95 mph	minimal
2	96–110 mph	moderate
3	111–130 mph	extensive
4	131–155 mph	extreme
5	156 or more mph	catastrophic

   a. Evaluate $g(140)$.   **b.** Evaluate $f(2)$.

   _____   _____

   c. Is g a function? Explain. _____

   _____

   d. Is f a function? Explain. _____

   _____

In 2 and 3, a. give a reasonable domain for the function and b. is the function discrete?

2. $f(x)$ = the number of sisters of person x

   a. _____   **b.** _____

3. $g(x)$ = the weight of a person of height x as measured in feet

   a. _____   **b.** _____

4. Let f be a real function with $f(x) = \dfrac{\sqrt{x}}{x - 5}$.

   a. What is the largest possible domain of f? _____

   b. Is $(25, .25)$ a point on the graph of f? Why or why not?

   _____

5. If $h(t) = 4(t - 2)^2 - 5$, what is the height of the graph of h when $t = 10$? _____

6. The graph of a function g is shown at the right.

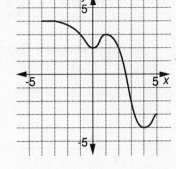

  a. Estimate $g(4)$.

  _____

  b. Estimate the interval(s) where g is constant.

  _____

  c. For what values of x is $-2 < g(x) < 2$? _____

  d. *True* or *false?* $g(-3) < g(5)$ _____

  e. What is the domain of g? _____

7. Graph $y = -x^2 + 14x - 45$ using a window $-10 \le x \le 10$ and $-10 \le y \le 10$. Now adjust the window so that the graph looks like the graph at the right. Describe this window with inequalities.

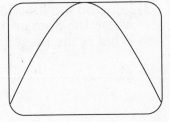

_____

_____

_____

_____

_____

LESSON **MASTER** **2–2**
QUESTIONS ON **SPUR** OBJECTIVES

■**PROPERTIES**   *Objective C (See pages 146–150 for objectives.)*
 1. Let $f(x) = 2x^2 + 14x + 21.5$.

   a. Complete the square to find the exact range.

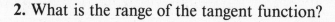

   b. Check your answer to part **a** by using an
   automatic grapher. Sketch the graph on
   the axes at the right.

 2. What is the range of the tangent function?

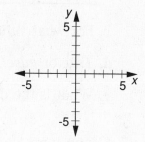

 3. Let g be the function defined by $g(x) = x^2$,
   where the domain is the set of integers.
   What is the range?

_____

■**USES**   *Objective F*
 4. A canning factory is going to cut up
   pineapples for processing. A pineapple is
   roughly cylindrical. It will be sliced in
   half lengthwise to test for freshness.
   Then the half cylinder will be trimmed
   to form a rectangular solid, as shown at
   the right. The maximum volume of
   pineapple is obtained when the area of
   the rectangular cross-section is a
   maximum. Assume the pineapple has a
   radius of 3 inches.

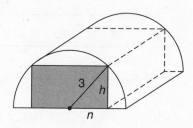

   a. Use the Pythagorean Theorem to express
   n, half the base of the rectangle, in terms
   of h.

   b. Write an equation to express A, the area
   of the rectangle, in terms of h.

Precalculus and Discrete Mathematics © Scott, Foresman and Company

c. Use an automatic grapher to graph your answer to part **b**. Sketch the graph on the axes at the right.

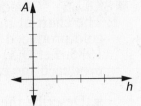

d. Find the dimensions of the rectangular cross-section that produce the maximum area.

_____

e. What is the maximum area?   _____

■ **REPRESENTATIONS**   *Objective G*

5. The entire graph of the function f is given at the right.

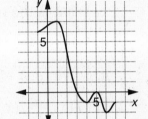

a. What is the domain of f?   _____

b. What is the range of f?   _____

c. Estimate the maximum and minimum values.

_____

_____

d. On what interval(s) is $f(x)$ nonpositive?   _____

e. Is f a discrete function? Why or why not?   _____

_____

_____

6. Sketch a graph with all of the following characteristics.

(a) The domain is $1 \leq x \leq 5$ for real numbers x.

(b) The range is $-3 \leq y \leq 3$ for real numbers y.

(c) $f(2)$ is the minimum value and $f(4)$ is the maximum value.

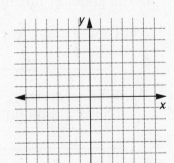

7. Use an automatic grapher to estimate the maximum or minimum values of $f(x) = x^3 + x^2 - 17x + 5$ on the interval $-5 \leq x \leq 5$.

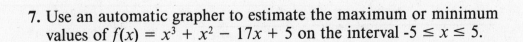

LESSON MASTER 2-3
QUESTIONS ON SPUR OBJECTIVES

■**SKILLS**   *Objective A (See pages 146–150 for objectives.)*

1. The chart at the right shows the amount of gold produced in the U.S. between 1970 and 1985. Let $G(x)$ be the amount of gold produced in year x.

Year	U.S. Gold Production in 1,000 oz
1970	1,743
1975	1,052
1979	964
1980	970
1981	1,379
1982	1,466
1983	2,003
1984	2,085
1985	2,475

   a. Describe the longest interval over which G is increasing. _____

   b. Describe the longest interval over which G is decreasing. _____

   c. What is the relative minimum? _____

   d. What is the relative maximum? _____

   e. Solve $G(x) = 2,003$. _____

2. Let $f(x) = -2(x + 1)^2 + 3$. Give the interval(s) on which f is **a.** decreasing and **b.** increasing.

   a. _____   **b.** _____

■**REPRESENTATIONS**   *Objective G*

3. Use an automatic grapher to estimate the relative maximum and relative minimum of the function $g(x) = x^3 + x^2 - 17x + 15$ on the interval $-5 \le x \le 3$.

_____

4. The graph of function h is given at the right.

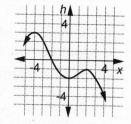

   a. Describe any intervals where h is increasing.

   _____

   b. Find any relative maximum or relative minimum values of h. _____

   _____

5. Graph $y = |x + 4|$ over $-10 \le x \le 10$. Describe all intervals on which the function is decreasing.

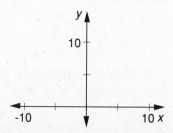

_____

Precalculus and Discrete Mathematics © Scott, Foresman and Company

LESSON MASTER 2-4
QUESTIONS ON SPUR OBJECTIVES

■SKILLS *Objective A (See pages 146–150 for objectives.)*
In 1 and 2, a formula for a sequence is given. a. Give the first four terms of the sequence, and b. tell if the sequence is increasing, decreasing, or neither.

1. $a_n = 5 + (-1)^n$

2. $b_n = \dfrac{2n + 1}{n^2}$

a. _____

b. _____

a. _____

b. _____

3. Give an example of a decreasing arithmetic sequence.

_____

In 4–6, a. tell if each sequence is arithmetic, geometric, harmonic, or none of these, and b. tell if it is increasing, decreasing, or neither.

4. $a_n = (1.01)^n$ a. _____   b. _____

5. $b_n = \dfrac{1}{n}$ a. _____   b. _____

6. $c_n = 3n - 7$ a. _____   b. _____

■PROPERTIES *Objective D*

7. Find $\lim\limits_{n \to \infty} a_n$ if $\begin{cases} a_1 = 8 \\ a_{k+1} = \dfrac{a_k}{10} \ \forall \ k \geq 1 \end{cases}$ _____

8. Use limit notation to describe the limit of $s_n = \left(-\frac{1}{2}\right)^{2n+1}$ as n increases without bound. _____

9. Let $\begin{cases} b_1 = 5 \\ b_{k+1} = \frac{1}{2} b_k \ \forall \ k \geq 1 \end{cases}$

   a. What is the limit of b_n as $n \to \infty$? _____

   b. For what value of n is b_n within .001 of the limit? _____

■REPRESENTATIONS *Objective G*

In 10 and 11, graph the first six terms of the sequence and find its limit as $n \to \infty$.

10. $a_n = \dfrac{2n^2 + 1}{n^2}$

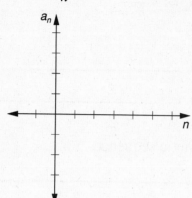

11. $b_n = 3 + \dfrac{(-1)^n}{n}$

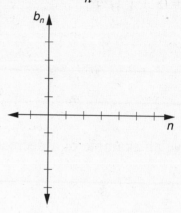

_____   _____

LESSON MASTER 2-5
QUESTIONS ON SPUR OBJECTIVES

■ **PROPERTIES** *Objective D (See pages 146–150 for objectives.)*

1. Consider the function $f(x) = \frac{x}{x+2}$.

   a. Complete the table below to give decimal approximations for function values as x becomes large.

x	10	100	1,000	10,000
$\frac{x}{x+2}$				

   b. What is $\lim\limits_{x \to \infty} f(x)$?   _____

   c. Write an equation of the horizontal asymptote of f.   _____

2. a. Let $g(x) = \frac{\sin x}{x}$. Find $\lim\limits_{x \to \infty} g(x)$ and $\lim\limits_{x \to -\infty} g(x)$.   _____

   b. For what values of x is $g(x)$ within .001 of the limit?   _____

   c. Is g even, odd, or neither?   _____

3. If h is an even function and $\lim\limits_{x \to \infty} h(x) = -3$, find $\lim\limits_{x \to -\infty} h(x)$.   _____

4. Describe the end behavior of $y = -6x^3$.

_____

■ **REPRESENTATIONS** *Objective G*

5. The function f is graphed at the right.

   a. Is f even, odd, or neither? _____

   b. Describe its end behavior.

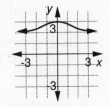

_____

   c. Write the equation of the horizontal asymptote.   _____

6. Sketch the graph of an odd function f that has a relative maximum at $x = -2$ such that $\lim\limits_{x \to \infty} f(x) = -1$.

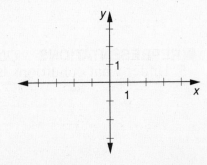

LESSON MASTER 2-6
QUESTIONS ON SPUR OBJECTIVES

■ **PROPERTIES** *Objective D (See pages 146–150 for objectives.)*
1. Contrast the end behavior of $f(x) = 5^x$ with that of $g(x) = 5^{-x}$.

_____

■ **USES** *Objective E*
2. A lake has been polluted by a certain chemical. To have the water safe for use, the concentration of that chemical must be one-tenth of its present level. If the chemical naturally dissipates so that 4% of it is lost each year, about how many years will it take for the lake water to become usable?

_____

3. $5,000 is invested in an oil drilling company that promises to pay 17% interest compounded continuously. At that rate, about how long will it take the investment to double?

_____

4. The table below lists the number of Americans in thousands traveling to foreign countries other than Mexico and Canada.

Year	1970	1975	1980	1985
Number of Travelers	5,260	6,354	8,163	12,766

   a. Use the Continuous Change Model to write a formula for the number $n(t)$ of American travelers t years after 1970, assuming an annual growth rate of 5.7%.

   _____

   b. Use your formula to predict how many Americans will travel abroad in the year 2010.

   _____

   c. Use your formula to calculate $n(10)$. Does this figure agree with the information in the chart?

_____

■ **REPRESENTATIONS** *Objective G*
5. Under what conditions is $f(x) = b^x$ an increasing function?

_____

      Precalculus and Discrete Mathematics © Scott, Foresman and Company

6. Graph both $f(x) = 2e^x$ and $g(x) = e^{2x}$ on the axes at the right. What qualities do these two functions have in common? (Consider the attributes given at the beginning of Lesson 2–6.)

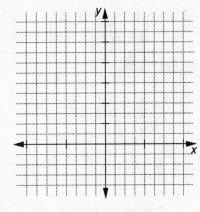

_____

_____

_____

_____

_____

_____

7. Use an automatic grapher to graph $h(x) = e^{x^2}$. Sketch the graph in the space at the right. Then analyze the function from the graph.

_____

_____

_____

_____

_____

_____

LESSON **MASTER 2-7**
QUESTIONS ON **SPUR** OBJECTIVES

■**SKILLS**   *Objective B (See pages 146–150 for objectives.)*
In 1–3, evaluate each expression.

1. $\log_2 8^2$

2. $\log_b \sqrt[3]{b}$

3. $\log_{10} \sqrt{1,000}$

_____   _____   _____

4. Express $\log_b \dfrac{n^3}{2w^4}$ *in terms of $\log_b n$ and $\log_b w$.*

_____

5. Let $\log_k 2 = .231$ and $\log_k 3 = .367$.

a. Use properties of logarithms to find $\log_k 6$. _____

b. Find the value of k and use it
to check your answer to part **a**. _____

6. Solve: $\log_3 x = 6$ _____

■**PROPERTIES**   *Objective D*
7. Explain why $\lim\limits_{x \to -\infty} \log_b x = 0$ is false for any $b > 0$ with $b \neq 1$.

_____

_____

■**USES**   *Objective E*
8. The sales of a certain new product increase over time according to
$s(t) = 105 + 200 \log (5t + 1)$ where $s(t)$ is the annual sales (in
thousands of dollars) after t years. About how many years does it
take for the annual sales to reach $500,000?

_____

Precalculus and Discrete Mathematics © Scott, Foresman and Company

9. One formula that relates the average weight
   w in pounds of girls to their average height h
   in inches is

   $$\log w = -2.86625 + 2.72158 \log h.$$

   a. Predict the weight of a girl who is 63 inches tall. _____

   b. Assume that a child's weight is normal if it is in a range of ±5% of
      the average. Give the range of normal weights for a girl who is 63
      inches tall.

   _____

■**REPRESENTATIONS**   *Objective G*

10. a. Graph the function $g(x) = \log_2 x$.

    b. Give the domain and range of g.

    _____

    _____

    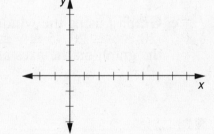

    c. Use the Change of Base Theorem
       to express g in terms of $\log_{10} x$.

    _____

    d. Compare the graph of g to the graph of $f(x) = \log_{10} x$.

    _____

    _____

    _____

    _____

NAME _____

LESSON **MASTER 2-8**
QUESTIONS ON **SPUR** OBJECTIVES

■**PROPERTIES** *Objective D (See pages 146–150 for objectives.)*
1. a. Graph $f(x) = 1 - \cos(.01x^2 - 1)^2$
on an automatic grapher using the
viewing window $-10 \le x \le 10$,
$-1 \le y \le 1$. Sketch the graph on
the axes at the right.

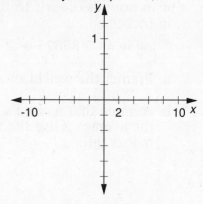

b. Describe the end behavior of *f*, based on your graph from part **a**.

_____

c. Graph *f* using the window
$-20 \le x \le 20$, $-5 \le y \le 5$. Sketch
the graph on the axes at the right.

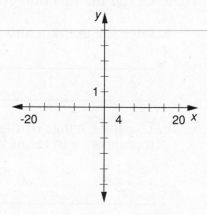

d. Does your graph from part **c** agree with your answer to part **b**?
Explain why or why not.

_____

_____

_____

■**USES** *Objective E*
2. An office building is topped by a radio
antenna. An observer on the ground 300 feet
from the building finds that the angle α to
the top of the antenna is 56°. The angle β to
the top of the building is 52°. About how tall
is the antenna?

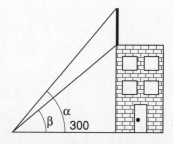

_____

Precalculus and Discrete Mathematics © Scott, Foresman and Company

3. The motion of a point P on a Ferris wheel is
approximated by $f(t) = 50 \sin (1.5\pi t) + 58$,
where t is the time in minutes and $f(t)$ is
the height in feet.

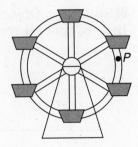

   a. Graph f.

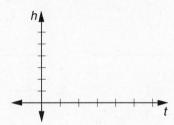

   b. What is the diameter of the Ferris wheel?   _____

   c. The lowest point on the wheel is how
      many feet above the ground?   _____

   d. How long does it take for the Ferris
      wheel to make one revolution?   _____

■**REPRESENTATIONS**   *Objective G*
In 4–6, tell whether each function is odd, even, or neither.

   4. $f(x) = \sin x$ **5.** $g(x) = |\sin x|$ **6.** $h(x) = \sin |x|$

   _____   _____   _____

7. Consider the function $f(x) = -\cos x$ on the interval $0 \le x \le 2\pi$.

   a. Over what interval is f decreasing?   _____

   b. Where do any maximum and minimum values occur?

   _____

LESSON MASTER 3-1
QUESTIONS ON SPUR OBJECTIVES

■**SKILLS** *Objective A (See pages 217–220 for objectives.)*
In 1–8, find all real solutions.

1. $\sqrt[5]{x^2 - 13} = 3$

2. $\sqrt{y + 5} = y - 7$

3. $\sqrt{x - 3} + 2 = \sqrt{2x + 1}$

4. $\dfrac{1}{z^2 + 2z} = \dfrac{1}{5z}$

5. $5^{3a - 3} = 25^a$ (Hint: $25 = 5^2$)

6. $e^{2x^2 - 6x} = e^{4x - 12}$

7. $\ln (t^2 - 10) = \ln (3t + 30)$

8. $\ln (y^2 - 14) = \ln (6y + 13)$

■**PROPERTIES** *Objective F*
In 9–11, tell whether the step is always reversible.

9. taking the square root of both sides _____

10. subtracting a variable from both sides _____

11. dividing both sides by a variable _____

■**USES** *Objective J*
12. A baseball is thrown straight up with an initial velocity of 44 feet per second. After how many seconds is it 33 feet above the ground? (Hint: Use $h = -\frac{1}{2}gt^2 + v_0 t$, where h is the height in feet, t is the time in seconds, g is the acceleration due to gravity in feet/second², 9.8 ft/s², and v_0 is the initial velocity in feet/second.)

Precalculus and Discrete Mathematics © Scott, Foresman and Company

LESSON MASTER 3-2
QUESTIONS ON SPUR OBJECTIVES

■**SKILLS**   *Objective A (See pages 217–220 for objectives.)*
In 1–4, solve each equation.

1. $e^x = 280$

2. $y^{2/5} = 16$

_____

_____

3. $(\sqrt{2t + 5})^3 = 27$

4. $8 + \log_5 m = 133$

_____

_____

■**SKILLS**   *Objective B*
5. Let $f(x) = 5x + 2$, $g(x) = x^2$, and $h(x) = \frac{1}{x}$. Give a simplified formula for each function.

a. $f \circ g$ **b.** $g \circ f$ **c.** $h \circ f$

_____   _____   _____

d. Does $g \circ h = h \circ g$?   _____

6. If r and s are real functions such that $r(x) = \sqrt{x}$ and $s(x) = \log x$, give the domains of $r \circ s$ and $s \circ r$.

_____

■**PROPERTIES**   *Objective G*
7. If $f(x) = \frac{x - 5}{7}$, give a formula for f^{-1}. _____

8. Prove that $g(x) = \sqrt[3]{x + 5}$ and $h(x) = x^3 - 5$ are inverses.

■**REPRESENTATIONS**   *Objective M*
9. Given the graph of f at the right, graph the inverse of f on the same grid.

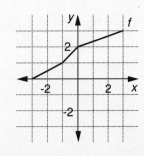

LESSON MASTER 3-3
QUESTIONS ON SPUR OBJECTIVES

■**SKILLS** *Objective B (See pages 217–220 for objectives.)*
For 1 and 2, formulas for *f* and *g* are given. Write simplified formulas for
a. *f* + *g*, b. *f* ∘ *g*, and c. $\frac{f}{g}$.

  1. $f(x) = e^x$ and $g(x) = e^{x+2}$

   a. _____

   b. _____   **c.** _____

  2. $f(x) = x^3 - 5x$ and $g(x) = \frac{1}{x}$

   a. _____

   b. _____   **c.** _____

  3. Using the formulas given in Question 2, give the domains of $\frac{f}{g}$ and $\frac{g}{f}$.

   _____

   _____

■**USES** *Objective K*
  4. Working at its slowest speed, a machine can produce 250 magnetic
disks per hour with a 98% efficiency rate (2% are defective). For each
step up in speed, the machine can produce 10 more disks per hour,
but its efficiency rate drops .5%.

   a. Write a formula for *n*, where $n(x)$ is the
total number of disks produced hourly
when the speed is increased *x* steps.   _____

   b. Write a formula for $e(x)$, the efficiency
rate when the speed is raised *x* steps.   _____

   c. Let $w(x)$ be the number of nondefective
disks produced per hour when the speed
is raised *x* steps. How are *w*, *n*, and *e*
related?   _____

   d. Write a formula for $w(x)$
in terms of *x*.   _____

   e. Graph the function *w* on the grid
at the right.

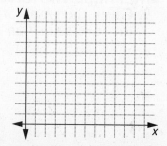

Precalculus and Discrete Mathematics © Scott, Foresman and Company

    f. At how many steps above the slowest
    speed should the machine be set to
    produce the maximum number of
    nondefective disks per hour?   _____

    g. What is the maximum number of
    nondefective disks that the machine can
    produce per hour?   _____

■**REPRESENTATIONS**   *Objective M*

5. The functions f and g are graphed at the
right. On the grids below, sketch the
graphs of

    a. $f + g$.   **b.** $f \cdot g$.

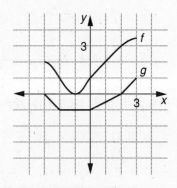

a.

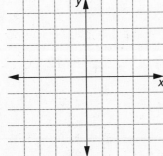

b.

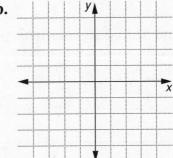

6. The graphs of two functions
f and $f + g$ are shown at the
right. Tell if $g(x)$ is positive,
negative, or zero when

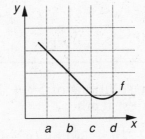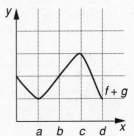

    a. $x = a$.   **b.** $x = b$.

_____   _____

    c. $x = c$.   **d.** $x = d$.

_____   _____

LESSON **MASTER 3-4**
QUESTIONS ON **SPUR** OBJECTIVES

■**SKILLS** *Objective C (See pages 217–220 for objectives.)*
1. Consider the equation $(\log_7 (x + 4))^2 - 8 \log_7 (x + 4) + 15 = 0$.

   a. Write the equation resulting from the
   substitution $u = \log_7 (x + 4)$.   _____

   b. Solve the equation you found in part **a**.   _____

   c. Substitute $u = \log_7 (x + 4)$ back into your results from part **b**
   and solve for x.

   _____

In 2 and 3, find the zeros of the function.

   2. $g(x) = x^2 - 36$ **3.** $h(x) = x^3 - 7x^2 - 8x$

   _____   _____

In 4 and 5, find all solutions.

   4. $(3k + 8)^3 - 2 = 3k + 6$ **5.** $0 = x^4 - 7x^2 + 12$

   _____   _____

6. Give exact values of the zeros of $f(x) = 2 \sin^2 x + \sin x - 1$ on
   $0 \le x \le 2\pi$.

   _____

7. Approximate the solutions of $5^{2x} + 18 =$
   $9 \cdot 5^x$ to the nearest tenth.   _____

8. a. Multiply $(n^2 + 7n + 30)$ by $(n - 4)$.   _____

   b. When spheres are stacked in a triangular pyramid with n layers,
   $s(n) = \frac{1}{6}n^3 + \frac{1}{2}n^2 + \frac{1}{3}n$ gives the number of spheres used. Use
   part **a** to help you find the number of layers that can be made
   with 20 spheres.

   _____

LESSON MASTER 3-5
QUESTIONS ON SPUR OBJECTIVES

■**SKILLS**   *Objective D (See pages 217–220 for objectives.)*
1. The function f is continuous on the interval $-3 \le x \le 3$. The chart below gives some values of f.

x	-3	-2	-1	0	1	2	3
$f(x)$	5	3	1	-.5	-2	1	9

Find consecutive integers a and b such that

a. $\exists \; x_1$ such that $a < x_1 < b$
and x_1 is a zero of f.   _____

b. $\exists \; x_2$ such that $a < x_2 < b$
and $f(x_2) = -1$.   _____

2. Consider the equation $\cos x = \frac{3}{2^{x^2}}$. Use the Intermediate Value Theorem to

a. find an interval of length 1 that
contains a solution.   _____

b. find an interval of length .1 that
contains a solution.   _____

■**PROPERTIES**   *Objective H*
3. Use the diagram at the right to fill in the blanks.

According to the Intermediate Value
Theorem, if it is known that g is a
continuous function and y_0 is between

_____ and _____,

then $\exists$ _____

such that _____.

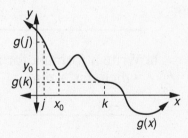

In 4–6, determine whether the function is continuous on the interval
$0 \le x \le \pi$. If not, tell where the function is discontinuous.

4. $f(x) = x$ _____

5. $g(x) = \frac{1}{x - 2}$ _____

6. $h(x) = \frac{1}{\cos x}$ _____

7. *Multiple choice*. A function is graphed at the right. On which interval is the function *not* continuous?

(a) $b \le x \le c$
(b) $0 \le x \le c$
(c) $0 \le x \le d$
(d) $c \le x \le d$ _____

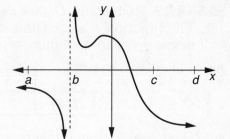

■**USES**   *Objective J*

8. For some cardiac tests, a dye is injected into a vein. The concentration of the dye can be approximated by $f(x) = -.003x^4 + .07x^3 - .026x^2 + .8x$, where $f(x)$ is the percent of dye in the bloodstream after x seconds. After about how many seconds does half the dye remain in the bloodstream?

_____

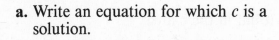

■**REPRESENTATIONS**   *Objective O*

9. Refer to the graphs of $f(x) = e^x$ and $g(x) = -x^2 + 2x + 4$ below.

a. Write an equation for which c is a solution.

_____

b. Write a formula for a function h for which c is a zero.

_____

c. Find an interval of length .1 that contains c.

_____

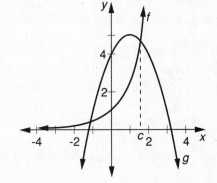

NAME _____

■**SKILLS** *Objective E (See pages 217–220 for objectives.)*
In 1–6, solve each inequality.

1. $4^x < 1024$

2. $\frac{1}{y-5} \geq 3.2$

_____   _____

3. $(a + 10)(a - 3) < 0$

4. $3b^2 + 10b \leq b^2 - b - 5$

_____   _____

5. $2x^2 - 2 \geq -x^2 - x$

6. $\log(2x - 8) > \log(6x + 9)$

_____   _____

7. When can the cube of a number be greater than twice its square?

_____

8. Find all solutions to $\cos x < \frac{1}{2}$ on the
interval $0 \leq x \leq 2\pi$.   _____

■**PROPERTIES** *Objective F*
9. Since $f: x \rightarrow x^{35}$ is an increasing function, if
$\sqrt[5]{x - 3} < \sqrt[7]{2 - x}$, what can you conclude? _____

■**USES** *Objective L*
10. The formula $R = e^{21.4b}$ relates the percent risk R of an automobile
accident to the percent b of the blood alcohol level of the driver. At
what value of b does a driver have at least a 50% chance of having an
accident?

_____

LESSON MASTER 3-7
QUESTIONS ON SPUR OBJECTIVES

■**SKILLS**   *Objective E (See pages 217–220 for objectives.)*
In 1–4, describe the solutions to the given inequality.

1. $3x^2 + 17x + 10 > 0$

2. $x^2 - 4x < 77$

_____

_____

3. $(x + 5)(x + 3)(2x - 1) > 0$

4. $x^3 + 2x^2 + x < 0$

_____

_____

■**USES**   *Objective L*

5. Midville School has 3,700 students but is decreasing in enrollment by about 3% per year. Westville has 2,100 students but is gaining about 50 students per year. If these trends continue, when will Westville have a larger enrollment?

_____

6. When a particular baseball is hit, its height y in feet after traveling x feet horizontally is given by $y = -.04x^2 + 1.4x + 3$. At the same time the baseball is hit, a football is kicked. Its path is described by $y = -.02x^2 + 1.1x$. For how many feet horizontally is the baseball higher than the football?

_____

■**REPRESENTATIONS**   *Objective O*

7. Let f and g be the functions graphed at the right.

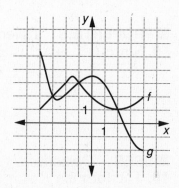

a. For which values of x is $f(x) > g(x)$?

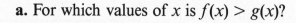

b. When is $g(x) > f(x)$?

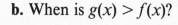

8. Use a graph to determine when $\sin x > (x - 1)^2$ on the interval $0 \le x \le \pi$. _____

LESSON MASTER 3-8
QUESTIONS ON SPUR OBJECTIVES

■**SKILLS** *Objective A (See pages 217–220 for objectives.)*
1. Interpret $|t - 15| = 9$ in terms of distance.

_____

In 2–5, solve the equation.

2. $|7 + 2q| = 19$ **3.** $|5 - x| = -6$

_____   _____

4. $|2b - 3| = 17$ **5.** $|4m + 21| = 2m + 7$

_____   _____

■**SKILLS** *Objective E*
In 6 and 7, write an absolute value inequality to describe each interval.

6.   **7.**

_____   _____

8. *Multiple choice.* Which of the following is equivalent
to the inequality $|3x - 25| < 10$?   _____

(a) $3x - 25 < -10$ and $3x - 25 < 10$
(b) $3x - 25 < -10$ or $3x - 25 < 10$
(c) $3x - 25 > -10$ and $3x - 25 < 10$
(d) $3x - 25 > -10$ or $3x - 25 < 10$

In 9 and 10, solve the inequality.

9. $|z - 12| > 2$ **10.** $|10y - 17| \leq 13$

_____   _____

■**USES** *Objective L*
11. A contractor estimates that a construction job will cost $27,500.
Suppose the actual cost is within $1,500 of the estimate. Describe
this situation

a. with absolute value.   _____

b. with a double inequality. _____

LESSON **MASTER** 3-9
QUESTIONS ON **SPUR** OBJECTIVES

■**PROPERTIES** *Objective I (See pages 217–220 for objectives.)*
1. How is the graph of $y = \sin 4x$ related to the graph of $y = \sin x$?

_____

In 2 and 3, give a. the amplitude, b. the period, and c. the phase shift.

2. $y = -5 \cos (2(x - \frac{\pi}{2}))$ **a.** _____

3. $y = 3 \sin (4x + \pi)$ **a.** _____

b. _____

b. _____

c. _____

c. _____

4. Consider the graph at the right.

a. Give the amplitude. _____

b. Give the period. _____

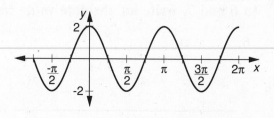

c. Write the equation as an
offspring of $y = \cos x$.

_____

d. Write the equation as an
offspring of $y = \sin x$.

_____

■**REPRESENTATIONS** *Objective N*
5. Write the equation of the result when
the graph of $y = |x|$ is transformed by
$S_{5, 1}$ and then $T_{-4, 0}$.

_____

6. a. Write an equation for the ellipse graphed at
the right.

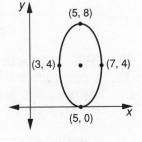

_____

b. If the graph is the result of applying $S_{a, b}$ and
then $T_{c, d}$ to the unit circle, what are the
values of a, b, c, and d?

_____

NAME _____

LESSON **MASTER** **4–1**
QUESTIONS ON **SPUR** OBJECTIVES

■**SKILLS**   *Objective E (See pages 283–286 for objectives.)*
1. Show that $x + 5$ is a factor of $x^2 + x - 20$.

_____

2. If $5x^2 - 8x - 21 = (x - 3) \cdot p(x)$, what is $p(x)$? _____

■**PROPERTIES**   *Objective F*
In 3–5, determine whether the statement is *true* or *false* and explain your answer.

3. -6 is a factor of 720.

_____

4. 21 is a factor of 98.

_____

5. $2x + 7y$ is a factor of $4x^2 - 49y^2$.

_____

6. Prove: *If a, b, and c are integers such that a is a factor of b and b^2 is a factor of c, then a is a factor of c.*

7. Prove: *If a(x), b(x), and c(x) are polynomials such that a(x) is a factor of b(x) and a factor of c(x), then a(x) is a factor of b(x) − c(x).*

8. Consider the conjecture *If a and b are integers and a is a factor of b, then a is a factor of $(b + 1)^2 - 1$.*

   a. Find values for a and b to illustrate this conjecture. _____

   _____

   b. Prove the conjecture.

Precalculus and Discrete Mathematics © Scott, Foresman and Company   **39**

LESSON **MASTER** 4–2
QUESTIONS ON **SPUR** OBJECTIVES

■**SKILLS**   *Objective A (See pages 283–286 for objectives.)*
In 1–4, values for n and d are given. Find values for q and r as defined in the Quotient-Remainder Theorem.

1. $n = 138, d = 23$ _____

2. $n = 15; d = 40$ _____

3. $n = -72; d = 13$ _____

4. $n = 247{,}291; d = 718$ _____

In 5–7, when n is divided by d, the quotient is 11 and the remainder is 5.

5. Can d be 4? Explain your answer. _____

_____

6. If $n = 93$, find the value of d.   7. If $d = 10$, find the value of n.

_____   _____

In 8–10, suppose n is an integer and n is divided by 9.

8. How many different remainders are possible? _____

9. Give two positive values of n for which
   $r = 7$.   _____

10. Give two negative values of n for which
    $r = 7$.   _____

11. Explain why every integer m can be written in exactly one of the
    following forms (where k is an integer):

    $m = 6k$, $m = 6k + 1$, $m = 6k + 2$, $m = 6k + 3$, $m = 6k + 4$,
    $m = 6k + 5$

_____

_____

_____

_____

_____

_____

■ **USES**   *Objective K*

12. A particular brand of pen is sold in three ways: individually (for $4 each), in boxes of 12 (for $45 per box), and in cases of 100 pens (for $320 per case). Suppose n pens are bought using c cases, b boxes, and i individual pens, in such a way that the total cost is minimized.

a. What are the values of c, b, and i if
$n = 88$?   _____

b. What are the values of c, b, and i if
$n = 362$?   _____

c. Are your answers to parts **a** and **b** unique? Why or why not?

_____

_____

_____

LESSON MASTER 4-3
QUESTIONS ON SPUR OBJECTIVES

■SKILLS *Objective D (See pages 283–286 for objectives.)*
1. Name three elements in each of the congruence classes modulo 4.

_____

_____

In 2–5, give the smallest positive integer that makes the congruence true.

2. $a \equiv 79 \pmod 3$ _____ **3.** $b \equiv 2013 \pmod{23}$ _____

4. $d \equiv 0 \pmod{13}$ _____ **5.** $e \equiv -7 \pmod{17}$ _____

6. *True* or *false?* An integer can belong to more than one congruence class for a given modulus. _____

7. Consider the congruence classes modulo 7: $R0, R1, \ldots, R6$. The product of an element of $R3$ and an element of $R6$ is in _____.

■PROPERTIES *Objective G*
8. Rewrite *x can be expressed as 7k + 3 for some integer k* using congruence notation. _____

9. If a leap year is defined as a year evenly divisible by 4 but not evenly divisible by 100, express leap year, y, as a solution to congruence sentences.

_____

10. If $m \equiv 4 \pmod{13}$ and $n \equiv 10 \pmod{13}$, write a congruence statement for

a. $m + n$. **b.** $m - n$.

_____ _____

c. mn. _____

■USES *Objective L*
11. Find the last three digits of 13^{13}. _____

In 12 and 13, fill in the missing digit in the ISBN number.

12. 0-466298-77-__ _____ **13.** 2-470132-5__-X _____

42

LESSON **MASTER** **4-4**
QUESTIONS ON **SPUR** OBJECTIVES

■**SKILLS** *Objective A (See pages 283–286 for objectives.)*
1. If $p(x) = q(x)d(x) + r(x)$, $p(x) = 3x^3 - 2x$, and $d(x) = x^2 - 3$, find $q(x)$ and $r(x)$.

$q(x) =$ _____ $r(x) =$ _____

2. a. Write an equation in the form $p(x) = q(x)d(x) + r(x)$ based on the long division at the right.

$$
\begin{array}{r}
2x - 4 \\
3x^2 + 5x\overline{)6x^3 - 2x^2 + 0x + 3} \\
\underline{6x^3 + 10x^2} \\
-12x^2 + 0x \\
\underline{-12x^2 - 20x} \\
20x + 3
\end{array}
$$

_____

_____

b. Simplify the expression on the right side of the equation from part **a** to show that it in fact equals the left side.

_____

3. Find k and m so that $-12x^2 + mx - 5 = (4x - 1)(kx + 2) - 3 \; \forall$ real numbers x.

$k =$ _____ $m =$ _____

■**SKILLS** *Objective C*
In 4–8, find the quotient $q(x)$ and the remainder $r(x)$ when the polynomial $p(x)$ is divided by the polynomial $d(x)$.

4. $p(x) = 4x^3 + 7x - 4$
$d(x) = 2x + 1$

5. $p(x) = x^5 - x^3 + 2$
$d(x) = x - 1$

$q(x) =$ _____ $q(x) =$ _____

$r(x) =$ _____ $r(x) =$ _____

6. $p(x) = 18x^3 - 13x^2 - 4x + 1$ 7. $p(x) = 4x^4 - 6x^3 + 6x^2 + 4$
   $d(x) = 9x - 2$ $d(x) = 2x^2 + x + 1$

   $q(x) =$ _____ $q(x) =$ _____

   $r(x) =$ _____ $r(x) =$ _____

8. $p(x) = x^5 + 5x^4 - 7x^3 - 15x^2 - 16x + 44$
   $d(x) = x^2 + 4x - 11$

   $q(x) =$ _____ $r(x) =$ _____

9. What is the length of a rectangle whose
   width is $x + 4$ units and whose area is
   $2x^3 + 10x^2 + 9x + 4$ square units?   _____

■ **PROPERTIES**   *Objective H*

10. Suppose that polynomials $m(x)$ and $n(x)$ have degrees 6 and 2,
    respectively. If $m(x)$ is divided by $n(x)$, what do you know about the
    degrees of the quotient and remainder polynomials?

    _____

    _____

    _____

11. Suppose that a polynomial $p(x)$ is divided by a polynomial $d(x)$, and
    that the quotient polynomial has degree 4 while the remainder
    polynomial has degree 2. What do you know about the degrees of
    polynomials $d(x)$ and $p(x)$?

    _____

    _____

Precalculus and Discrete Mathematics © Scott, Foresman and Company

LESSON MASTER 4-5
QUESTIONS ON SPUR OBJECTIVES

■ **SKILLS**   *Objective B (See pages 283–286 for objectives.)*
In 1–4, use synthetic substitution to find p(c) for the given polynomial and value of c.

1. $p(x) = 5x^3 - x^2 + 9$; $c = 3$

2. $p(x) = 4x^3 + 6x - 11$; $c = 0.5$

$p(c) =$ _____

$p(c) =$ _____

3. $p(x) = 3x^4 - x^3 + 6x$; $c = 2.1$

4. $p(x) = x^5 + x^4 - x^3$; $c = -0.2$

$p(c) =$ _____

$p(c) =$ _____

5. *Multiple choice.* Which is not a zero of $x^3 - 5x^2 - 12x + 36$?

   (a) 6   (b) 2   (c) -3   (d) 3   _____

6. What is the value of b if $p(x) = x^4 - 5x^2 - 7x + b$ and $p(-2) = 5$?

$b =$ _____

■ **SKILLS**   *Objective C*
In 7–10, use synthetic division to find the quotient q(x) and the remainder r(x) when the given polynomial p(x) is divided by the polynomial d(x).

7. $p(x) = 3x^3 + 2x^2 + x$
    $d(x) = x + 1$

8. $p(x) = x^5 - 1$
    $d(x) = x - 1$

$q(x) =$ _____

$q(x) =$ _____

$r(x) =$ _____

$r(x) =$ _____

9. $p(x) = x^4 + 3x^3 - 2x + 60$
    $d(x) = x + 4$

10. $p(x) = 2x^3 + 5x^2 + 2x$
    $d(x) = 2x + 1$

$q(x) =$ _____

$q(x) =$ _____

$r(x) =$ _____

$r(x) =$ _____

LESSON **MASTER** **4-6**
QUESTIONS ON **SPUR** OBJECTIVES

■**PROPERTIES**   *Objective H (See pages 283–286 for objectives.)*

1. If $x^2 - 4$ is a factor of a given polynomial
$p(x)$, find the value(s) of c for which
$p(c) = 0$.   _____

2. If 3, 7, and -2 are the zeros of a cubic polynomial $c(x)$, give a
possible formula for $c(x)$.

_____

_____

3. Suppose $p(t) = t^4 - 3t^2 - t + 14$. Find $p(3)$ by dividing $p(t)$ by
$d(t) = t - 3$.

$p(3) =$ _____

4. If -1 is a zero of $p(x) = x^3 - 5x^2 + 2x + 8$, find the remaining zeros
of $p(x)$.

_____

5. *Multiple choice.* If the graph of a polynomial
$p(x)$ crosses the x-axis exactly two times, then _____.

(a) $p(x)$ is of degree 2
(b) $p(x)$ is of degree greater than 2
(c) $p(x)$ is of degree 2 or more
(d) $p(x)$ may have more than two real zeros

6. *True* or *false?* If $t(c) = 0$ and $p(x) = q(x)t(x)$,
then $p(c) = 0$.   _____

7. If $p(x)$ and $q(x)$ are polynomials such that $p(x) = q(x)(x + 3) - 2$,

then you can conclude that $p($_____$) =$ _____

Precalculus and Discrete Mathematics © Scott, Foresman and Company

LESSON MASTER 4-7
QUESTIONS ON SPUR OBJECTIVES

■ **REPRESENTATIONS**   *Objective M (See pages 283–286 for objectives.)*
In 1 and 2, find the base-2 representation of the number.

1. 40   _____

2. 129   _____

In 3 and 4, find the base-10 representation of the number.

3. 110110_2 _____

4. 1000001_2 _____

In 5 and 6, perform the following steps:
   a. Find the binary representation of r.
   b. Find the binary representation of t.
   c. Use your answers to parts a and b to find the base-2 representation of $r + t$.
   d. Convert your answer from part c into base 10.

5. $r = 23, t = 24$

6. $r = 62, t = 7$

   a. _____

   b. _____

   c. _____

   d. _____

   a. _____

   b. _____

   c. _____

   d. _____

7. Express 94 in base n where

   a. $n = 2$.

   b. $n = 8$.

   c. $n = 4$.

   _____   _____   _____

LESSON MASTER 4-8
QUESTIONS ON SPUR OBJECTIVES

■**SKILLS** *Objective E (See pages 283–286 for objectives.)*
In 1–6, factor into prime factors over the real numbers.

1. $6y^2 + 17y + 5$

2. $25n^4 - 30n^2 + 9$

_____   _____

3. $x^4 - 2x^2 - 8$

4. $7x^2 - 49x + 42$

_____   _____

5. $p(x) = 2x^3 + 7x^2 - 14x + 5$, given that $x - 1$ is a factor of $p(x)$

_____

6. $(x^2 + xy)(3x^2 + y^2) - (x^2 + xy)(2x^2 + 2y^2)$

_____

■**PROPERTIES** *Objective I*
7. *True* or *false?* In a proof by contradiction, the assumption which begins the proof is proved to be true.

_____

Precalculus and Discrete Mathematics © Scott, Foresman and Company

NAME _____

Lesson MASTER 4–8 (page 2)

8. Consider the statement *There is no largest real number less than one.*

   a. To write a proof by contradiction, with what assumption would you start?

   _____

   b. Complete the proof.

   c. What does this tell you about the number $0.\overline{9}$? Justify your answer.

   _____

   _____

■**PROPERTIES**   *Objective J*

9. a. List the numbers that must be tested as factors to determine whether 907 is prime.

   _____

   b. Is 907 prime?   _____

10. a. *Multiple choice.* Which prime factorization is not equivalent to the others?

   (a) $2 \cdot 2 \cdot 2 \cdot 3 \cdot 11 \cdot 19$ (b) $2^3 \cdot 2 \cdot 3 \cdot 19 \cdot 11$
   (c) $19 \cdot 2^3 \cdot 3 \cdot 11$ (d) $2^3 \cdot 3 \cdot 11 \cdot 19$ _____

   b. Which of the above represents a standard prime factorization?   _____

In 11 and 12, give the standard prime factorization of the number.

11. 360 _____   **12.** 1938 _____

13. *True* or *false?* In the context of the Fundamental Theorem of Arithmetic, $3 \cdot 5 \cdot 7$ and $7 \cdot 5 \cdot 3$ would be considered distinct factorizations.   _____

LESSON MASTER 5-1

QUESTIONS ON SPUR OBJECTIVES

■**SKILLS** *Objective A (See pages 341–344 for objectives.)*
In 1–6, a. simplify and b. state any restrictions on the variables.

1. $\dfrac{3}{p^2 + 6p + 5} - \dfrac{4}{p^2 + 2p - 15}$

2. $\dfrac{2r - 3}{2r + 3} + \dfrac{7}{r}$

a. _____

b. _____

a. _____

b. _____

3. $\dfrac{4x^2 - 13x - 12}{2x^2 + 3x - 2} \div \dfrac{x - 4}{2x^2 - 5x + 2}$

4. $\dfrac{\frac{1}{x} + \frac{3}{x^2}}{\frac{9}{x^2} - 1}$

a. _____

b. _____

a. _____

b. _____

5. $\dfrac{4}{y^2 - 4} + \dfrac{6}{2y^2 - 7y + 6}$

6. $\dfrac{5}{n^2 + n - 12} - \dfrac{2}{n^2 + 6n + 8}$

a. _____

b. _____

a. _____

b. _____

7. **a.** Prove that the equation $\dfrac{4x}{4x - 3} + \dfrac{3}{3 - 4x} = 1$ is an identity.

b. What is the domain of the identity?

_____

■SKILLS   *Objective B*

In 8–11, show that the given number is rational by expressing it as a ratio of two integers.

8. $\sqrt{\frac{1}{4}}$ _____

9. $0.4\overline{18}$ _____

10. 3.232 _____

11. $3.23\overline{2}$ _____

■PROPERTIES   *Objective F*

12. *Prove:* If a rational number is divided by a nonzero rational number, the result is a rational number.

In 13 and 14, determine whether the statement is *true* or *false*. Justify your answer.

13. All whole numbers are rational numbers.

_____

14. The reciprocal of any nonzero rational number is rational.

_____

■USES   *Objective I*

15. It takes 100 experienced construction workers N days to construct a large office building. It will take 80 novice workers $2N - 30$ days to construct the same building.

   a. Write an expression for the fraction of work done on a single day by the 100 experienced workers.   _____

   b. Write an expression for the fraction of work done on a single day by the 80 novice workers.   _____

   c. Write and simplify a rational expression that represents the fraction of work done on a single day by both groups of workers working together.   _____

   d. What restrictions must be placed on N?   _____

NAME _____

LESSON **MASTER 5-2**
QUESTIONS ON **SPUR** OBJECTIVES

■**SKILLS** *Objective B (See pages 341–344 for objectives.)*
1. If a real number is irrational, then its decimal representation is either

_____ or _____.

In 2–5, identify each number as rational or irrational. Justify your answer.

2. $\frac{1}{2 - \sqrt{3}}$

3. $\sqrt{841}$

_____   _____

_____   _____

4. 2.1212212221 . . .

5. -5.1$\overline{37}$

_____   _____

_____   _____

■**SKILLS** *Objective C*
In 6–8, rationalize the denominator.

6. $\frac{11\sqrt{2}}{1 - \sqrt{2}}$

7. $\frac{-5\sqrt{3}}{\sqrt{7} - \sqrt{3}}$

8. $\frac{\sqrt{a} - \sqrt{b}}{\sqrt{a} + \sqrt{b}}$

_____

9. Rationalize the *numerator* in the expression
$\frac{\sqrt{3} + \sqrt{2}}{2}$.

_____

■**PROPERTIES** *Objective F*
10. Prove that $\sqrt{17}$ is irrational.

11. a. *True* or *false*? The quotient of two
irrational numbers is irrational.   _____

b. If true, prove the statement. Otherwise give a counterexample.

12. Prove that if a and b are integers and a is not a perfect square, then
$\sqrt{a} + b$ is irrational.

LESSON **MASTER 5–3**
QUESTIONS ON **SPUR** OBJECTIVES

■**PROPERTIES**   *Objective G (See pages 341–344 for objectives.)*
  1. Refer to the graph of f at the right.

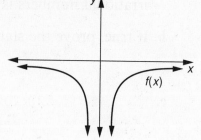

  a. Explain in words what happens to $f(x)$ as x approaches zero.

  _____

  _____

  b. Use limit notation to describe the behavior of f as x approaches zero for positive values of x.

  _____

  c. Use limit notation to describe the behavior of f as x approaches zero for negative values of x.

  _____

  d. Describe, in words, the end behavior of f.

  _____

  e. Describe, using limit notation, the end behavior of f.

  _____

  2. Consider the functions g and h where $g(x) = \frac{2}{x-3}$ and $h(x) = \frac{2}{x}$.

  a. What transformation maps the graph of h to the graph of g? ____

  b. Describe, using limit notation, the behavior of g near any vertical asymptotes.

  _____

  c. Describe, using limit notation, the end behavior of g.

  _____

■**REPRESENTATIONS**   *Objective J*
  3. Let f be the function $f(x) = \frac{1}{x+1}$.

  a. Graph f.

  b. Write an equation for the vertical asymptote to the graph of f.

  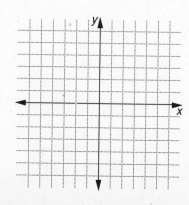

  _____

Precalculus and Discrete Mathematics © Scott, Foresman and Company

4. a. Graph the function g where $g(x) = \frac{-1}{x^4}$.

b. Use limit notation to describe the end behavior of g.

_____

c. Use limit notation to describe the behavior of g near any vertical asymptotes.

_____

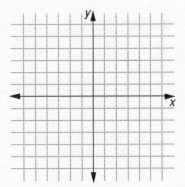

5. Describe, in words, the difference between the graphs of $f(x) = \frac{1}{x^{2k}}$ and $g(x) = \frac{1}{x^{2k+1}}$ for positive integers k.

_____

_____

_____

■**REPRESENTATIONS** *Objective K*

In 6 and 7, a. write an equation for the graph's vertical asymptote and b. use limit notation to describe the behavior of the function near the vertical asymptote.

6.

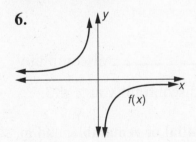

7.

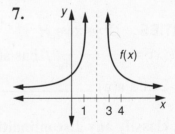

a. _____   **a.** _____

b. _____   **b.** _____

8. Let f be the function defined by $f(x) = \frac{1}{x^n}$ such that $\lim_{x \to 0^-} f(x) = \infty$.

a. Sketch a possible graph of f.

b. Is n even or odd?   _____

c. Find $\lim_{x \to 0^+} f(x)$.   _____

LESSON MASTER 5-4
QUESTIONS ON SPUR OBJECTIVES

■ **PROPERTIES**   *Objective G (See pages 341–344 for objectives.)*

1. Consider the function g defined by $g(y) = \dfrac{-2y}{4y^2 - 9}$.

   a. Identify the vertical asymptotes of the
     graph of g. _____

   b. Use limit notation to describe the behavior of g near the
     asymptotes.

   _____

   _____

   c. Use limit notation to describe the end behavior of g.

   _____

2. Given $f(x) = \dfrac{x + 4}{x^2 + 2x - 8}$, find

   a. $\lim\limits_{x \to -4^-} f(x)$. _____   **b.** $\lim\limits_{x \to -4^+} f(x)$. _____

   c. $\lim\limits_{x \to 2^-} f(x)$. _____   **d.** $\lim\limits_{x \to 2^+} f(x)$. _____

■ **PROPERTIES**   *Objective H*

3. Given $f(x) = \dfrac{x + 2}{x^2 - x - 6}$, f has a(n) _____ discontinuity
   at $x = -2$ and a(n) _____ discontinuity at $x = 3$.

**In 4 and 5, classify any discontinuities as essential or removable, and at
each removable discontinuity, redefine the function to make it continuous.**

4. $f(a) = \dfrac{2a^2 + a - 3}{a + 1}$ **5.** $f(b) = \dfrac{2b^2 + b - 3}{b - 1}$

   _____   _____

   _____   _____

6. Find a rule for a function that has a removable discontinuity at
   $x = -2$ and no essential discontinuities.

_____

■ **REPRESENTATIONS** *Objective J*
In 7–10, sketch a graph of the function, indicating holes at the removable discontinuities and dashed lines for any asymptotes.

7. $g(x) = \dfrac{2x^2 + 7x}{x + 3}$

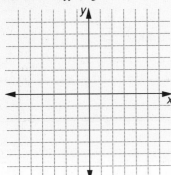

8. $f(x) = \dfrac{x^2 + 2x}{x^3 - 4x}$

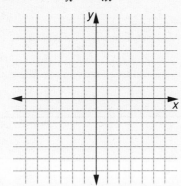

9. $h(x) = \dfrac{x^2 + 5x - 6}{x + 6}$

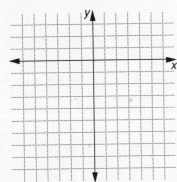

10. $f(x) = \dfrac{x - 2}{x^2 - 4}$

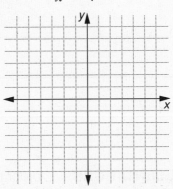

■ **REPRESENTATIONS** *Objective K*
In 11 and 12, a. find equations for any vertical asymptotes, b. use limit notation to describe the behavior of the function near any asymptote, and c. use limit notation to describe the behavior of the function near any removable discontinuity.

11. the function in Question 8   a. _____

    b. _____   c. _____

12. the function graphed at the right

    a. _____

    b. _____

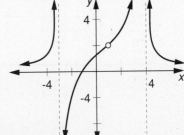

       _____

    c. _____

NAME _____

■**PROPERTIES** *Objective G (See pages 341–344 for objectives.)*
In 1–4, a. find a constant function, linear function, power function, or
reciprocal of a power function whose end behavior resembles that of the
given function, b. use limit notation to describe the end behavior, and c.
use limit notation to describe the behavior near any vertical asymptotes.

1. $f(x) = \dfrac{3x^2 + 2x + 1}{5x - 2x^3}$

a. _____

b. _____

c. _____

2. $g(x) = \dfrac{2x^2 - 5}{5x^2 + 2}$

a. _____

b. _____

c. _____

3. $h(x) = \dfrac{x^2 + x - 1}{x - 1}$

a. _____

b. _____

c. _____

4. $f(t) = t^5 + 12t^3 - 4t - \dfrac{2}{t}$

a. _____

b. _____

c. _____

■**REPRESENTATIONS** *Objective J*
In 5–7, a. find the *x*- and *y*-intercepts of the graph of the function and
b. sketch the graph.

5. the function in Question 1

a. _____

b.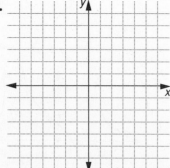

6. the function in Question 2

a. _____

b.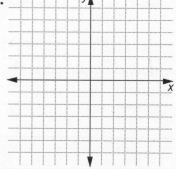

Precalculus and Discrete Mathematics © Scott, Foresman and Company

7. the function in Question 3

a. _____

_____

b.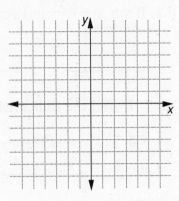

■**REPRESENTATIONS**   *Objective K*
**In 8–10, find an equation for each asymptote of the graph of the function
and state whether the asymptote is vertical, horizontal, or oblique.**

8. the function in Question 2

_____

_____

9. the function in Question 3

_____

_____

10. the function graphed at the right

_____

_____

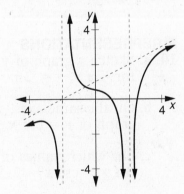

11. Sketch the graph of a function with
asymptotes $y = -x + 4$ and $x = 3$,
$\lim\limits_{x \to 3^-} f(x) = -\infty$, and $\lim\limits_{x \to 3^+} f(x) = \infty$.

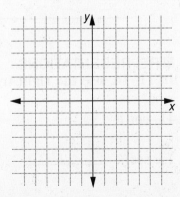

LESSON MASTER 5–6
QUESTIONS ON SPUR OBJECTIVES

■ **SKILLS** *Objective D (See pages 341–344 for objectives.)*

1. If $\sin x = \frac{-\sqrt{3}}{2}$ and $\cos x = -\frac{1}{2}$, find the value of $\tan x$, $\sec x$, $\cot x$, and $\csc x$.

_____   _____   _____   _____

In 2–7, find the indicated value.

2. $\cot \frac{7\pi}{6}$ _____

3. $\sec -\frac{3\pi}{2}$ _____

4. $\csc \frac{\pi}{2}$ _____

5. $\tan \pi$ _____

6. $\sec \frac{3\pi}{4}$ _____

7. $\tan -\frac{\pi}{4}$ _____

■ **PROPERTIES** *Objective H*

8. Consider the cotangent function $f\colon x \to \cot x$. For what values of x does this function have essential discontinuities?

_____

9. What transformation can be applied to the graph of the function $\csc x$ so that the image has essential discontinuities at $x = \frac{n\pi}{2}$ ∀ integers n?

_____

■ **REPRESENTATIONS** *Objective J*

10. **a.** Sketch a graph of $y = \cot x$ for $-2\pi < x < 2\pi$.

b. On the same axes, sketch a graph of $y = \csc x$.

c. For which values of x is $\cot x > \csc x$?

_____

_____

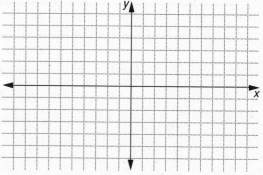

■ **REPRESENTATIONS** *Objective L*
In 11–14, use the right triangle below to find the indicated value.

11. $\cot \theta$ _____

12. $\csc \phi$ _____

13. $\sec \theta$ _____

14. $\tan \phi$ _____

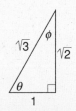

Precalculus and Discrete Mathematics © Scott, Foresman and Company

LESSON MASTER 5-7
QUESTIONS ON SPUR OBJECTIVES

■ **SKILLS** *Objective E (See pages 341–344 for objectives.)*
In 1–6, solve each equation.

1. $\dfrac{1}{y-3} = \dfrac{y}{y+4} + \dfrac{7y}{(y+4)(y-3)}$

2. $\dfrac{8}{t+3} + \dfrac{t}{t-3} = \dfrac{-2}{t^2-9}$

_____

3. $\dfrac{r}{r-1} + \dfrac{r-1}{r} = 1$

4. $2 + \dfrac{20}{s^2-s-6} = \dfrac{-3}{s-3}$

_____

5. $\dfrac{z+3}{z-6} + \dfrac{z}{3z-4} = \dfrac{2z^2-3}{3z^2-22z+24}$

6. $\dfrac{x}{2x-1} = \dfrac{6}{5x+7} + \dfrac{x^2-x+1}{10x^2+9x-7}$

_____

■ **USES** *Objective I*

7. A tired swimmer takes 30 minutes longer to return to shore from a pier as it took to swim from shore to the pier. The pier is 1 km from shore and the swimmer's average speed returning is 3 km/h less than the swimmer's average speed going out to the pier. What is the swimmer's average speed going out to the pier?

_____

8. In an electrical circuit, if two resistors with resistances R_1 and R_2 are connected in parallel, then the equivalent resistance, R, is found using the equation $\frac{1}{R} = \frac{1}{R_1} + \frac{1}{R_2}$. If R_1 is 5 ohms less than R_2 and R is one-third of R_2, what are the values of R_1, R_2, and R?

_____

LESSON MASTER 6-1
QUESTIONS ON SPUR OBJECTIVES

■**REPRESENTATIONS**   *Objective G (See pages 396–398 for objectives.)*
In 1–6, use an automatic grapher to determine whether the equation
appears to be an identity. If so, conjure the domain of the identity. If not,
give a counterexample.

1. $1 + \cos^2 x = 2 \sin^2 \left(x + \frac{\pi}{2}\right)$ **2.** $\tan y = \cot \left(\frac{\pi}{2} - y\right)$

_____   _____

_____   _____

3. $\sin x \cdot \tan x = \sec x + \cos x$ **4.** $\sin x \cdot \tan x = \sec x - \cos x$

_____   _____

_____   _____

5. $\sin 3z = 3 \sin z \cos z$ **6.** $\csc u = \text{-}\csc (\pi + u)$

_____   _____

_____   _____

7. Use an automatic grapher to decide whether $\tan (\alpha + \beta) = \tan \alpha +$
$\tan \beta$, for $\alpha = \frac{\pi}{4}$, $\alpha = \frac{\pi}{2}$, and a value of your choice for α.

_____

8. *True* or *false*? Identities can be proved using an automatic grapher.

_____

LESSON MASTER 6-2
QUESTIONS ON SPUR OBJECTIVES

■**SKILLS** *Objective A (See pages 396–398 for objectives.)*

1. Suppose x is in the interval $\frac{\pi}{2} < x < \pi$ and $\sin x = \frac{\sqrt{2}}{\sqrt{3}}$. Use trigonometric identities to find each value.

   a. sec x _____

   b. tan x _____

   c. cox x _____

   d. csc x _____

2. If $\sin \alpha = -.8$ and $\tan \alpha = 2.1$, find sec α. _____

■**PROPERTIES** *Objective D*
In 3–5, prove the identity and specify its domain.

3. $\sec x \cdot \cos x = \sin x \csc x$

4. $\frac{1}{1 + \cos x} + \frac{1}{1 - \cos x} = 2 \csc^2 x$

5. $\cot x \cdot \sin x \cdot \sec x = \cos^2 x + \sin^2 x$

6. Fill in the blank to make an identity: $\cos x \cdot \cot x + \sin x =$ _____.

■**REPRESENTATIONS** *Objective G*
In 7 and 8, use an automatic grapher to conjecture whether the equation is an identity. If so, prove it and identify its domain. If not, give a counterexample.

7. $\cot 2x + \cot x = \cot 3x$

8. $\frac{\cos x \cot x}{1 - \sin x} = 1 + \csc x$

LESSON MASTER 6-3
QUESTIONS ON SPUR OBJECTIVES

■**SKILLS** *Objective A (See pages 396–398 for objectives.)*
1. Suppose $0 < \alpha < \frac{\pi}{2} < \beta < \pi$, $\cos \alpha = .75$, and $\sin \beta = .3$. Find the following values.

   a. $\sin \alpha$ _____   **b.** $\cos \beta$ _____

   c. $\cos (\alpha + \beta)$ _____   **d.** $\cos (\alpha - \beta)$ _____

In 2–4, express the following in terms of rational numbers and radicals.

2. $\cos \left(\frac{\pi}{4} + \frac{\pi}{6} \right)$ 3. $\cos \frac{11\pi}{12}$

_____   _____

4. $\cos \frac{\pi}{9} \cos \frac{2\pi}{9} - \sin \frac{\pi}{9} \sin \frac{2\pi}{9}$

_____

5. Find the cosine of $\frac{\pi}{12}$:

   a. by writing $\frac{\pi}{12}$ as $\frac{\pi}{4} - \frac{\pi}{6}$.   **b.** by writing $\frac{\pi}{12}$ as $\frac{\pi}{3} - \frac{\pi}{4}$.

   _____   _____

6. Simplify $\cos \left(\frac{\pi}{2} + x \right) + \cos \left(\frac{\pi}{2} - x \right)$.   _____

■ **PROPERTIES** *Objective D*

In 7–9, prove the identity and specify the domain.

7. $-2 \sin x \sin y = \cos (x + y) - \cos (x - y)$

8. $\cos (\pi - x) = -\cos x$

9. $\sin x = \cos \left(x + \frac{3\pi}{2}\right)$

NAME _____

LESSON **MASTER 6–4**
QUESTIONS ON **SPUR** OBJECTIVES

■**SKILLS**   *Objective A (See pages 396–398 for objectives.)*
In 1–4, express the following in terms of rational numbers and radicals.

1. $\sin\left(\frac{2\pi}{3} - \frac{\pi}{4}\right)$

2. $\tan\frac{7\pi}{12}$

_____   _____

3. $\dfrac{\tan\frac{3\pi}{16} + \tan\frac{\pi}{16}}{1 - \tan\frac{3\pi}{16}\tan\frac{\pi}{16}}$

4. $\sin\frac{13\pi}{12}$

_____   _____

5. Given that $\sin \alpha = \frac{2}{3}$, find $\sin(\pi - \alpha)$.   _____

In 6–9, suppose r is in the interval $0 < r < \frac{\pi}{2}$ with $\cos r = \frac{3}{5}$ and s is in the interval $\pi < s < \frac{3\pi}{2}$ with $\sin s = -\frac{1}{4}$. Use this information to find each value.

6. $\sin(s - r)$

7. $\tan(r + s)$

_____   _____

8. $\sin(\pi + s - r)$

9. $\tan(\pi + s - r)$

_____   _____

66   *Continued*   *Precalculus and Discrete Mathematics* © Scott, Foresman and Company

■**PROPERTIES**   *Objective D*

In 10–13, prove the identity and specify its domain.

10. $\sin\left(\frac{3\pi}{2} + x\right) = -\cos x$

11. $\tan x = -\tan(\pi - x)$

12. $\sin(x + y)\cos(x - y) = \sin x \cos x + \sin y \cos y$

13. $\sin(x + y) + \cos(x - y) = (\sin x + \cos x)(\sin y + \cos y)$
      (Compare this identity to the one in Question 12.)

LESSON **MASTER** 6-5
QUESTIONS ON **SPUR** OBJECTIVES

■**SKILLS** · *Objective A (See pages 396–398 for objectives.)*

1. Given $0 < x < \frac{\pi}{2}$ and $\cos x = \frac{8}{17}$, find $\sin 2x$ and $\sin \frac{x}{2}$. _____

_____

In 2 and 3, express the following in terms of rational numbers and radicals.

2. $\cos \frac{\pi}{8}$ 3. $\sin \frac{\pi}{12}$

_____   _____

4. **a.** Use the identity for $\cos (\alpha - \beta)$ to find $\cos \frac{7\pi}{12}$. _____

  b. Use the identity $\cos 2\alpha = 2 \cos^2 \alpha - 1$ to find $\cos \frac{7\pi}{12}$. _____

  c. Show that your answers to parts **a** and **b** are equal.

    Precalculus and Discrete Mathematics © Scott, Foresman and Company

■ PROPERTIES   *Objective D*

5. *Multiple choice.* Which expression equals cos $2x$ for all x? _____

(a) $1 - 2 \cos^2 x$ (b) $\sin^2 x - \cos^2 x$

(c) $2 \sin^2 x - 1$ (d) $2 \cos^2 x - 1$

In 6–9, prove the identity and specify its domain.

6. $(\sin x + \cos x)^2 = \sin 2x + 1$

7. $1 - \tan^2 \theta = \dfrac{2 \tan \theta}{\tan 2\theta}$

8. $4 \sin^2 \alpha \cos^2 \alpha + (\cos^2 \alpha - \sin^2 \alpha)^2 = 1$

9. $2 \sin \beta \csc 2\beta = \sec \beta$

LESSON **MASTER** 6-6
QUESTIONS ON **SPUR** OBJECTIVES

■**SKILLS** *Objective B* *(See pages 396–398 for objectives.)*
1. Let $f(x) = \tan^{-1}(x)$.

   a. Within what interval must x lie?

   b. Within what interval must $f(x)$ lie?

   _____

   _____

In 2–5, compute without using a calculator.

2. $\sin^{-1}\left(\frac{-\sqrt{3}}{2}\right)$ _____

3. $\tan(\tan^{-1} 0)$ _____

4. $\cos(\sin^{-1} 1)$ _____

5. $\sin\left(\tan^{-1}\left(\tan\frac{\pi}{6}\right)\right)$ _____

In 6 and 7, use $\triangle ABC$ to evaluate the expression.

6. $\sin\left(\tan^{-1}\left(\frac{a}{b}\right)\right)$ _____

7. $\cos^{-1}\left(\frac{a}{c}\right)$ _____

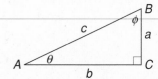

■**USES** *Objective E*
8. Snell's Law of Refraction states that when a light ray passes from one medium into a second one, its path bends so that the angles α and β (shown in the diagram) obey $\frac{\sin \alpha}{\sin \beta} = C$, where C is a constant called the *index of refraction*. If the index of refraction is 1.24, and a ray of light strikes the liquid at an angle of incidence of $\alpha = 65°$, find the angle of refraction β. _____

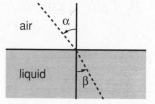

9. Suppose that the sun, Earth, and Jupiter are positioned as shown in the diagram at the right.

   a. If Jupiter is x km from the sun and Earth is 150 million km from the sun, give an expression for the angle θ formed by the sight lines from Earth to the other two bodies.

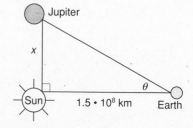

   _____

   b. If $x = 7.8 \cdot 10^8$ km, find θ. _____

Precalculus and Discrete Mathematics © Scott, Foresman and Company

LESSON MASTER 6-7
QUESTIONS ON SPUR OBJECTIVES

■SKILLS *Objective C (See pages 396–398 for objectives.)*
In 1–4, solve without a calculator over the interval $0 \leq x \leq 2\pi$.

1. $\csc x = \frac{2\sqrt{3}}{3}$

2. $\tan x \leq -\sqrt{3}$

_____   _____

3. $\sec 2x = 2$

4. $(\sin x)(2 \sin x - 1) < 0$

_____   _____

In 5 and 6, solve over the reals using a calculator or automatic grapher, if necessary.

5. $\sec^2 x + \csc^2 x = \sec^2 x \csc^2 x$

6. $7 \sin^2 \phi + 10 \sin \phi + 3 = 0$

■ **USES**　*Objective F*

7. Two jugglers toss bowling pins to each other with an initial velocity v_0 of 35 ft/s. The horizontal distance R that the bowling pins travel is approximated by the equation $R = \frac{v_0^2}{32} \sin 2\theta$. At what angle should the pins be thrown if the jugglers are standing 30 ft apart?

_____

■ **REPRESENTATIONS**　*Objective H*

8. Use an automatic grapher to approximate to the nearest tenth all solutions to $\tan x + \sin x = 1.7$ over the interval $0 \leq x \leq 2\pi$.

_____

9. Refer to the graph below of $g(x) = x$ and $h(x) = \tan^2 x$.

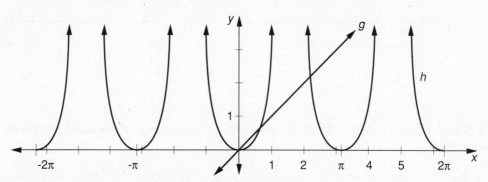

a. Solve $\tan^2 x = x$ over the interval $-\pi \leq x \leq \pi$.

_____

b. Solve $\tan^2 x < x$ over the interval $-\pi \leq x \leq \pi$.

_____

LESSON MASTER 7–1
QUESTIONS ON SPUR OBJECTIVES

■SKILLS   *Objective A (See pages 462–464 for objectives.)*
In 1–6, write the first five terms of the sequence defined by the given formula.

1. $d_n = n^3 + 4n^2 - 3n + 1$

2. $\begin{cases} a_1 = 4 \\ a_{k+1} = -3a_k - 7 \ \forall \ k \geq 1 \end{cases}$

_____   _____

3. $a_n = 2\left\lceil \dfrac{n}{3} \right\rceil$

4. $b_n = (-1)^n \cdot \dfrac{n(n+1)}{2}$

_____   _____

5. $f_n = \begin{cases} \cos n\pi, & n \text{ even} \\ \sin n\pi, & n \text{ odd} \end{cases}$

6. $c_n = 3\left\lfloor \dfrac{n}{3} \right\rfloor$

_____   _____

7. Let a be the sequence defined by $a_n = (-2)^{n+1}$.

  a. Which term is greater: a_7 or a_8? _____

  b. Given two consecutive integers, how can one tell which will yield the greater term of the sequence?

_____

8. Let b be the sequence defined by
$\begin{cases} b_1 = 2 \\ b_{k+1} = 3b_k - 2 \ \forall \ k \geq 1. \end{cases}$ Find b_6. _____

9. Which of the sequences in Questions 1–7 are defined recursively? _____

10. If 5, a, b, c, d, 14 are consecutive terms of an arithmetic sequence, find a, b, c, and d. _____

■USES *Objective H*

10. A leading brand of soap advertises that it is $99\frac{44}{100}$% pure. Suppose that in the manufacturing process, the soap is initially 80% pure, and is then put through a series of chemical processes to purify it further, each step removing 40% of the existing impurities. Let A_n represent the percent of impurities present after the nth step.

a. Write a recursive definition
for the sequence A.   _____

b. Find A_3.   _____

c. Find n so that the soap is at least $99\frac{44}{100}$% pure. _____

11. A phone company suggests that you call two friends, with instructions for each of them to call two of their friends. If this process is continued, how many friends will receive a call as the seventeenth in the line of calls?

_____

12. Suppose an economist suggests that the government adopt an income tax system consisting of income brackets of equal size, and in which the tax rate increases by a constant amount from one bracket to the next. A possible tax table for this system is given below.

Income Bracket	Annual Income (in dollars)	Tax Rate (in percent)
1	0 – 20,000	12
2	20,001 – 40,000	16.5
3	40,001 – 60,000	21
4	60,001 – 80,000	25.5

a. If the tax rate in the nth income bracket is R_n, write a recursive definition for R_n.

_____

_____

b. Find R_8.   _____

c. If the maximum tax rate were 48 percent, what level of income would be taxed at this rate?

_____

d. Suppose the tax rates change so that the lowest rate is 9 percent, with an increase of 5.1 percent from one bracket to the next. At what rate would someone who earned $136,000 annually be taxed? Is this more or less than under the originally proposed system?

_____

Precalculus and Discrete Mathematics © Scott, Foresman and Company

NAME _____

LESSON MASTER 7-2
QUESTIONS ON **SPUR** OBJECTIVES

■SKILLS *Objective B (See pages 462–464 for objectives.)*
In 1–4, a. write the first five terms of the sequence and b. determine an explicit formula that is suggested by the pattern of numbers in part a.

1. $\begin{cases} a_1 = 2 \\ a_{k+1} = 3a_k \ \forall \ k \geq 1 \end{cases}$

a. _____

b. _____

2. $\begin{cases} d_1 = -1 \\ d_{k+1} = d_k + 5 \ \forall \ k \geq 1 \end{cases}$

a. _____

b. _____

3. $\begin{cases} a_1 = 1 \\ a_{k+1} = (k+1)a_k \ \forall \ k \geq 1 \end{cases}$

a. _____

b. _____

4. $\begin{cases} x_1 = 3 \\ x_2 = 5 \\ x_{k+1} = x_k + 2x_{k-1} - 2 \ \forall \ k \geq 1 \end{cases}$
(Hint: Subtract 1 from each term to see the pattern.)

a. _____

b. _____

5. Conjecture an explicit formula for S_n, the sum of the first n positive odd integers.

_____

■REPRESENTATIONS *Objective J*
6. a. List the terms generated by the program at the right.

_____

_____

```
10  FOR N=0 TO 6
20     C=5N*(N+1)
30     PRINT C
40  NEXT N
```

b. Does the program use a recursive or explicit formula? What is this formula?

_____

7. Complete the program at the right so it uses a recursive formula to generate the first seven terms of the sequence defined by $a_n = \frac{n}{2} + 3$ $\forall \ n \geq 1$.

```
10  TERM = _____
20  PRINT TERM
30  FOR K = _____
40     TERM = _____
50     PRINT TERM
60  NEXT K
```

Precalculus and Discrete Mathematics © Scott, Foresman and Company

75

LESSON MASTER 7-3
QUESTIONS ON SPUR OBJECTIVES

■ **SKILLS** *Objective C (See pages 462–464 for objectives.)*

1. If $n = 3$, find $\displaystyle\sum_{k=-1}^{n} k^2 + 3k$. _____

In 2 and 3, write using summation notation.

2. $7 + 14 + 21 + 28 + 35 + 42$ _____

3. $-\dfrac{2}{(k+1)^2} - \dfrac{1}{(k+1)} + 0 + (k+1) + 2(k+1)^2$ _____

4. **a.** Rewrite the equation $1^3 + 2^3 + 3^3 + 4^3 + \ldots + n^3 = (1 + 2 + 3 + 4 + \ldots + n)^2$ using summation notation.

_____

   b. Show that the equation is true for $n = 5$. _____

■ **SKILLS** *Objective D*

5. **a.** Express $\displaystyle\sum_{j=0}^{11} (j^4 - j)$ in terms of $\displaystyle\sum_{j=0}^{10} (j^4 - j)$. _____

   b. Given that $\displaystyle\sum_{j=0}^{10} (j^4 - j) = 25{,}278$, find $\displaystyle\sum_{j=0}^{11} (j^4 - j)$. _____

6. Let $S(k)$ be the statement: $\displaystyle\sum_{j=1}^{k} j^3 = \tfrac{1}{4}k^2(k+1)^2$.

   a. Find $\displaystyle\sum_{j=1}^{5} j^3$ and show that $S(5)$ is true.

_____

   b. Rewrite $\displaystyle\sum_{j=1}^{k+1} j^3$ in terms of $\displaystyle\sum_{j=1}^{k} j^3$. _____

   c. Use your answers to parts **a** and **b** to find $\displaystyle\sum_{j=1}^{6} j^3$. _____

   d. Use the answer to part **c** to determine if $S(6)$ is true.

_____

Precalculus and Discrete Mathematics © Scott, Foresman and Company

■**PROPERTIES**   *Objective F*

7. Prove that the sequence defined by $\begin{cases} a_1 = \frac{1}{2} \\ a_{k+1} = \frac{a_k}{k+2} \ \forall \ k \geq 1 \end{cases}$

has explicit formula $a_n = \frac{1}{(n+1)!}$.

8. Prove that the sequence defined by $\begin{cases} x_1 = 3 \\ x_{k+1} = \frac{x_k}{4} \ \forall \ k \geq 1 \end{cases}$

has explicit formula $x_n = \frac{3}{4^{n-1}}$.

■**REPRESENTATIONS**   *Objective J*

9. Consider the computer program below.

```
10  INPUT N
20  SUM = 0
30  FOR K = 4 TO N
40     TERM = K/(K + 1)
50     SUM = SUM + TERM
60  NEXT K
70  PRINT SUM
```

a. Use summation notation to express the
sum computed by this program.   _____

b. If 7 is input for N, what output is
generated?   _____

10. How would you change the program in Question 9 so it would

compute $\displaystyle\sum_{k=n}^{15} \frac{n-k}{k}$?

_____

LESSON **MASTER** 7–4
QUESTIONS ON **SPUR** OBJECTIVES

■ **PROPERTIES** *Objective F (See pages 462–464 for objectives.)*

1. Prove that the sequence defined by $\begin{cases} a_1 = 2 \\ a_{k+1} = a_k + k + 1 \ \forall \ k \geq 1 \end{cases}$

   has explicit formula $a_n = \frac{n^2}{2} + \frac{n}{2} + 1$.

2. Identify the basis step and the inductive step in your proof for Question 1.

   basis: _____

   inductive: _____

3. Find an explicit formula for the sequence defined by
   $\begin{cases} a_1 = 2 \\ a_{k+1} = 3a_k \ \forall \ k \geq 1 \end{cases}$. Use mathematical induction to prove that your formula is correct.

Precalculus and Discrete Mathematics © Scott, Foresman and Company

■**PROPERTIES** *Objective G*

In 4–6, use mathematical induction to prove that $S(n)$ is true for all positive integers n, or find a counterexample.

4. $S(n)$: $3 + 9 + 15 + \ldots + (6n - 3) = 3n^2$

5. $S(n)$: $\displaystyle\sum_{i=0}^{n} 2^i = 2^{n+1} - 1$

6. $S(n)$: $(a + b)^n = a^n + b^n$

LESSON MASTER 7-5
QUESTIONS ON SPUR OBJECTIVES

■**PROPERTIES**   *Objective G (See pages 462–464 for objectives.)*
1. Let $P(n)$ be a statement in n. What can be concluded in each of the following instances?

   a. $P(1)$ is true and $P(k) \Rightarrow P(k + 1)$.

   _____

   b. $P(1)$ is true and $P(k)$ does not imply $P(k + 1)$.

   _____

   c. $P(6)$ is true and $P(k) \Rightarrow P(k + 1)$.

   _____

In 2 and 3, use mathematical induction to prove that the statement is true.

2. 4 is a factor of $5^n - 1$ ∀ positive integers n.

3. 3 is a factor of $n^3 + 8n$ ∀ positive integers n.

4. a. Show that $x + y$ is a factor of $x^3 + y^3$.

b. Use mathematical induction to prove that $x + y$ is a factor of $x^{2n-1} + y^{2n-1}$ ∀ positive integers n. (Hint: In the inductive step, add and subtract $x^2 y^{2k-1}$.)

LESSON MASTER 7-6
QUESTIONS ON SPUR OBJECTIVES

■ **SKILLS**   *Objective E (See pages 462–464 for objectives.)*
In 1–3, a. **find the value of the series for** $n = 4$ **and b. find the limit of the series as** $n \to \infty$.

1. $\displaystyle\sum_{k=0}^{n} \frac{2}{7^k}$ 2. $\displaystyle\sum_{k=1}^{n} 4^k$ 3. $\displaystyle\sum_{k=1}^{n} c(.9)^k$

a. _____   a. _____   a. _____

b. _____   b. _____   b. _____

4. Let b be the sequence defined by $\begin{cases} b_1 = 2 \\ b_{k+1} = \frac{3}{4}b_k \ \forall \ k \ge 1. \end{cases}$
Let S_n be the nth partial sum of the sequence.

a. Find a formula for S_n.

b. Find S_6.

c. Find $\displaystyle\lim_{n\to\infty} S_n$.   _____

5. Give an example of a series which converges
and whose seventh term is greater than $\frac{1}{2}$.

6. Consider the finite geometric series
$a + 2a + 4a + \ldots + 512a.$

a. Use sigma notation to express the series. _____

b. If the value of the series is 613.8, find a. _____

Precalculus and Discrete Mathematics © Scott, Foresman and Company

■REPRESENTATIONS *Objective J*

7. Consider the computer program below.

```
10  TERM = 3
20  PRINT TERM
30  SUM = TERM
40  FOR K = 2 TO 15
50     TERM = 2 * (TERM)/3
60     PRINT TERM
70     SUM = SUM + TERM
80  NEXT K
90  PRINT SUM
```

a. Use summation notation to write the
   sum that is calculated by the program.   _____

b. Use the formula for the sum of the terms
   of a finite geometric series to find the sum
   in part **a**.   _____

c. What would the sum approach if the 15 in
   line 40 were changed to a larger and larger
   number?   _____

8. What changes would have to be made to the program in Question 7
   to compute the partial sums of the sequence defined by $a_n = 2(.3)^n$?

NAME _____

LESSON **MASTER 7-7**
QUESTIONS ON **SPUR** OBJECTIVES

■**PROPERTIES** *Objective G (See pages 462–464 for objectives.)*
1. The Strong Form of Mathematical Induction differs from the original

form only in the _____ step.

In 2–4, use the Strong Form of Mathematical Induction.

2. Consider the sequence defined recursively by
$$\begin{cases} a_1 = 3 \\ a_2 = -12 \\ a_{k+1} = a_k - 4a_{k-1} \ \forall \text{ integers } k \geq 2. \end{cases}$$
Prove that every term of the sequence is a multiple of 3.

3. Consider the sequence defined recursively by
$$\begin{cases} a_1 = 2 \\ a_2 = 4 \\ a_{k+1} = 2a_k - 3a_{k-1} \ \forall \text{ integers } k \geq 2. \end{cases}$$
Prove that every term of the sequence is an even integer.

Precalculus and Discrete Mathematics © Scott, Foresman and Company

NAME _____
Lesson MASTER 7-7 (page 2)

4. Let c be a fixed integer. Prove that every term of the sequence
defined by
$$\begin{cases} b_1 & = c \\ b_2 & = 2c \\ b_{k+1} & = 2b_k + b_{k-1} \ \forall \text{ integers } k \geq 2 \end{cases}$$
is divisible by c.

Precalculus and Discrete Mathematics © Scott, Foresman and Company

85

LESSON MASTER 7-8
QUESTIONS ON SPUR OBJECTIVES

■ **USES** *Objective I (See pages 462–464 for objectives.)*
In 1–5, use the specified algorithm to arrange the given list in increasing order. Show all intermediate steps.

1. -7, 3, 0, 1 (Bubblesort)

2. 9, 4, -2, 10, 8 (Quicksort)

3. 2, -3, .5, -7, -6 (Quicksort)

4. 1, 3, 5, 7, 2, 4, 6 (Bubblesort)

5. -3, -2, -1, 7, 1, 2, 3 (Quicksort)

6. For a list of four numbers, what is the maximum number of passes needed for the Bubblesort algorithm to arrange them in increasing order? _____

7. Is the Quicksort algorithm recursive or iterative? _____

Precalculus and Discrete Mathematics © Scott, Foresman and Company

LESSON MASTER 8-1
QUESTIONS ON SPUR OBJECTIVES

■SKILLS   *Objective A (See pages 534–536 for objectives.)*
In 1 and 2, rewrite the complex number as an ordered pair.

1. $3 + 5i$ _____

2. $-i - 2$ _____

In 3 and 4, rewrite the complex number in $a + bi$ form.

3. $(-5, 0)$ _____

4. $\left(\frac{1}{4}, -1\right)$ _____

5. If the real part and the imaginary part of a
complex number are 7 and 15, respectively,
write the number in $a + bi$ form.   _____

■SKILLS   *Objective B*
In 6–10, perform the indicated operation. Write the result in $a + bi$ form.

6. $\sqrt{-4} \cdot \sqrt{-81}$ _____

7. $\frac{6 - 2\sqrt{9}}{3}$ _____

8. $(12 - 3i) - i(5 + 7i)$

9. $\frac{5i}{1 - i} + 3 - 4i$

10. $(5 - 8i)(2 + 7i)$ _____

In 11 and 12, express the solutions in $a + bi$ form.

11. $z^2 = -45$

12. $-3 + 2i + w = 8 - 9i$

_____   _____

■PROPERTIES   *Objective F*
13. Let $z = 6 - 2i$. Verify that $z \cdot \bar{z}$ is a real number.

14. Let $z = a + bi$. Prove that $\bar{\bar{z}} = z$.

15. Prove that for all complex numbers u, v, and w, $(u + w)v = uv + wv$.

■**USES**   *Objective H*

16. If the voltage in an AC circuit is 120V and the current is $6 + 3i$ amps, find the impedance.

_____

17. Two AC circuits with impedances of $9 + 16i$ ohms and $-6 + 8i$ ohms are connected in series.

a. Find the total impedance.

_____

b. If the total voltage is 10 volts, find the current.

_____

■**REPRESENTATIONS**   *Objective I*

In 18 and 19, let $A = 0$, $B = -2i$, and $C = -4 + 2i$.

18. a. Graph A, B, and C on the same complex plane.

b. Find the area of $\triangle ABC$.

_____

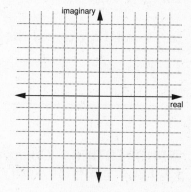

19. Let f be the function defined by $f(z) = (-2 + i)z$. Graph the points $f(A)$, $f(B)$, and $f(C)$ in the same complex plane.

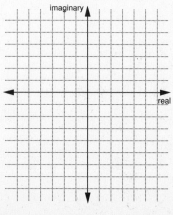

88

LESSON MASTER 8-2
QUESTIONS ON SPUR OBJECTIVES

■ **SKILLS** *Objective C (See pages 534–536 for objectives.)*
In 1 and 2, give one pair of polar coordinates for each (x, y) pair.

1. $(1, \sqrt{3})$ _____ 2. $(-5, -12)$ _____

3. If $P = \left[r, \frac{7\pi}{4}\right] = (5, y)$, $r =$ _____ and $y =$ _____.

4. Suppose $P = \left[10, \frac{\pi}{4}\right]$. Give another polar coordinate representation for P:

   a. with $r < 0$; _____

   b. with $r > 0$, $\theta < 0$. _____

In 5 and 6, find the rectangular coordinates for the point P whose polar coordinates are given.

5. $[5\sqrt{2}, 225°]$ _____ 6. $[-4, -\frac{\pi}{3}]$ _____

■ **REPRESENTATIONS** *Objective I*

7. Plot the following points on the polar grid at the right.

   a. $[1, 45°]$ b. $\left[-4, -\frac{\pi}{2}\right]$

   c. $\left[0, -\frac{3\pi}{2}\right]$ d. $\left[-3, -\frac{2\pi}{3}\right]$

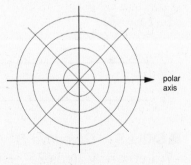

8. On the polar grid, sketch all solutions to the equation $r = 3$.

9. Give two polar representations of the point P graphed below.

   _____

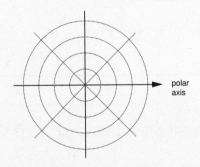

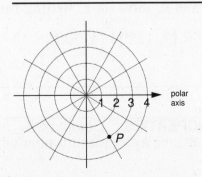

LESSON MASTER 8-3
QUESTIONS ON SPUR OBJECTIVES

■ **SKILLS** *Objective A (See pages 534–536 for objectives.)*
In 1–4, the complex number is written in either binomial, rectangular, polar, or trigonometric form. Write it in the other three forms.

1. 10

2. $\left[-3, \frac{3\pi}{2}\right]$

_____

_____

_____

3. $(7\sqrt{3}, -7)$

4. $4 [\cos (-120°) + i \sin (-120°)]$

_____

_____

_____

In 5 and 6, find the modulus and the argument θ $(0 \le \theta < 2\pi)$ of the complex number.

5. $15 - 4i$

6. $a - ai$ where $a > 0$

_____

_____

■ **SKILLS** *Objective B*
7. Let $z = \sqrt{3}(\cos 25° + i \sin 25°)$ and $w = \sqrt{2}(\cos 60° + i \sin 60°)$.

a. Find z^2.

b. Find $z \cdot w$.

_____

_____

In 8 and 9, solve for z, writing the answer in polar form.

8. $z = [3, 115°] \cdot [4, 290°]$

9. $[8, 50°] \cdot z = [6, 172°]$

_____

_____

■ **PROPERTIES** *Objective F*
10. Let z be a complex number with argument θ. Show that $z \cdot [1, -2\theta] = \bar{z}$.

     Precalculus and Discrete Mathematics © Scott, Foresman and Company

11. What does multiplying a complex number by a real number do to its polar representation?

_____

_____

_____

■ **REPRESENTATIONS**   *Objective I*

12. Let $G = 0$, $H = -2 - 3i$, $I = 3 - i$, and $J = H + I$.

a. Sketch quadrilateral *GHJI* in the complex plane.

b. What kind of figure is *GHJI*?   _____

c. Prove your answer to part **b**.

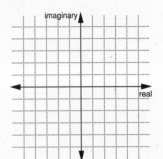

13. Illustrate the multiplication of $z = 2(\cos 75° + i \sin 75°)$ by $w = 4(\cos 45° + i \sin 45°)$ with a diagram showing the appropriate size transformation and rotation.

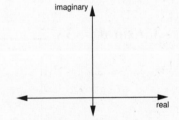

14. a. Graph $\triangle ABC$ in the complex plane where $A = 0$, $B = 3 - 4i$, and $C = -2 - i$.

b. Let A', B', and C' be the images of A, B, and C under the transformation $f: z \rightarrow (-1 + i)z$. Graph $\triangle A'B'C'$.

c. Find the ratio of similitude of $\triangle A'B'C'$ to $\triangle ABC$ and relate it to the Geometric Multiplication Theorem.

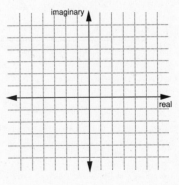

_____

_____

d. How does the argument of C' compare to that of C? Use the Geometric Multiplication Theorem.

_____

LESSON **MASTER 8–4**
QUESTIONS ON **SPUR** OBJECTIVES

■**REPRESENTATIONS**   *Objective J (See pages 534–536 for objectives.)*
In 1–6, sketch the graph of the polar equation and identify the type of
curve obtained.

1. $r = 5$ _____

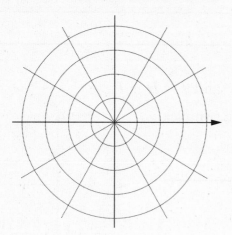

2. $\theta = 60°$ _____

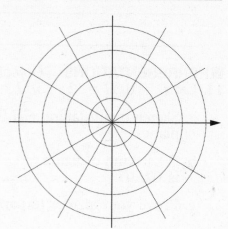

3. $r \sin \theta = -3$ _____

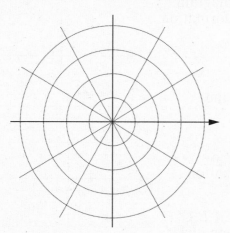

4. $r = 2 + 2 \cos \theta$ _____

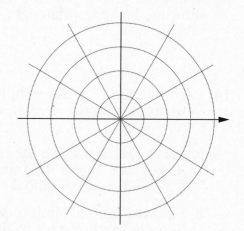

Precalculus and Discrete Mathematics © Scott, Foresman and Company

5. a. Sketch the rectangular graph of the equation $r = 1 + 3 \sin \theta$.

b. Use the rectangular graph in part **a** to sketch its polar graph.

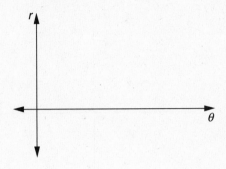

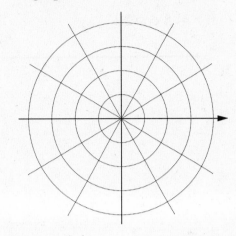

c. Identify the type of curve that results in part **b.** _____

6. a. Sketch the graph of $r = 5 \cos \theta$.

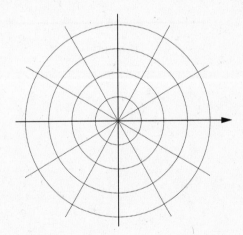

b. Prove that the graph is a circle and find its center.

LESSON MASTER 8-5
QUESTIONS ON SPUR OBJECTIVES

■**REPRESENTATIONS**   *Objective J (See pages 534–536 for objectives.)*
In 1–3, sketch the graph of the polar equation and identify the type of curve obtained.

1. $r = 5 \cos 2\theta$

_____

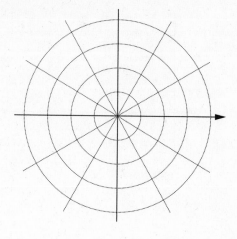

2. $r = \frac{3}{2}\theta + 2$

_____

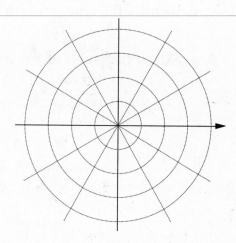

3. $r = 5^{\theta}$

_____

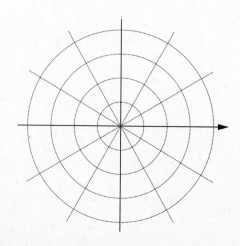

    Precalculus and Discrete Mathematics © Scott, Foresman and Company

4. a. Graph the three-leafed rose
curve $r = 6 \sin 3\theta$.

b. Does it have any reflection
symmetries? Prove that your
answer is correct.

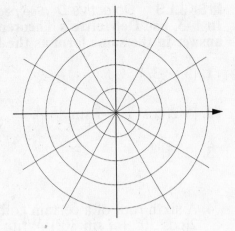

5. a. Write an equation for a five-leafed rose
with leaves of length 2.5 which is
reflection-symmetric over the polar axis. _____

b. Graph this curve.

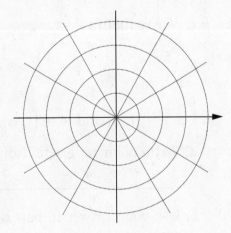

LESSON MASTER 8-6
QUESTIONS ON SPUR OBJECTIVES

■SKILLS   *Objective D (See pages 534–536 for objectives.)*
In 1–3, use DeMoivre's Theorem to compute the power. Write your answer in the same form as the base.

1. $(3 + 3i)^5$ _____

2. $\left[\sqrt{2}\left(\cos \frac{3\pi}{4} + i \sin \frac{3\pi}{4}\right)\right]^4$ _____

3. $\left[2, \frac{\pi}{2}\right]^{10}$ _____

4. A sixth root of a certain complex number z is $2(\cos 30° + i \sin 30°)$. Write z in $a + bi$ form.   _____

■PROPERTIES   *Objective F*
5. Let $z = [3, -12°]$.

   a. Write a polar representation of z^5.   _____

   b. Use your answer to part **a** to find a polar representation for $(z^5)^4$.   _____

   c. Verify that $(z^5)^4 = z^{20}$.

6. Let $z = [r, \theta]$ and $w = [s, \phi]$, and let n be a positive integer.

   a. Write polar representations for z^n, w^n, and $z \cdot w$.

   _____

   b. Use your answer to part **a** to prove that $z^n \cdot w^n = (z \cdot w)^n$.

   Precalculus and Discrete Mathematics © Scott, Foresman and Company

■**REPRESENTATIONS**   *Objective K*

7. a. Graph z^1, z^2, z^3, z^4, z^5, and z^6 when $z = \frac{3}{4}\left(\cos\frac{\pi}{3} + i\sin\frac{\pi}{3}\right)$.

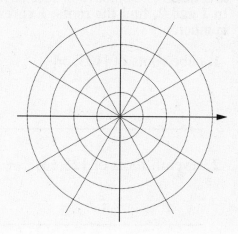

   b. Is the sequence of points getting closer to or farther from the origin?

   _____

8. Give the polar coordinates of the points w^1, w^2, w^3, w^4, and w^5 where the first four are graphed below.

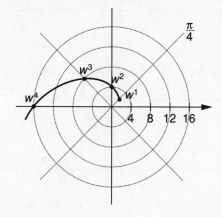

$w^1 = $ _____

$w^2 = $ _____

$w^3 = $ _____

$w^4 = $ _____

$w^5 = $ _____

NAME _____

QUESTIONS ON **SPUR** OBJECTIVES

■**SKILLS**   *Objective D (See pages 534–536 for objectives.)*
In 1 and 2, find the roots. Express them in the same form as the given number.

1. cube roots of $[125, \pi]$

_____

2. seventh roots of $128\left(\cos \frac{\pi}{3} + i \sin \frac{\pi}{3}\right)$

_____

_____

_____

3. The fifth power of some complex number z is 243. Find all possible values of z.

_____

In 4–6, solve the equation over the set of complex numbers. Express the solutions in $a + bi$ form.

4. $x^6 = -1$ **5.** $z^8 = 16$

_____   _____

6. $(z - 1)^8 = 16$ (Hint: Use your answer to Question 5.)

_____

98   *Continued*   *Precalculus and Discrete Mathematics © Scott, Foresman and Company*

7. A sixth root of a certain complex number is $\sqrt{2}(\cos 108° + i \sin 108°)$. Find the complex number and its other sixth roots.

_____

_____

_____

_____

■**REPRESENTATIONS**   *Objective K*

8. Graph the sixth roots of -1 on a complex plane. (Refer to Question 4.)

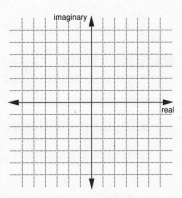

9. a. The seventh roots of $128\left(\cos \frac{\pi}{3} + i \sin \frac{\pi}{3}\right)$ form the vertices of what figure? (Refer to Question 2.)   _____

b. Graph the figure.

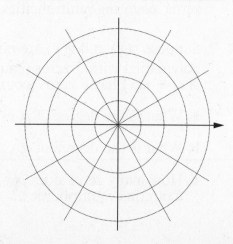

NAME _____

LESSON MASTER 8-8
QUESTIONS ON SPUR OBJECTIVES

■**SKILLS** *Objective E (See pages 534–536 for objectives.)*
In 1–3, find all zeros and their multiplicities for the given polynomial.

1. $f(x) = 2x^5 + x^4 - 3x^3$

2. $g(x) = (x - 1)^4 (x + 3)^2 (x^2 + 1)^5$

_____   _____

_____   _____

3. $p(r) = r^3 + 3r^2 - 9r + 5$ given that 1 is a zero of $p(r)$

_____

4. Give a polynomial of degree 3 that has the zeros 3, i, and $-i$.

_____

■**PROPERTIES** *Objective G*
5. A polynomial $g(x)$ has the following zeros: 2, 1, i, $-i$, and $\frac{1}{2}$. The 1 has multiplicity 3, and the other zeros have multiplicity 1.

a. What is the degree of $g(x)$?   _____

b. Write a possible formula for $g(x)$ in factored form.

_____

6. According to the Fundamental Theorem of Algebra,

$p(x) = 6x^{12} - x^4 + 10x^3 + 5$ has exactly _____ complex zeros, counting multiplicities.

7. Suppose $p(x)$ and $g(x)$ are polynomials such that $\frac{p(x)}{q(x)}$ is a polynomial with 5 zeros (counting multiplicities), and $p(x) + q(x)$ has 7 zeros (counting multiplicities).

a. What is the degree of $p(x)$?   _____

b. What is the degree of $q(x)$?   _____

c. How many zeros does $p(x)q(x)$ have (counting multiplicities)?   _____

Precalculus and Discrete Mathematics © Scott, Foresman and Company

LESSON **MASTER 8-9**
QUESTIONS ON **SPUR** OBJECTIVES

■**SKILLS** *Objective E (See pages 534–536 for objectives.)*

1. a. Find the zeros and corresponding multiplicities of
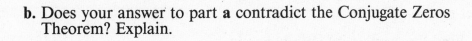
$p(x) = (2x^2 + ix - 5)^2$.

_____

b. Does your answer to part **a** contradict the Conjugate Zeros Theorem? Explain.

_____

_____

2. If $-i$ is a zero of $p(x) = x^4 - 5x^3 + 5x^2 - 5x + 4$, find the remaining zeros.   _____

3. Two of the zeros of the polynomial
$f(t) = t^4 - 4t^3 + 9t^2 - 16t + 20$ are $2 - i$ and $2i$. Find the remaining zeros of $f(t)$.   _____

■**PROPERTIES** *Objective G*

4. Does there exist a polynomial $p(x)$ with real coefficients which has exactly five zeros: $2i$, $-2i$, $3 + i$, $3 - i$, and $11i$? Justify your answer.

_____

5. What is the smallest possible degree of a polynomial $p(x)$ with real coefficients if $1 + 2i$, $7 - 5i$, and 2 are zeros of $p(x)$?   _____

6. Use the Conjugate Zeros Theorem to prove: Every polynomial of odd degree with real coefficients has at least one real zero.

7. Find a polynomial of smallest degree with real coefficients that has zeros $2 - 3i$ and 0.

_____

8. Suppose $p(x)$ is a polynomial with real coefficients such that $p(x) = (x + 2 + i)q(x)$ where $q(x)$ is a polynomial. Give a factor of $q(x)$.   _____

LESSON MASTER 9–1
QUESTIONS ON SPUR OBJECTIVES

■ **SKILLS** *Objective A (See pages 581–584 for objectives.)*

1. Find the average rate of change in
   $f(x) = 2x^3 + 5x - 4$ from $x = -2$ to $x = 5$.   _____

2. Find the average rate of change in
   $h(x) = x^2 + 25$ over the interval $-3 \le x \le 3$.   _____

3. Let $g(x) = \frac{1}{2}t^2 + 6t$.

   a. Find the average rate of change in g
   from t to $t + \Delta t$.   _____

   b. Use your answer to part **a** to find the
   average rate of change in g from 0 to 2.   _____

■ **USES** *Objective D*

4. A ball is thrown upward from a height of 4.5 feet with an initial
   velocity of 21 feet per second. If only the effect of gravity is
   considered, then its height (in feet) after t seconds is given by the
   equation $u(t) = -16t^2 + 21t + 4.5$.

   a. Find a formula for the average
   velocity from $t = \frac{1}{2}$ to $t = \frac{1}{2} + \Delta t$.   _____

   b. Use the formula from part **a** to find the average velocity from
   $t = \frac{1}{2}$ to $t = 4\frac{1}{2}$. Include appropriate units with your answer.

   _____

■ **REPRESENTATIONS** *Objective G*

5. Refer to the graph of f at the right.

   a. Find the average rate of change
   in f from A to C.

   _____

   b. Over what interval is the average
   rate of change in f zero?

   _____

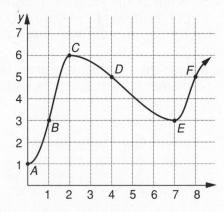

   c. Over what interval is the average rate of change $\frac{2}{3}$?   _____

   d. Find the average rate of change in f over the
   interval $0 \le x \le 8$.   _____

6. Suppose P and Q are points on the graph of
   the function g, with $P = (-4, b)$ and $Q =$
   $(6, 1)$. If the average rate of change in g from
   $x = -4$ to $x = 6$ is -2, find b.   _____

Precalculus and Discrete Mathematics © Scott, Foresman and Company

LESSON **MASTER** 9-2
QUESTIONS ON **SPUR** OBJECTIVES

■**SKILLS** *Objective B (See pages 581–584 for objectives.)*
In 1–3, find the derivative of the function at the given point.

1. $f(x) = 2x^2 - x + 5$; $(0, 5)$ _____

2. $g(x) = 20x + 17$; $(.6, 29)$ _____

3. $h(y) = -15$; $(18, -15)$ _____

4. Let $f(x) = -x^3 + 3x$. Use the definition of derivative to compute $f'(1)$ and $f'\left(\frac{3}{2}\right)$.

_____

■**USES** *Objective D*
5. Suppose that the profit (in cents per pound) a grocer makes in a day from selling hamburger at a price of s cents per pound is given by $P(s) = -s^2 + 320s - 5000$.

a. Find the derivative when $s = 120$. _____

b. What does your answer to part **a** mean?

_____

_____

_____

■**USES** *Objective E*
6. Suppose the distance in meters that a car has travelled at time t (in seconds) is given by $s(t) = 4t^2 + 3t$. Find its instantaneous velocity at time $t = \frac{1}{4}$. _____

7. A ball is dropped from the roof of a house 25 feet high. The height (in feet) of the ball above the ground at time t seconds is given by $h(t) = -16t^2 + 25$.

a. What is the instantaneous velocity of the ball at time $t = .5$ seconds? _____

b. At what time t does the ball hit the ground? _____

c. What is the instantaneous velocity of the ball at the moment it hits the ground? _____

■ **REPRESENTATIONS**   *Objective H*

8. Refer to the graph of f at the right. Estimate $f'(x)$ for each value of x given below.

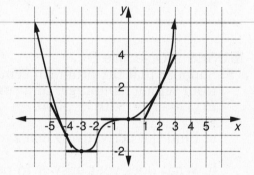

a. $x = 0$ _____

b. $x = 2$ _____

c. $x = -3$ _____

d. $x = -4$ _____

LESSON MASTER 9-3
QUESTIONS ON SPUR OBJECTIVES

■**SKILLS**   *Objective B (See pages 581–584 for objectives.)*
In 1–4, find the derivative of the function whose formula is given.

1. $f(x) = -6x$

2. $p(x) = 2x^2 - 6$

_____

_____

3. $q(x) = \frac{1}{2}x^2 - 4x + 650$

4. $g(x) = 620$

_____

_____

■**USES**   *Objective D*

5. If $500 is invested at an interest rate of 6% compounded continuously, the amount in the account after t years is $A(t) = 500e^{.06t}$ dollars. The derivative of A is $A'(t) = 30e^{.06t}$.

   a. Find the amount in the account after 10 years. _____

   b. Find $A'(10)$. _____

   c. What does the answer to part **b** mean?

_____

_____

6. A piece of metal expands by heat so that the surface area at time t (in minutes) is $A(t) = \frac{\pi}{10}t^2 + \frac{1}{6}t + 3$.

   a. Find the surface area at $t = 10$ minutes. _____

   b. Find the derivative of $A(t)$. _____

   c. Find the instantaneous rate of change of the surface area when $t = 10$ minutes. _____

   d. Calculate $A'(2)$. _____

   e. What is the initial rate of change of the surface area (that is, at $t = 0$)? _____

■**USES** *Objective E*

7. A particle moves so that the distance *s* traveled in meters at time *t* seconds is given by $s(t) = t^2 + 3t - 2$.

a. Find the average velocity between 2 and 3 seconds.
_____

b. What is the instantaneous velocity of the particle at time $t = 6$?
_____

c. What is the initial velocity of the particle?
_____

■**REPRESENTATIONS** *Objective H*

8. The function *g* is graphed at the right.

a. Estimate the values of $g'(x)$ when $x = -5, -4, -2, 0,$ and 2.

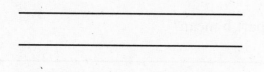

_____

_____

_____

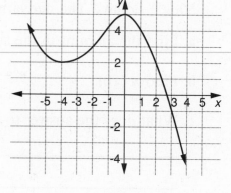

b. Use this information and the graph of *g* to sketch a graph of g'.

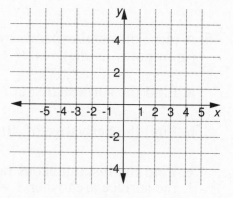

Precalculus and Discrete Mathematics © Scott, Foresman and Company

LESSON MASTER 9-4
QUESTIONS ON SPUR OBJECTIVES

■ **USES** *Objective D (See pages 581–584 for objectives.)*
1. A pot of water is being heated on a stove. The temperature (in degrees Fahrenheit) of the water after t minutes is given by $F(t) = 212 - 140e^{-.5t}$. For this function, $F'(t) = 70e^{-.5t}$ and $F''(t) = -35e^{-.5t}$.

   a. What units should be used to measure $F''(t)$? _____

   b. What units should be used to measure $F''(t)$? _____

   c. How fast is the temperature changing at time $t = 2$ minutes? _____

   d. How fast is the rate of heating changing at time $t = 2$ minutes? _____

   e. How fast is the temperature changing at time $t = 3$ minutes? _____

■ **USES** *Objective E*
2. A kite which is 125 feet high is rising vertically. The height of the kite after t minutes is given by $h(t) = 2t^2 + 6t + 125$.

   a. How fast is the string being played out when $t = 2$ minutes?

   _____

   b. What is the vertical acceleration of the kite at $t = 10$ minutes?

   _____

   c. Is the velocity of the kite changing at a constant rate? _____

3. A ball thrown directly upward with a speed of 96 ft/sec moves according to the equation $h(t) = 96t - 16t^2$, where h is the height of the ball in feet and t is the time in seconds after the ball is thrown.

   a. Find the velocity of the ball 2 seconds after it is thrown. _____

   b. For how many seconds does the ball rise? _____

   c. What is the highest height reached by the ball? _____

   d. Find its acceleration at time t. _____

4. If the position of a particle at time t is given by $s(t) = (2t + 3)^2$, find its velocity and acceleration at time $t = 0$. _____

LESSON **MASTER   9-5**
QUESTIONS ON **SPUR** OBJECTIVES

■**PROPERTIES**   *Objective C (See pages 581–584 for objectives.)*
1. Suppose f is a function such that $f(x) = \frac{1}{3}x^3 - \frac{1}{2}x^2 - 2x$. Then $f'(x) = x^2 - x - 2$. Use the first derivative to find

   a. the interval(s) on which f is increasing, _____

   b. the interval(s) on which f is decreasing, _____

   c. the points at which f may have a
   relative maximum or minimum.   _____

2. Suppose $f(x) = 2x^3 + x - 620$. Then $f'(x) = 6x^2 + 1$. Is f increasing on the set of all real numbers? Justify your answer.

   _____

■**USES**   *Objective F*
3. What rectangle with the largest area can be formed using 80 ft of fencing?

   _____

■**REPRESENTATIONS**   *Objective I*
4. The derivative g' of a function g is graphed at the right.

   a. Where is g increasing? decreasing?

   _____

   _____

   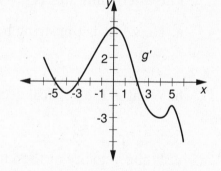

   b. Where may g have a relative
   maximum or minimum?   _____

5. Consider the function f graphed at right.

   a. On what interval(s) is $f'(x)$ positive?

   _____

   b. On what interval(s) is $f'(x)$ negative?

   _____

   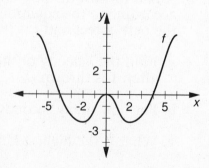

   c. For what value(s) of x is $f'(x) = 0$?   _____

   d. Is $f''(x)$ greater than or less than 0 on the
   interval $-4 < x < -2$?   _____

108

LESSON **MASTER 10–1**
QUESTIONS ON **SPUR** OBJECTIVES

■**SKILLS**   *Objective A (See pages 636–638 for objectives.)*
In 1–5, describe the essential features of the problem.

1. The coach of a volleyball team chooses six starting players from a group of nine people. How many different starting teams are possible?

_____

2. A department store offers a free monogramming service for customers who purchase a set of bath towels. If the monogram consists of three letters, how many different monograms are possible?

_____

3. The winner of a contest held by a record store is allowed to pick a total of 10 free albums from any of five different musical categories: reggae, classical, country, jazz, and rock. How many different selections are possible?

_____

4. Five married couples attend an opera performance together. If they wish to be seated in a row of 10 seats so that each person is sitting next to his or her spouse, how many different seating arrangements are possible?

_____

5. How many numbers between 100 and 999 have at least one digit that is a seven?

_____

6. Ten Olympic swimmers compete for gold (1st place), silver (2nd place), and bronze (3rd place) medals in a 400-meter freestyle event. In how many different ways can the three medals be awarded?

_____

LESSON MASTER 10-2
QUESTIONS ON SPUR OBJECTIVES

■USES   *Objective F (See pages 636–638 for objectives.)*

1. At a pharmacy, toothbrushes are available in
c different colors, three different firmnesses
(hard, medium, and soft), and two different
sizes (adult and youth). How many different
kinds of toothbrushes are available?   _____

2. How many numbers between 1,000 and
9,999 inclusive have at least one digit that is
a seven?   _____

3. If Roger owns 12 shirts, 4 belts, and 10 pairs
of pants, how many more shirts must he buy
in order to have at least 600 different outfits?   _____

4. How many 6-letter codewords can be made from the letters F, G, H,
I, J, K, and L:

   a. if the letters can be repeated?   _____

   b. if the letters cannot be repeated?   _____

5. A mother, a father, and their seven children
plan to have a family portrait taken. If one
parent is to stand at each end of the row, in
how many ways can the family members be
arranged?   _____

6. a. How many 3-digit numbers contain at least one six?   _____

   b. What is the probability of choosing one of
the numbers in part a which has exactly
two sixes?   _____

7. How many lines of output are produced by the following computer
program?

```
10   FOR I = 0 TO 7
20     FOR J = 1 TO 3
30       FOR K = 2 TO 6
40         PRINT I * J * K
50       NEXT K
60     NEXT J
70   NEXT I
```
_____

■REPRESENTATIONS   *Objective I*

8. Draw a possibility tree to count the number
of different 3-letter codewords that can be
made from the letters A, B, and C if only the
C may be repeated.   _____

9. Jack, Patrice, Lydia, and Miguel are the finalists in a statewide
science fair. First and second prizes will be awarded.

   a. Draw a possibility tree to determine all possible distributions of
   the awards.

   b. In how many of these distributions does
   Patrice receive 2nd prize?   _____

NAME _____

■**SKILLS**   *Objective B (See pages 636–638 for objectives.)*
In 1 and 2, evaluate the expressions.

1. $P(18, 4)$ _____   2. $P(12, 3)$ _____

3. $P(7, 4) \cdot P(3, 1) = P(\text{_____} , \text{_____})$

4. Find n so that $P(13, n) = \frac{13!}{4!}$.   _____

■**PROPERTIES**   *Objective D*
5. Verify that $P(7, 6) = P(7, 7)$ and generalize your result.

6. If $(n - 4)! = (n - 4) \cdot x!$, what is x?   _____

■**USES**   *Objective F*
7. Each player of a certain board game must choose a different token to move around the board. If there are 8 tokens, in how many different ways can 5 players choose them?   _____

8. Nine high school swim teams are competing in a 400-meter freestyle event. The pool contains 10 lanes. If the two swimmers from Lincoln High must swim in adjacent lanes and one swimmer from each of the other schools fill the remaining eight lanes, how many different arrangements of the swimmers are possible?   _____

Precalculus and Discrete Mathematics © Scott, Foresman and Company

LESSON **MASTER** **10–4**
QUESTIONS ON **SPUR** OBJECTIVES

■**SKILLS** *Objective B (See pages 636–638 for objectives.)*
In 1 and 2, evaluate the expressions.

1. $C(12, 8)$ _____

2. $\binom{11}{6}$ _____

3. Find integers r and n such that $C(n, 2) = \frac{7!}{r! \cdot 2}$. _____

4. $C(7, 2) \cdot 2! = P(\underline{\hspace{2cm}}, \underline{\hspace{2cm}})$

■**PROPERTIES** *Objective D*

5. Show that $\binom{10}{4} = \binom{10}{6}$.

6. Prove that $\forall$ positive integers n, $C(n, n) = 1$.

■**USES** *Objective G*

7. Suppose there are seven points in a plane, with no three points collinear. How many distinct triangles can be formed which have these points as vertices? _____

8. In a standard deck of 52 playing cards, how many different 4-card hands contain exactly one card from each of the four suits? _____

9. A choir director is to assemble a choir consisting of 4 girls and 5 boys. If 9 girls and 12 boys audition, how many different choirs are possible? _____

10. **a.** A questionnaire for a psychology experiment consists of 10 questions. Each one asks the subject to pick two words out of a group of five which he or she feels are most closely related. How many different responses are possible? _____

   b. A second version of the questionnaire contains 15 questions, each with four words. Which version has a greater number of possible responses?

   _____

LESSON **MASTER** **10–5**
QUESTIONS ON **SPUR** OBJECTIVES

■SKILLS *Objective C (See pages 636–638 for objectives.)*
In 1–3, expand using the Binomial Theorem.

1. $(y + z)^6$

_____

2. $(3a - 2b)^5$

_____

3. $(x + 2)^4$

_____

4. What is the coefficient of the x^3y^4 term in the
expansion of $(2x - 4y)^7$? _____

5. Find the tenth term of $(x - 3y)^{12}$. _____

6. a. What combination is the coefficient of the
$x^{12}y^8$ term in the expansion of $(x + y)^{20}$? _____

b. What is this coefficient? _____

7. Express as the power of a binomial: $\sum_{k=0}^{9} \binom{9}{k} y^{9-k} 3^k$. _____

8. The coefficients of which terms in the expansion of $(x + y)^8$ are
equal?

_____

 Precalculus and Discrete Mathematics © Scott, Foresman and Company

LESSON MASTER 10-6
QUESTIONS ON SPUR OBJECTIVES

■ **PROPERTIES** *Objective E (See pages 636–638 for objectives.)*

1. The number of 4-element subsets that can be formed from a set with 7 elements is given by the combination _____.

2. How is $_7C_5 + {_7C_6} + {_7C_7}$ related to the number of subsets that can be formed from a set?

_____

_____

_____

■ **USES** *Objective G*

3. In how many ways is it possible to obtain at least five heads in 13 tosses of a coin? _____

4. An "all-you-can-eat" buffet table contains 10 meat dishes. How many different combinations of meat dishes are possible, assuming that each customer chooses at least one? _____

■ **USES** *Objective H*

5. If the "DON'T WALK" symbol on a pedestrian signal is lit for 40 seconds per minute, and the "WALK" symbol is lit for 20 seconds per minute, what is the probability that the signal will say "WALK" two out of six times that it is approached? _____

6. A soft drink manufacturer gives away prizes by printing the name of the prize on the inside of some of the cans. If 6% of the cans produced result in a prize, what is the probability that in a 24-can case,

a. exactly three cans result in a prize? _____

b. no more than one can results in a prize? _____

LESSON **MASTER** **10-7**
QUESTIONS ON **SPUR** OBJECTIVES

■**USES**   *Objective G (See pages 636–638 for objectives.)*

1. How many terms are there in the expansion of $(m + n + p)^{11}$?

_____

2. How many positive integers less than 10,000 have digits which add to 16?

_____

3. The spinner for a game consists of a circle with five sections, colored red, blue, yellow, purple, and green. If an outcome is defined as a certain number of occurrences of each color, how many different outcomes are possible in seven spins?

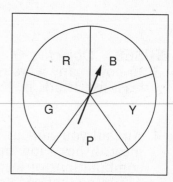

_____

4. a. How many integers from 1 to 999 have the property that the sum of their digits is 9?

_____

b. How many of these have exactly one five?

_____

LESSON MASTER 11-1
QUESTIONS ON SPUR OBJECTIVES

■ **USES**   *Objective E (See pages 694–698 for objectives.)*
In 1–4, suppose that a reporter conducts a poll of voters regarding a plan to construct a new sports stadium using city funds. Of those polled, 77% are people who vote regularly, while 23% vote only occasionally. Of the regular voters, 42% are in favor of the plan to construct the stadium. Among the occasional voters, 54% favor its construction.

1. Draw a probability tree to represent this situation.

2. If 1,500 voters respond, how many are
regular voters not in favor of the plan?   _____

3. Which category contains the largest percentage of respondents?

_____

4. What is the probability that a randomly
chosen voter who is not in favor of the plan
is a regular voter?   _____

5. Suppose the process of conducting an archaeological dig involves the following tasks:

Task	Description	Time Required (Days)	Prerequisite Tasks
A	choose a site	1	none
B	organize a team	3	none
C	travel to site	1	A, B
D	set up equipment	2	C
E	dig	8	D
F	keep journal of findings	9	D
G	write a report of findings	12	E, F

a. Sketch a directed graph to represent the situation.

b. What is the minimal time required to
conduct the entire dig?   _____

■ **USES** *Objective G*
In 6 and 7, the vertices of the graph at the
right represent traffic lights and the edges
represent streets.

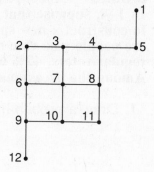

6. Draw a path that will allow a maintenance
   person to pass each light exactly once.

7. Suppose light 8 and the part of the street
   connecting it to light 7 are removed (so
   lights 4 and 11 are connected directly).
   Would a path satisfying Question 6 still be
   possible?

_____

118

LESSON **MASTER** **11-2**
QUESTIONS ON **SPUR** OBJECTIVES

■**SKILLS** *Objective A (See pages 694–698 for objectives.)*
In 1–3, draw a graph with the specified characteristics.

1. two vertices and three edges

2. an isolated vertex, two loops, and three edges

3. two parallel edges, three vertices, and a loop

4. Draw the graph G defined as follows:

set of vertices: $\{v_1, v_2, v_3, v_4, v_5\}$; edge-endpoint function:
set of edges: $\{e_1, e_2, e_3, e_4\}$

edge	endpoints
e_1	$\{v_1\}$
e_2	$\{v_2, v_4\}$
e_3	$\{v_3, v_5\}$
e_4	$\{v_1, v_3\}$

■**PROPERTIES** *Objective B*

5. A graph consists of a finite set of _____, a finite set

of _____, and a _____ that maps

each _____ to a set of either one or two _____.

6. Use the graph at the right.

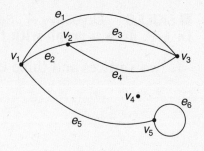

   a. Identify any isolated vertices.

   _____

   b. Identify all edges adjacent to e_3.

   _____

   c. Identify any loops.   _____

   d. Give the edge-endpoint function
      table for the graph.

_____

■**REPRESENTATIONS**   *Objective I*

7. Write the adjacency matrix for the
   directed graph below.

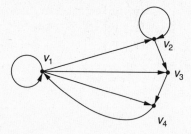

_____

8. What does the sum of the components of
the matrix for a directed graph represent? _____

9. Draw an undirected graph with the
following adjacency matrix.

$$
\begin{array}{c}
\;\; v_1 \;\; v_2 \;\; v_3 \\
\begin{array}{c} v_1 \\ v_2 \\ v_3 \end{array}
\left[\begin{array}{ccc}
0 & 0 & 1 \\
0 & 2 & 0 \\
1 & 0 & 2
\end{array}\right]
\end{array}
$$

LESSON MASTER 11-3
QUESTIONS ON **SPUR** OBJECTIVES

■**SKILLS**   *Objective A   (See pages 694–698 for objectives.)*
1. Draw a graph with four vertices of the following degrees: 1, 3, 3, and 5.

2. Draw a simple graph with three vertices of degrees 1, 2, and 1.

■**PROPERTIES**   *Objective B*
3. *Fill in the blank with the word* even *or* odd. Every graph has an

_____ number of vertices of _____ degree.

4. A graph has four edges. What is its total degree? _____

5. Refer to the graph below.

   a. Give the degree of each vertex. _____

   b. Give the total degree of the graph. _____

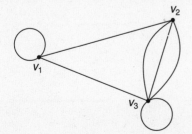

NAME _____

Lesson MASTER 11-3 (page 2)

■ **PROPERTIES** *Objective C*
In 6 and 7, either draw a graph with the given properties or explain why no such graph exists.

6. a graph with five vertices of degrees 1, 2, 2, 3, and 5

7. a graph with six vertices of degrees 1, 1, 2, 3, 4, and 5

■ **USES** *Objective F*
8. Thirty-three parents meet at a graduation ceremony. Is it possible for each parent to shake hands with exactly seven other parents? Explain.

_____

_____

_____

_____

9. The instructor of a Spanish class requests that each one of the 12 students in the class meet with three other students, one at a time, to practice speaking Spanish.

   a. Draw a graph
   to represent
   this situation.

   b. How many different pairings result? _____

122   *Precalculus and Discrete Mathematics* © Scott, Foresman and Company

LESSON MASTER 11-4
QUESTIONS ON **SPUR** OBJECTIVES

■**SKILLS** *Objective A (See pages 694–698 for objectives.)*
1. Draw a graph with 4 vertices, one loop, and 2 parallel edges, and which has an Euler circuit. Identify the circuit.

_____

_____

2. Consider the graph at the right below. Describe, if possible:

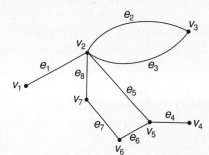

   a. a walk from v_1 to v_4,

   _____

   b. a path from v_4 to v_7,

   _____

   c. an Euler circuit starting at v_1,

   _____

   d. a walk from v_1 to v_4 that is not a path. _____

In 3–5, determine whether or not the graph is connected.

3. 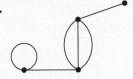   4.   5.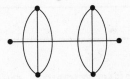

_____   _____   _____

6. Consider the graph at the right.

   a. Give each edge whose removal (by itself) would keep the graph connected.

   _____

   b. What is the maximum number of edges that can be removed simultaneously while keeping the graph connected?

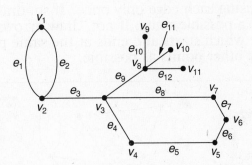

   _____

■**PROPERTIES**   *Objective D*

7. Consider the statement: *If every vertex of a graph has even degree, then the graph has an Euler circuit.*

a. Write the converse of the statement.

_____

_____

b. Which is true, the statement or its converse?   _____

c. What additional characteristic, if possessed by the graph, makes both statements true?   _____

In 8 and 9, determine whether or not the graph described has an Euler circuit. Justify your answer.

8.

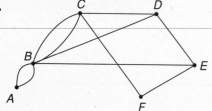

9. the graph with adjacency matrix

$$
\begin{array}{c}
 & \begin{array}{cccc} v_1 & v_2 & v_3 & v_4 \end{array} \\
\begin{array}{c} v_1 \\ v_2 \\ v_3 \\ v_4 \end{array} &
\begin{bmatrix}
2 & 0 & 0 & 4 \\
0 & 2 & 1 & 0 \\
0 & 1 & 2 & 0 \\
4 & 0 & 0 & 2
\end{bmatrix}
\end{array}
$$

_____   _____

_____   _____

■**REPRESENTATIONS**   *Objective G*

10. Suppose a pirate finds a treasure map like the one below. If the treasure is at one end of the points marked, is it possible for the pirate to search at every point, starting and ending at the same point and using each edge only once? If so, draw arrows on the map to show a possible route. If not, draw arrows on the map to show a route which starts and ends at the same point and passes through as many other points as possible.

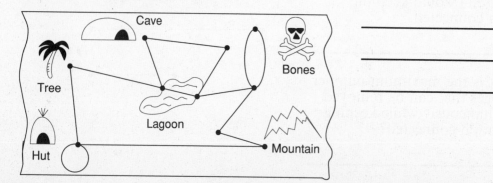

_____

_____

_____

LESSON MASTER 11-5
QUESTIONS ON **SPUR** OBJECTIVES

■**SKILLS**   *Objective A (See pages 694–698 for objectives.)*
1. Draw a simple graph with four vertices and three walks of length 2
   from v_1 to v_2.

■**PROPERTIES**   *Objective B*
2. Refer to the graph at the right.

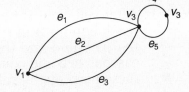

   a. How many walks of
   length 3 are there
   from v_1 to v_2?   _____

   b. List four of these walks.

   _____

   c. What is the length of the longest path from v_1 to v_2?   _____

■**REPRESENTATIONS**   *Objective J*

3. The adjacency matrix for an undirected graph is $\begin{bmatrix} 1 & 0 & 1 \\ 0 & 2 & 3 \\ 1 & 3 & 0 \end{bmatrix}$.

   a. How many walks of length 2 go from v_1 to v_3?   _____

   b. How many walks of length 2 start from v_2?   _____

4. **a.** Give the adjacency matrix for the
      directed graph at the right.

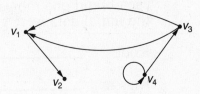

   _____

   b. How many walks of length 3 start at v_4?   _____

LESSON MASTER 11-6

QUESTIONS ON SPUR OBJECTIVES

■USES *Objective H (See pages 694–698 for objectives.)*

1. In a chemical experiment, molecules of a liquid are changing phase in a flask. It is known that from one minute to the next, 80% of the molecules remain liquid, while 20% become gaseous. At the same time, 40% of the gaseous molecules become liquid. The rest remain gaseous.

   a. Give T, the transition matrix.

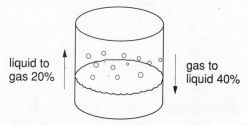

liquid to
gas 20%

gas to
liquid 40%

   _____

   b. After sufficient time, the substance will reach equilibrium so that the percent that is liquid and the percent that is gaseous become constant. Estimate these percents by calculating T^8.

   _____

   c. Find the exact percents by solving a system of equations.

   _____

2. At a particular time, it was found that 25% of adults drank Kool Cola, 20% drank Klassic Cola, and 55% preferred Fizzy Cola. The Kool Cola Company's surveys showed that people switched brands each month according to the directed graph below.

   a. Based on these data, what percent of the adults drank each brand one month after the initial data were gathered?

   Kool: _____

   Klassic: _____

   Fizzy: _____

   b. What percent would eventually drink each brand after a long period of time?

   Kool: _____ Klassic: _____ Fizzy: _____

.8

Kool

.1   .05

.15   .2

.3

Klassic   Fizzy

.6   .1   .7

Precalculus and Discrete Mathematics © Scott, Foresman and Company

LESSON MASTER 12–1
QUESTIONS ON SPUR OBJECTIVES

■ SKILLS *Objective A (See pages 756–758 for objectives.)*
In 1 and 2, find the magnitude and direction of the given vector.

1. (2, -3) _____   **2.** (-5, -12) _____

3. Find a polar representation of the vector (12, 16). _____

■ USES *Objective G*

4. A plane's velocity is represented by [550, 160°], where the magnitude is measured in miles per hour and the direction is in degrees counter-clockwise from due east.

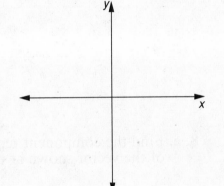

   a. Sketch the vector for the velocity.

   b. Give the vector in component form.

   _____

   c. Interpret the components.

   _____

   _____

5. A fish is caught at the end of a 15-meter fishline. Its angle with the horizontal is 37°. Assume the fishline is taut.

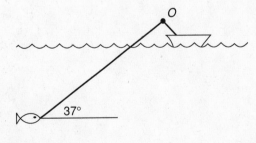

   a. Write a polar representation for the fish's position, using the end of the fishing rod (point *O*) as the origin.

   _____

   b. Compute a component representation. _____

   c. Interpret the components.

   _____

   _____

■REPRESENTATIONS   *Objective I*

6. Suppose $A = (1, -2)$ and $B = (x, y)$ are points
in a plane and $\vec{v}$ is the vector from A to B.
If $\vec{v} = \left[6, \frac{\pi}{3}\right]$, find the coordinates of B. _____

7. Find the component representation of
$[3, 210°]$ and sketch the vector.

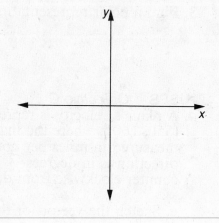

_____

8. a. Find the component representation
of the vector shown at the right.

_____

b. Sketch the vector in standard
position.

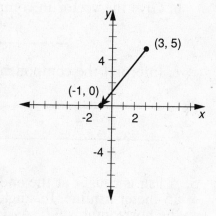

LESSON MASTER 12-2
QUESTIONS ON SPUR OBJECTIVES

■**SKILLS**   *Objective B (See pages 756–758 for objectives.)*
In 1–4, let $\vec{u} = (0, -5)$, $\vec{v} = (2, 3)$, and $\vec{w} = (-1, -6)$. Find the sum or difference.

1. $\vec{u} + \vec{v}$ _____

2. $-\vec{w}$ _____

3. $\vec{v} - \vec{w}$ _____

4. $\vec{v} - \vec{u} + \vec{w}$ _____

In 5 and 6, let $\vec{s} = [3, 15°]$ and $\vec{t} = [2, 160°]$. Compute and express the answer in its polar representation.

5. $\vec{s} + \vec{t}$ _____

6. $-\vec{s}$ _____

■**PROPERTIES**   *Objective E*

7. If $\vec{u} + \vec{v}$ is the zero vector, prove that $\vec{v}$ is the opposite of $\vec{u}$.

8. Show that $\vec{v} = (2 \cos 215°, 2 \sin 215°)$ is the opposite of $\vec{u} = (2 \cos 35°, 2 \sin 35°)$.

■ **USES** *Objective H*

9. Two people push a disabled car with the forces shown at the right.

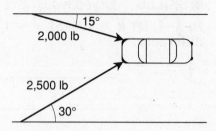

   2,000 lb 15°

   2,500 lb 30°

   a. Give the resultant force in polar form.

   _____

   b. Interpret your answer to part **a.**

   _____

   _____

   c. How much more forward force (to the right) is provided by the person exerting 2,500 lb of force than the person exerting 2,000 lb of force?

   _____

10. Relative to the water, a boat is moving with a speed of 20 mph in the direction 15° west of north. Due to the current which is moving in the direction 60° south of east, the boat is actually heading north relative to the land.

   a. Find the speed of the current.

   _____

   b. Find the speed of the boat moving north.

   _____

■ **REPRESENTATIONS** *Objective J*

11. The vectors $\vec{v}$ and $\vec{w}$ are shown at the right. Sketch the following.

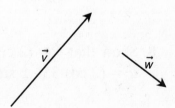

   a. $\vec{v} + \vec{w}$

   b. $-\vec{w}$

   c. $\vec{w} - \vec{v}$

LESSON MASTER 12-3
QUESTIONS ON **SPUR** OBJECTIVES

■**SKILLS** *Objective B (See pages 756–758 for objectives.)*
In 1–4, let $\vec{u} = (6, -2)$ and $\vec{v} = (-1, 5)$, and compute.

1. $\frac{1}{2}\vec{u}$ _____

2. $2\vec{v}$ _____

3. $\frac{1}{2}\vec{u} + 2\vec{v}$ _____

4. $2\vec{u} - 3\vec{v}$ _____

■**PROPERTIES** *Objective E*

5. Show that $\vec{v} = (3, 7)$ and $\vec{u} = (-18, -42)$ are parallel.

6. Show that the line passing through $(-1, 2)$ and $(3, 4)$ is parallel to the vector $\vec{v} = (-2, -1)$.

■**PROPERTIES** *Objective F*
In 7–10, determine whether or not $\vec{u}$ and $\vec{v}$ are parallel.

7. $\vec{u} = (2, -3)$, $\vec{v} = (4, 6)$ _____

8. $\vec{u} = \left(-1, -\frac{1}{2}\right)$, $\vec{v} = (10, 5)$ _____

9. $\vec{u} = (7, 3)$, $\vec{v} = (7, 3)$ _____

10. $\vec{u} = [3, 20°]$, $\vec{v} = [5, 200°]$ _____

■**REPRESENTATIONS** *Objective I*
11. Sketch $\vec{v} = (5, 1)$ and $-2\vec{v}$ on the same set of axes.

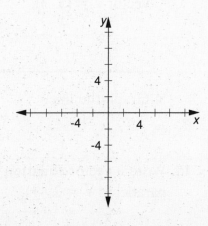

12. a. Give the endpoint of a vector $\vec{w}$ which
has polar representation [2, 150°] and
starts at the point (-1, 1).

_____

b. Give the endpoint of the vector $3\vec{w}$ if
it starts at (-1, 1).

_____

c. Sketch both vectors.

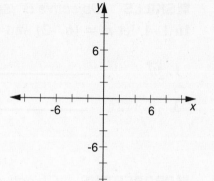

■ REPRESENTATIONS *Objective J*

13. Given the vectors $\vec{u}$ and $\vec{v}$ shown at the
right. Sketch the following.

a. $2\vec{u}$

b. $-3\vec{v}$ **c.** $2\vec{u} - 3\vec{v}$

■ REPRESENTATIONS *Objective L*

14. a. Find parametric equations of the line
through (-3, 5) that is parallel to the
vector $\vec{v} = (3, 3)$.

_____

b. Graph the line.

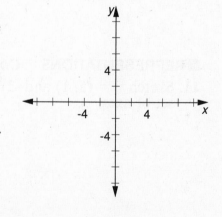

15. Write a vector equation for the line through $P = (-5, 2)$ that is
parallel to $\vec{v} = 2, -1$).

_____

LESSON **MASTER** **12-4**
QUESTIONS ON **SPUR** OBJECTIVES

■**SKILLS**   *Objective B (See pages 756–758 for objectives.)*
In 1–3, let $\vec{u} = (5, 10)$, $\vec{v} = (-1, 3)$, and $\vec{w} = (4, 7)$, and compute.

1. $\vec{u} \cdot \vec{v}$ _____   2. $(\vec{u} \cdot \vec{v})\vec{w}$ _____

3. $(\vec{u} + \vec{v}) \cdot (\vec{v} - \vec{w})$ _____

■**SKILLS**   *Objective D*
In 4–6, find the measure of the angle between the two vectors.

4. $(-1, 1)$ and $(4, 2)$ _____   5. $(0, 8)$ and $(-4, 0)$ _____

6. $[18, 63°]$ and $[42, 172°]$ _____

■**PROPERTIES**   *Objective E*
7. Show that $\vec{v} = (20, 18)$ and $\vec{u} = (-6, 10)$ are not orthogonal.

8. If $\vec{u}$ and $\vec{v}$ are vectors in a plane, prove that $(\vec{u} + \vec{v}) \cdot (\vec{u} - \vec{v}) = \vec{u} \cdot \vec{u} - \vec{v} \cdot \vec{v}$.

■ **PROPERTIES**   *Objective F*

In 9–11, determine whether $\vec{u}$ and $\vec{v}$ are perpendicular, parallel, or neither.

9. $\vec{u} = (-2, 1)$, $\vec{v} = (10, -5)$ _____

10. $\vec{u} = (3, -4)$, $\vec{v} = (6, 2)$ _____

11. $\vec{u} = (7, -3)$, $\vec{v} = (-6, -14)$ _____

■ **REPRESENTATIONS**   *Objective L*

In 12 and 13, let $\vec{v} = (4, -4)$. Write a vector equation for the line through $P = (-1, 8)$ that is

12. parallel to $\vec{v}$.

13. perpendicular to $\vec{v}$.   _____

Precalculus and Discrete Mathematics © Scott, Foresman and Company

LESSON MASTER 12–5
QUESTIONS ON SPUR OBJECTIVES

■ **REPRESENTATIONS** *Objective M (See pages 756–758 for objectives.)*

1. Give an equation that describes the *xy*-plane. _____

2. Write an equation for the sphere with radius 6 and center (6, 0, -1).

   _____

3. Let *M* be the plane parallel to the *xz*-plane
   that is 2 units in the positive direction from
   the *xz*-plane. Give a system of two linear
   equations that describes the intersection of
   M and the *yz*-plane. _____

4. Find the center and radius of the sphere with equation
   $x^2 + y^2 + z^2 - 4x + 6z = 12$.

   _____

5. **a.** Sketch *A*(2, 8, 0) and *B*(0, 1, 2,) in
      three-dimensional space.

   b. Write an equation for the sphere
      with center *A* and radius $\overline{AB}$.

   _____

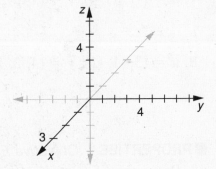

6. Write a system of two linear equations that
   describes the line parallel to the *x*-axis
   passing through the point (9, -4, 7). _____

NAME _____

■**SKILLS**   *Objective C (See pages 756–758 for objectives.)*
In 1–5, let $\vec{u} = (-1, 2, 5)$ and $\vec{v} = (3, -4, -6)$, and compute.

1. $\vec{u} + \vec{v}$ _____   2. $7\vec{u} - 2\vec{v}$ _____

3. $|\vec{v}|$ _____   4. $\vec{u} \cdot \vec{v}$ _____

5. Find a vector orthogonal to both $\vec{u}$ and $\vec{v}$. _____

■**SKILLS**   *Objective D*
In 6–8, find the measure of the angle between the two vectors.

6. $\vec{u} = (2, 0, 3)$, $\vec{v} = (9, -5, -6)$ _____

7. $\vec{u} = (-7, 1, -4)$, $\vec{v} = (14, -2, 8)$ _____

8. $\vec{u} = (3, -1, -1)$, $\vec{v} = (4, 2, 5)$ _____

■**PROPERTIES**   *Objective E*
9. Prove that if $\vec{u}$, $\vec{v}$, and $\vec{w}$ are vectors in three-dimensional space, then
$\vec{u} \cdot (\vec{v} + \vec{w}) = \vec{u} \cdot \vec{v} + \vec{u} \cdot \vec{w}$.

Precalculus and Discrete Mathematics © Scott, Foresman and Company

■ **PROPERTIES** *Objective F*
In 10 and 11, determine whether $\vec{u}$ and $\vec{v}$ are perpendicular, parallel, or neither.

10. $\vec{u} = (4, 1, 2)$ and $\vec{v} = (-1, 2, 1)$ _____

11. $\vec{u} = (-1, 3, -5)$ and $\vec{v} = (2, -6, 10)$ _____

12. Let $\vec{v} = (x, 4, 3)$ and $\vec{u} = (x - 4, 4, -4)$. If
$\vec{u}$ and $\vec{v}$ are orthogonal, find x. _____

■ **REPRESENTATIONS** *Objective K*
In 13 and 14, let $\vec{u} = (-1, 5, 3)$ and $\vec{v} = (2, 7, 0)$.

13. Sketch the vectors $\vec{u}$ and $\vec{v}$.

14. Find $\vec{u} - \vec{v}$ and sketch the vector
$\vec{u} - \vec{v}$ in standard position on the
same graph as vectors $\vec{u}$ and $\vec{v}$.

_____

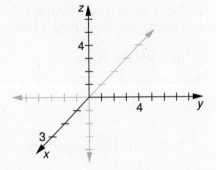

LESSON MASTER 12-7
QUESTIONS ON **SPUR** OBJECTIVES

■**REPRESENTATIONS**   *Objective M* *(See pages 756–758 for objectives.)*

1. **a.** Find the intercepts of the plane
defined by the equation
$x + 4y + 2z = 8$.

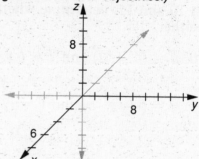

_____

b. Sketch the plane.

2. Find a vector equation for the line through (2, -1, 3) that is
perpendicular to the plane given by $x - 4y + 2z = 8$.

_____

3. Let l be a line passing through the two points (7, 12, -8) and
(-4, 6, -9). Describe l with

a. a vector equation.   _____

b. parametric equations.   _____

4. Find a vector perpendicular to the plane
defined by the equation $2x + 5y - 3z = 30$.   _____

5. Find parametric equations for the line in
3-space through the point (6, -3, 5) that is
parallel to the vector (-4, 12, -7).   _____

6. Find an equation for the plane that is perpendicular to $\vec{u} =$
(-3, -2, 14) and that contains the point (7, 0, -1).

_____

7. Let N be the plane defined by the
equation $4x - 3y - 6z = 12$.

  a. Sketch N.

  b. Show that $(3, 2, -1)$ is a point on
the plane.

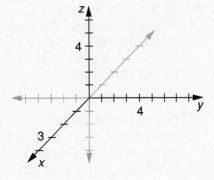

  c. Show that the vector $\vec{u} = (-2, 1.5, 3)$ is perpendicular to N.

  d. Find an equation for the plane K that is parallel to N and passes
through the point $(2, 3, -1)$.

_____

LESSON **MASTER** **13–1**
QUESTIONS ON **SPUR** OBJECTIVES

■**USES** *Objective D (See pages 810–813 for objectives.)*

1. What is the total distance traveled by a car which travels at a rate of 65 mph for 1.5 hours, 15 mph for 30 minutes, and 40 mph for 45 minutes?

_____

2. Use summation notation to express the total distance traveled by an object whose rate-time graph is given at the right.

_____

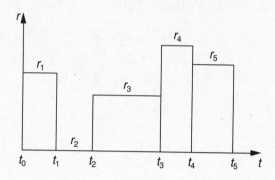

3. Suppose a space probe travels on a straight line with an initial speed of 100 m/sec and a constant acceleration of 9.8 m/sec^2. Then its velocity at time t seconds is given by $100 + 9.8t$. Find the distance it will have traveled in 10 seconds.

_____

■**USES** *Objective F*

In 4 and 5, each rate-time graph depicts a runner competing in a track event. From the graph, estimate the distance of the race.

4. _____

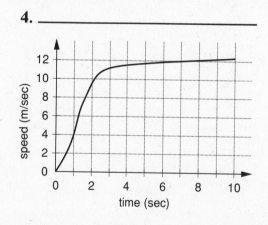

5. _____

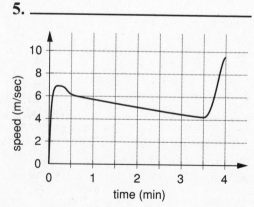

LESSON MASTER 13-2
QUESTIONS ON SPUR OBJECTIVES

■ **SKILLS** *Objective A (See pages 810–813 for objectives.)*
1. For the function $f(x) = 3x^3 - 1$, calculate the Riemann sum over the interval $0 \le x \le 2$ for $\Delta x = .25$ when

   a. z_i = the left endpoint of the ith subinterval. _____

   b. z_i = the right endpoint of the ith subinterval. _____

2. **a.** For the function $g(x) = 2 \sin x$, evaluate

   the Riemann sum $\displaystyle\sum_{i=1}^{n} g(z_i)\Delta x$ over the _____

   interval from 0 to $\frac{\pi}{2}$ with $n = 4, 8$, and 16. _____
   Let z_i be the right endpoint of the ith
   subinterval. _____

   b. Which value of n provides an answer that is nearest the area under the graph of g? Why?

   _____

   _____

   c. To what value might you expect the Reimann
   sum to converge as n grows larger and larger? _____

3. Use a computer or programmable calculator to evaluate the Reimann sum for the function $g(x) = x^2(\sin x - 2 \cos x)$ over the interval from 0 to $\frac{\pi}{2}$ with $n = 10, 50, 100$, and 500. Choose z_i to be the right endpoint of the ith subinterval.

   _____

■ **USES** *Objective D*

4. The graph below indicates the velocity of a train during a 1 hour interval.

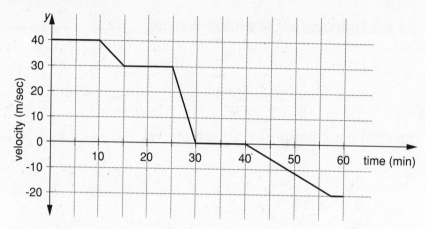

a. How far did the train travel in the first half hour? _____

b. At the end of the hour, what is the train's distance from its position at the beginning of the interval? _____

5. A cyclist accelerates from 36 ft/sec to 60 ft/sec during the last 5 seconds of the race. The cyclist's velocity t seconds after beginning to accelerate is given by $v(t) = .96t^2 + 36$. Estimate the distance the cyclist travels during these 5 seconds using a Riemann sum where $n = 5$ and

a. z_i = the right endpoint of the ith subinterval. _____

b. z_i = the left endpoint of the ith subinterval. _____

c. Which of the above answers is closer to the exact distance? Why? (Hint: Sketch the velocity-time graph.)

_____

_____

Precalculus and Discrete Mathematics © Scott, Foresman and Company

LESSON MASTER 13-3
QUESTIONS ON SPUR OBJECTIVES

■SKILLS *Objective B (See pages 810–813 for objectives.)*
In 1–4, find the exact value of the definite integral.

1. $\int_2^5 4\,dx$ _____

2. $\int_{-1}^3 x\,dx$ _____

3. $\int_0^5 \sqrt{25 - x^2}\,dx$ _____

4. $\int_0^2 (2x + 2)\,dx$ _____

5. Estimate the value of $\int_3^5 \sqrt{25 - x^2}\,dx$
   to the nearest hundredth.   _____

■REPRESENTATIONS *Objective G*
In 6–9, express the shaded area using integral notation.

6.
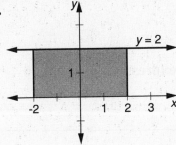

7.
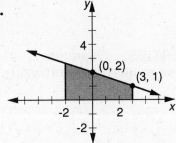

_____   _____

8.
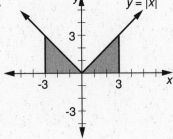

9.
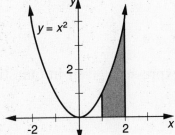

_____   _____

LESSON **MASTER** **13-4**
QUESTIONS ON **SPUR** OBJECTIVES

■**SKILLS**   *Objective B (See pages 810–813 for objectives.)*
In 1–4, evaluate the definite integrals.

1. $\int_3^7 3(x - 2)\, dx$

2. $\int_2^5 (2x + 2)\, dx + 2\int_5^{10} (x + 1)\, dx$

_____   _____

3. $\int_a^b 4\, dx + \int_b^c 4\, dx$

4. $\int_a^b 5x\, dx + \int_a^b 4x\, dx$

_____   _____

■**PROPERTIES**   *Objective C*
In 5–8, use properties of integrals to write the expression as a single integral.

5. $\int_0^5 (x^2 + 2)\, dx + 3\int_0^5 x\, dx$ _____

6. $\int_0^3 (x + 4)\, dx + \int_3^5 (x + 4)\, dx$ _____

7. the expression given in Question 2   _____

8. the expression given in Question 4   _____

■**USES** *Objective E*

9. A candy manufacturer has two machines which produce a chocolate mixture at different rates. Let $f(t)$ and $g(t)$ represent the production rates (in gallons per hour) of the two machines at time t (in hours).

a. Use integral notation in two different ways to write the total output of chocolate mixture during their first 12 hours of operation.

_____

t	$f(t)$	$g(t)$
0	3.50	2.00
2	3.00	2.15
4	2.75	3.00
6	3.15	2.75
8	3.05	2.85
10	3.50	3.00
12	3.40	2.75

b. Approximate the value of your answer to part **a** by evaluating the appropriate Riemann sum, first using the left endpoints as the x_i's and then using the right endpoints as the x_i's.

_____

■**REPRESENTATIONS** *Objective H*

In 10 and 11, express the area of each shaded region using integral notation and find its value.

10.

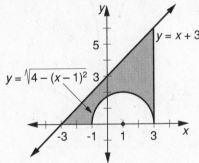

$y = x + 3$

$y = \sqrt{4 - (x-1)^2}$

11.

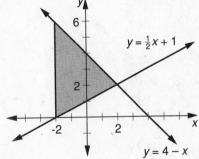

$y = \frac{1}{2}x + 1$

$y = 4 - x$

_____   _____

_____   _____

LESSON MASTER 13-5
QUESTIONS ON SPUR OBJECTIVES

■**SKILLS** *Objective B (See pages 810–813 for objectives.)*
In 1–3, evaluate the integral.

1. $\int_0^{15} x^2\,dx - \int_{10}^{15} x^2\,dx$

2. $\int_{-3}^{5} (x^2 + 4)\,dx$

_____   _____

3. $\int_2^{10} (x^2 + 5x + 2)\,dx$ _____

■**USES** *Objective D*

4. Suppose a car accelerates from 0 to 100 ft/sec in 5 seconds so that its velocity in ft/sec after t seconds is given by $v(t) = .25(t - 5)^2 + 100$. What is the total distance traveled in the 5-second interval?   _____

■**REPRESENTATIVES** *Objective H*
In 5 and 6, express the area of the shaded region using integral notation and find its value.

5.

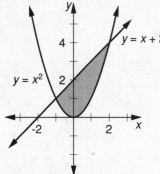

6.

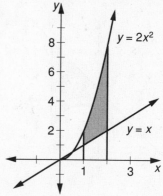

a. _____   a. _____

b. _____   b. _____

LESSON **MASTER 13-6**
QUESTIONS ON **SPUR** OBJECTIVES

■**USES** *Objective E (See pages 810–813 for objectives.)*

1. How much water is required to completely fill five glasses, each of which is formed by rotating the line $f(x) = \frac{1}{2}x + 1$ from $x = 0$ to $x = 10$ around the x-axis? All coordinates are in centimeters. Give your answer in liters.

_____

2. The parabolic cross-section of a trough is 2 feet wide and 2 feet high. If the trough is 9 feet long, find its volume.

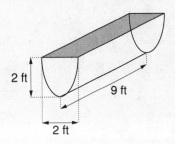

_____

■**REPRESENTATIONS** *Objective I*
In 3 and 4, a. sketch a graph of the region described and b. calculate the volume of the solid generated when the region is revolved about the x-axis.

3. the region bounded by the x-axis, the y-axis, and the line $y = -\frac{5}{4}x + 5$

a.   **b.** _____

4. the region bounded by the lines $y = 4 - \frac{x}{2}$, $x = 2$, $x = 4$, and the x-axis

a.   **b.** _____

LESSON MASTER 1-1
QUESTIONS ON **SPUR** OBJECTIVES

■ **SKILLS** *Objective A (See pages 74–78 for objectives.)*
1. Is the following statement universal, existential, or neither?

  The sum of two integers is also an integer. _____ **universal**

■ **SKILLS** *Objective B*
2. Consider the following statement.

  All countries have national anthems.

  Rewrite this statement by filling in the blanks.

  ∀ **countries** ∃ **an anthem** ____ such that
  it is the national anthem of the country.

■ **SKILLS** *Objective D*
In 3–5, tell if the statement is true or false.

3. ∀ *real numbers x, sin x ≤ 1.* _____ **true**

4. ∃ *a real number r such that r = -r.* _____ **true**

5. ∀ *real numbers y, log (y²) = (log y)².* _____ **false**

■ **PROPERTIES** *Objective E*
6. *Multiple choice.* If the statement ∃ *x in S such that p(x)* is true, then _____ **(c)**

  (a) *p(x)* is true for all *x* in *S*.
  (b) *p(x)* is true for more than one *x* in *S*.
  (c) *p(x)* is true for at least one *x* in *S*.
  (d) *p(x)* is never true.

■ **PROPERTIES** *Objective F*
7. Use universal instantiation and the true statement

  ∀ *nonnegative integers x,* $\sqrt{4x} = 2\sqrt{x}$

  to simplify $\sqrt{28}$. _____ $2\sqrt{7}$

■ **PROPERTIES** *Objective H*
8. Consider the following statement.

  The result of doubling a number is always less than the result of squaring it.

  a. Write this sentence in the form ∀ *x in S, p(x).*
  ∀ x in the set of numbers, 2x < x².

  b. Give a counterexample to show that the statement is false.
  Let x = 1. Then 2 · 1 ≮ 1².

In 9 and 10, prove or disprove.

9. ∃ *n such that* $\frac{8}{n}$ *is an integer.*
  Let n = 1. Then $\frac{8}{1}$ is an integer, so the statement is true.

10. ∀ *n,* $\frac{8}{n}$ *is an integer.*
  Let n = 5. $\frac{8}{5}$ is not an integer, so the statement is false.

■ **USES** *Objective I*
In 11 and 12, tell if the sentence is a statement. If it is, determine whether it is *true* or *false*.

11. *All guitars are powered by electricity.* **statement; false**

12. *He is wearing a blue shirt today.* **not a statement**

LESSON MASTER 1-2
QUESTIONS ON **SPUR** OBJECTIVES

■ **SKILLS** *Objective C (See pages 74–78 for objectives.)*
In 1–4, write the negation of the statement.

1. *All diamonds are made of carbon.*
  There exists a diamond that is not made of carbon.

2. ∀ *real numbers x, -3 < x.*
  ∃ x such that -3 ≥ x.

3. *Some equations have no solutions.*
  All equations have at least one solution.

4. ∃ *a real number x such that ∀ real numbers y, x is a factor of y.*
  ∀ real numbers x, ∃ a real number y such that x is not a factor of y.

■ **SKILLS** *Objective D*
5. Let *p: No parallelograms have more than two lines of symmetry.*
  a. Write *p.* **There is a parallelogram with more than two lines of symmetry.**

  b. Which is true, *p* or *~p*? _____ **~p**

■ **PROPERTIES** *Objective E*
6. *True or false?* The negation of a statement *For all x in S, p(x)* is the statement *For no x in S, p(x).* _____ **false**

7. Let *p: ∃ y in R such that q(y).* Write *~p.* **∀ y in R, ~q(y)**

8. If a statement is false, what can be said about its negation? **The negation is true.**

9. The negation of an existential statement is an _____ **universal** statement.

■ **USES** *Objective I*
In 10 and 11, tell which is true, the statement or its negation.

10. ∀ *months m, the name for m begins with a consonant.* **negation**

11. ∀ *states s, ∃ a city c such that c is the capital of s.* **statement**

LESSON MASTER 1-3
QUESTIONS ON **SPUR** OBJECTIVES

■ **SKILLS** *Objective B (See pages 74–78 for objectives.)*
In 1 and 2, express the inequality by writing out each implied *and, or,* and *not.*

1. 20 ≤ *a* < 52
  (a = 20 or a > 20) and (a < 52)

2. *n* ≯ 6.2
  not (n > 6.2)

■ **SKILLS** *Objective C*
In 3–5, use De Morgan's Laws to write the negation of the statement.

3. *35 is divisible by 5 and 6.*
  35 is not divisible by 5 or 35 is not divisible by 6.

4. *I will come Thursday or Friday.*
  I will not come Thurs. and I will not come Fri.

5. *x > -2 or x < -16*
  x ≤ -2 and x ≥ -16 (-16 ≤ x ≤ -2)

■ **SKILLS** *Objective D*
6. Let *p(x): x ≤ 12* and *q(x): x is even.* Is the following statement true?

  not (p(9) or q(9)) _____ **no**

■ **PROPERTIES** *Objective E*
7. According to De Morgan's Laws, what is the negation of *p and q*? **~p or ~q**

8. *True or false?* The negation of an *or* statement is an *and* statement. _____ **true**

■ **PROPERTIES** *Objective H*
9. Find a counterexample to show the following statement is false.

  ∀ *positive real numbers x, log x > 0 and log x³ = 3 log x.*
  Let x = $\frac{1}{10}$. log $\frac{1}{10}$ = log 10⁻¹ = -1 log 10 = -1 ≯ 0

■ **USES** *Objective I*
10. According to the United States Constitution, those persons "who shall not have attained to the age of thirty-five years, and been fourteen years a resident within the United States" are ineligible to be President. Let *t: A person is at least thirty-five years old,* and *f: A person has been a resident of the United States for fourteen years.*

   a. Use the symbols *t, f,* and ~ to describe an ineligible person, as given in the above quote.   ~(t and f)

   b. Use De Morgan's Law to rewrite your answer to part **a.**   (~t) or (~f)

■ **USES** *Objective K*
11. Rewrite the following line of a program using De Morgan's Laws.

   100 IF NOT (A=B AND C<>0) THEN PRINT "ERROR"
   100 IF A<>B OR C=0 THEN PRINT "ERROR"

■ **REPRESENTATIONS** *Objective M*
12. Complete the truth table below.

p	q	~q	p or ~q	q and (p or ~q)
T	T	F	T	T
T	F	T	T	F
F	T	F	T	F
F	F	T	T	F

13. Write the truth table for ~(~p and q).

p	q	~p	(~p) and q	~(~p and q)
T	T	F	F	T
T	F	F	F	T
F	T	T	T	F
F	F	T	F	T

■ **REPRESENTATIONS** *Objective L (See pages 74–78 for objectives.)*
1. Consider the following network.

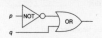

   a. Write the logical expression that corresponds to the network.   (not p) or q

   b. Write an input-output table for the network.

p	q	not p	Output (not p) or q
1	1	0	1
1	0	0	0
0	1	1	1
0	0	1	1

2. Fill in the input-output table below for this network.

p	q	r	~p	(~p) and q	~((~p) and q)	~(~p and q) or r
1	1	1	0	0	1	1
1	1	0	0	0	1	1
1	0	1	0	0	1	1
1	0	0	0	0	1	1
0	1	1	1	1	0	1
0	1	0	1	1	0	0
0	0	1	1	0	1	1
0	0	0	1	0	1	1

---

3. Suppose an AND gate costs 3¢, an OR gate 2¢, and a NOT gate 1¢.

   a. What is the cost of the network in Question 2?   7¢

   b. Draw a network that has the same output signals as those in Question 2, but has a lower cost.

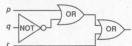

4. What is the output signal produced by the network below if *p* carries a signal of 1, *q* a signal of 0, and *r* a signal of 0?   1

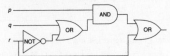

5. Use input-output tables to show that the two networks are functionally equivalent.

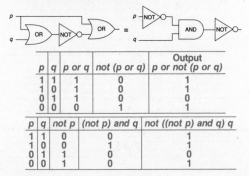

p	q	p or q	not (p or q)	Output p or not (p or q)
1	1	1	0	1
1	0	1	0	1
0	1	1	0	0
0	0	0	1	1

p	q	not p	(not p) and q	not ((not p) and q) q
1	1	0	0	1
1	0	0	0	1
0	1	1	1	0
0	0	1	0	1

■ **SKILLS** *Objective A (See pages 74–78 for objectives.)*
1. Consider these four statements.

   (1) *If the air conditioning is on, then Ed is cold.*
   (2) *If Ed is cold, then the air conditioning is on.*
   (3) *If the air conditioning is not on, then Ed is not cold.*
   (4) *If Ed is not cold, then the air conditioning is not on.*

   a. Name a pair of statements that are contrapositives of each other.
      [(1) and (4)] or [(2) and (3)]

   b. Which statement is the converse of (3)?   (4)

■ **SKILLS** *Objective B*
2. The union of which two statements from Question 1 is equivalent to the following statement?

   Ed is cold if and only if the air conditioning is on.   (1) and (2)

3. Write the inverse of the following statement.

   If a parabola has equation $y - k = a(x - h)^2$*, then its vertex is (h, k).*
   If a parabola does not have equation $y - k = a(x - h)^2$, then its vertex is not (h, k).

4. Write the following statement in if-then form, using the symbol ∀.

   All numbers divisible by 12 are even.
   ∀ numbers n, if n is divisible by 12, then n is even.

■ **SKILLS** *Objective C*
5. Write the negation of the following statement.

   If an object is on the moon, then its weight is about $\frac{1}{6}$ *its weight on Earth.* There is an object on the moon whose weight is not $\frac{1}{6}$ its weight on earth.

6. Let *p:* ∀ real numbers *x,* if $x^2 = 20$, then $x \neq \sqrt{20}$.

   a. Write ~p.   ∃ a real number x such that if $x^2 = 20$, then $x \neq \sqrt{20}$.

   b. Which is true, *p* or ~p? Justify your answer.   ~p is true, because if x = -√20 then $x^2 = 20$ but $x \neq \sqrt{20}$.

■ SKILLS   Objective D
7. Let $p(x)$: $|x + 2| < 5$ and $q(x)$: $x + 2 < 5$. Is
   the statement $\forall x$, if $p(x)$, then $q(x)$ true? _____ **yes**

■ PROPERTIES   Objective E
8. Under what conditions is the following statement false?

   If the team plays at home, then it wins.

   when the team plays at home and does not win

9. *Multiple choice.* A conditional statement is
   logically equivalent to its

   (a) converse. (b) inverse. (c) contrapositive. _____ **(c)**

■ USES   Objective I
10. Find a counterexample to the following statement.

    If a food is nutritious, then it tastes good.

    sample: Liver is nutritious, and some people

    think it doesn't taste good.

■ USES   Objective K
11. Consider the computer program below.

```
10  INPUT A
20  IF (A > -10) AND (A < -5) THEN PRINT "TRUE"
30  END
```

    a. What is the output if the input is $A = -2$? **no output**

    b. Write line 25 so that the program will print FALSE for all cases in
       which A is not in the interval $-10 < A < -5$.
       25 IF (A<=-10) OR (A>=-5) THEN PRINT "FALSE"

■ REPRESENTATIONS   Objective M
12. Write a truth table for the expression $p \Rightarrow \sim q$.

p	q	$\sim q$	$p \Rightarrow \sim q$
T	T	F	F
T	F	T	T
F	T	F	T
F	F	T	T

■ PROPERTIES   Objective G   (See pages 74–78 for objectives.)
In 1–4, each match symbolic statement with one of the terms below.
   (a) Law of Detachment   (b) Law of Indirect Reasoning
   (c) transitivity   (d) invalid argument

1. $a \Rightarrow b$ 2. $g \Rightarrow k$ 3. $n \Rightarrow p$ 4. $d \Rightarrow e$
    $\sim b$ k $p \Rightarrow r$ d
    $\therefore \sim a$ $\therefore g$ $\therefore n \Rightarrow r$ $\therefore e$
    (b)   **(d)**   **(c)**   **(a)**

■ PROPERTIES   Objective H
In 5 and 6, draw a valid conclusion from the given premises.

5. *If an instrument is in the percussion section, then it is placed in the
   back of the orchestra.*
   *If an instrument is played with a stick, then it is in the percussion
   section.*
   ∴ If an instrument is played with a stick, then it is
   placed in the back of the orchestra.

6. *If a figure is a square, then it has four sides.*
   A pentagon does not have four sides.
   ∴ A pentagon is not a square.

7. Below are two statements from a Lewis Carroll puzzle. Put each
   statement into if-then form, then draw a valid conclusion. (You may
   need to use the Contrapositive Theorem.)

   No bald person needs a hairbrush.   No lizards have hair.
   If a person is bald, then (s)he doesn't need a hairbrush.
   If it is a lizard, then it has no hair (it is bald).
   ∴ If it is a lizard, then it doesn't need a hairbrush.

■ USES   Objective J
In 8 and 9, tell if the argument is valid   (a) Law of Detachment
or invalid. If it is valid, tell which of   (b) Law of Indirect Reasoning
the laws at the right it follows.   (c) Law of Transitivity

8. *If a state was one of the thirteen original colonies,
   then it was settled by Europeans prior to 1776.
   California was settled by the Spanish in 1769.
   ∴ California was one of the thirteen original colonies.* **invalid**

9. *What goes up must come down.
   A rocket goes up.
   ∴ The rocket must come down.* **valid, (a)**

■ PROPERTIES   Objective H   (See pages 74–78 for objectives.)
1. Show that $14x + 6y$ is even if x and y are integers.
   $14x + 6y = 2(7x + 3y)$. Since x and y are integers,
   $7x + 3y$ is an integer because the integers are
   closed under addition and multiplication.
   Therefore, $14x + 6y$ is even.

2. Show that $\forall$ integers a, $20a + 7$ is odd.
   $20a + 7 = 20a + 6 + 1 = 2(10a + 3) + 1$. Since
   a is an integer, $10a + 3$ is an integer, so
   $2(10a + 3) + 1$ is odd.

3. Supply the missing steps in the proof of the following theorem.

   *If m is an even integer and n is any integer that is a multiple of 3,
   then $m \cdot n$ is a multiple of 6.*

   Suppose **m is an even integer and n is an integer**
   that is a multiple of 3
   Then there exists an integer r such that $m =$ **$2r$**
   according to **the definition of even number** According to
   the definition of multiple, there exists an integer s such that $n = 3s$.
   By substituting, $m \cdot n =$ **$(2r) \cdot (3s)$** $= 6 \cdot$ **rs**
   Because **rs** is an integer, $m \cdot n$ is a multiple of 6.

In 4 and 5, give a direct proof of the statement.

4. If m and n are odd integers, then $m - n$ is even.
   Suppose m and n are odd integers. Then ∃ integers
   r and s such that $m = 2r + 1$ and $n = 2s + 1$. By
   substituting, $m - n = (2r + 1) - (2s + 1) = 2r -$
   $2s = 2(r - s)$. Since $r - s$ is an integer, $m - n$ is
   even.

5. If m is even, m^3 is a multiple of 8.
   Suppose m is an even integer. Then ∃ an integer
   r such that $m = 2r$. By substituting, $m^3 = (2r)^3 = 8r^3$.
   Since r^3 is an integer, m^3 is a multiple of 8.

■ PROPERTIES   Objective G   (See pages 74–78 for objectives.)
In 1 and 2, a. is the argument valid? b. is the conclusion true?

1. *If $a < 5$, then $a^2 < 25$.
   $-8 < 5$
   ∴ $64 < 25$*
   a. _____ **yes**   b. _____ **no**

2. *If the freezing point of water is 212°F, then the moon is made of
   green cheese.
   The moon is not made of green cheese.
   ∴ The freezing point of water is 212°F.*
   a. **no**   b. **no**

3. Under what conditions is an argument guaranteed to produce a true
   conclusion?
   when the premises are true and the argument is valid

4. Joe noticed the following facts:
   3, 4, and 5 form a Pythagorean triple, and $3 \cdot 4 \cdot 5$ is divisible by
   60.
   5, 12, and 13 form a Pythagorean triple, and $5 \cdot 12 \cdot 13$ is divisible
   by 60.
   7, 24, and 25 form a Pythagorean triple, and $7 \cdot 24 \cdot 25$ is divisible
   by 60.
   Joe concluded that if a, b, and c form a Pythagorean triple, then abc
   is divisible by 60. Is Joe's conclusion valid? Why or why not?
   No, it is an example of Improper Induction.

5. Give an example of a valid argument that has a false conclusion.
   sample: If an American has "Ronald" as his first
   name, then he was once president. Mr.
   McDonald is an American whose first name is
   Ronald. ∴ Mr. McDonald was once president.

6. Give an example of an invalid argument that has a true conclusion.
   sample: If an American has "Ronald" as his first
   name, then he was once president. Mr. Reagan
   was once president. ∴ Mr. Reagan's first name is
   Ronald.

■ **USES**   *Objective J*

7. a. Write a symbolic form for the argument below.

If a year is divisible by 10, then the U.S. census is taken that year.
The census was taken last year.
∴ Last year was divisible by 10.

$p \Rightarrow q$
q
$\therefore p$

b. Is the argument valid?

no

8. Consider the following statement.

All math teachers can balance a checkbook.

a. Illustrate this situation with a diagram.

people who can balance a checkbook

math teachers

b. Write the converse of the given statement.

Anyone who can balance a checkbook is a math teacher.

c. Write the inverse of the given statement.

Anyone who is not a math teacher cannot balance a checkbook.

d. Suppose Mr. Smith is not a math teacher. Name the type of argument that would lead to the conclusion that Mr. Smith cannot balance a checkbook.

inverse error

e. Is the type of argument named in part **d** valid?

no

■ **PROPERTIES**   *Objective C*   (See pages 146–150 for objectives.)

1. The table below shows how hurricanes are classified according to their strength. Let c = category, w = wind speed, f: category → wind speed, and g: wind speed → category.

Category	Sustained Winds	Damage
1	74–95 mph	minimal
2	96–110 mph	moderate
3	111–130 mph	extensive
4	131–155 mph	extreme
5	156 or more mph	catastrophic

a. Evaluate $g(140)$.   **b.** Evaluate $f(2)$.

4   96–110 mph

c. Is g a function? Explain.   Yes, to each wind speed there corresponds exactly one category.

d. Is f a function? Explain.   No, to each category there corresponds more than one wind speed.

In 2 and 3, a. give a reasonable domain for the function and **b.** is the function discrete?

2. $f(x)$ = the number of sisters of person x

a. set of all people on Earth   **b.** yes

3. $g(x)$ = the weight of a person of height x as measured in feet

a. $\{x : x \geq 1\}$ **b.** no

4. Let f be a real function with $f(x) = \frac{\sqrt{x}}{x-5}$.

a. What is the largest possible domain of f? $\{x : x \geq 0 \text{ and } x \neq 5\}$

b. Is $(25, .25)$ a point on the graph of f? Why or why not?
Yes, because $f(25) = .25$.

5. If $h(t) = 4(t-2)^2 - 5$, what is the height of the graph of h when $t = 10$?   251

---

6. The graph of a function g is shown at the right.

a. Estimate $g(4)$.

-4

b. Estimate the interval(s) where g is constant.

$-4 \leq x \leq -3$

c. For what values of x is $-2 < g(x) < 2$?

$2 < x < 3$

d. *True* or *false*? $g(-3) < g(5)$

false

e. What is the domain of g?

$-4 \leq x \leq 5$

7. Graph $y = -x^2 + 14x - 45$ using a window $-10 \leq x \leq 10$ and $-10 \leq y \leq 10$. Now adjust the window so that the graph looks like the graph at the right. Describe this window with inequalities.

sample: $3 \leq x \leq 11$ and

$-12 < y \leq 4$. The x interval

must be centered about 7, the maximum y must

be 4, and the minimum y must be the value of

the function for x at the endpoints of its interval.

■ **PROPERTIES**   *Objective C*   (See pages 146–150 for objectives.)

1. Let $f(x) = 2x^2 + 14x + 21.5$.

a. Complete the square to find the exact range.

$f(x) = 2(x + 3.5)^2 - 3;\ \{y : y \geq -3\}$

b. Check your answer to part **a** by using an automatic grapher. Sketch the graph on the axes at the right.

2. What is the range of the tangent function?
set of all real numbers

3. Let g be the function defined by $g(x) = x^2$, where the domain is the set of integers. What is the range?
set of all nonnegative perfect squares

■ **USES**   *Objective F*

4. A canning factory is going to cut up pineapples for processing. A pineapple is roughly cylindrical. It will be sliced in half lengthwise to test for freshness. Then the half cylinder will be trimmed to form a rectangular solid, as shown at the right. The maximum volume of pineapple is obtained when the area of the rectangular cross-section is a maximum. Assume the pineapple has a radius of 3 inches.

a. Use the Pythagorean Theorem to express n, half the base of the rectangle, in terms of h.

$n = \sqrt{9 - h^2}$

b. Write an equation to express A, the area of the rectangle, in terms of h.

$A = 2h\sqrt{9 - h^2}$

c. Use an automatic grapher to graph your answer to part b. Sketch the graph on the axes at the right.

d. Find the dimensions of the rectangular cross-section that produce the maximum area.
$h \approx 2.1$ in., $2n \approx 4.2$ in.

e. What is the maximum area?
≈ 8.8 in.

■ **REPRESENTATIONS** *Objective G*
5. The entire graph of the function f is given at the right.
   a. What is the domain of f? $-1 \le x \le 7$
   b. What is the range of f? $-2 \le y \le 7$
   c. Estimate the maximum and minimum values.
      max = 7 at $x = 1$, min = 2 at $x = 6$
   d. On what interval(s) is $f(x)$ nonpositive? $3 \le x \le 7$
   e. Is f a discrete function? Why or why not? No, the domain includes all reals between -1 and 7, and this is not a discrete set.

6. Sketch a graph with all of the following characteristics.
   (a) The domain is $1 \le x \le 5$ for real numbers x.
   (b) The range is $-3 \le y \le 3$ for real numbers y.
   (c) $f(2)$ is the minimum value and $f(4)$ is the maximum value.
   Answers will vary, but must have $f(2) = -3$ and $f(4) = 3$.

7. Use an automatic grapher to estimate the maximum or minimum values of $f(x) = x^3 + x^2 - 17x + 5$ on the interval $-5 \le x \le 5$.
   max = 70 (at $x = 5$), min $\approx$ -17 (at $x \approx$ 2)

LESSON MASTER 2-3
QUESTIONS ON SPUR OBJECTIVES

■ **SKILLS** *Objective A* (See pages 146–150 for objectives.)
1. The chart at the right shows the amount of gold produced in the U.S. between 1970 and 1985. Let $G(x)$ be the amount of gold produced in year x.

Year	U.S. Gold Production in 1,000 oz
1970	1,743
1975	1,052
1979	964
1980	970
1981	1,379
1982	1,466
1983	2,003
1984	2,085
1985	2,475

   a. Describe the longest interval over which G is increasing. $1979 \le x \le 1985$
   b. Describe the longest interval over which G is decreasing. $1970 \le x \le 1979$
   c. What is the relative minimum? 964
   d. What is the relative maximum? 1,743 and 2,475
   e. Solve $G(x) = 2,003$. $x = 1983$

2. Let $f(x) = -2(x + 1)^2 + 3$. Give the interval(s) on which f is
   a. decreasing and b. increasing.
   a. $x > -1$ b. $x < -1$

■ **REPRESENTATIONS** *Objective G*
3. Use an automatic grapher to estimate the relative maximum and relative minimum of the function $g(x) = x^3 + x^2 - 17x + 15$ on the interval $-5 \le x \le 3$.
   rel. max. $\approx$ 48.5 at $x \approx$ -2.7, rel. min. $\approx$ -7 at $x \approx$ 2.1

4. The graph of function h is given at the right.

   a. Describe any intervals where h is increasing.
      $x < -4, 0 < x < 2$
   b. Find any relative maximum or relative minimum values of h. rel max: 3 (at x = -4) and -1 (at x = 2); rel min: -2 (at x = 0)

5. Graph $y = |x + 4|$ over $-10 \le x \le 10$. Describe all intervals on which the function is decreasing. $x < -4$

LESSON MASTER 2-4
QUESTIONS ON SPUR OBJECTIVES

■ **SKILLS** *Objective A* (See pages 146–150 for objectives.)
In 1 and 2, a formula for a sequence is given. a. Give the first four terms of the sequence, and b. tell if the sequence is increasing, decreasing, or neither.

1. $a_n = 5 + (-1)^n$
   a. 4, 6, 4, 6
   b. neither

2. $b_n = \frac{2n + 1}{n^2}$
   a. 3, $\frac{5}{4}$, $\frac{7}{9}$, $\frac{9}{16}$
   b. decreasing

3. Give an example of a decreasing arithmetic sequence.
   sample: 5, 3, 1, -1, . . . ; that is, $c_n = 7 - 2n$

In 4–6, a. tell if each sequence is arithmetic, geometric, harmonic, or none of these, and b. tell if it is increasing, decreasing, or neither.

4. $a_n = (1.01)^n$ a. geometric   b. increasing
5. $b_n = \frac{1}{n}$ a. harmonic   b. decreasing
6. $c_n = 3n - 7$ a. arithmetic   b. increasing

■ **PROPERTIES** *Objective D*
7. Find $\lim_{n \to \infty} a_n$ if $\begin{cases} a_1 = 8 \\ a_{k+1} = \frac{a_k}{10} \ \forall\ k \ge 1 \end{cases}$ 0

8. Use limit notation to describe the limit of $s_n = \left(-\frac{1}{2}\right)^{2n+1}$ as n increases without bound. $\lim_{n \to \infty} \left(-\frac{1}{2}\right)^{2n+1} = 0$

9. Let $\begin{cases} b_1 = 5 \\ b_{k+1} = \frac{1}{2} b_k \ \forall\ k \ge 1 \end{cases}$.
   a. What is the limit of b_n as $n \to \infty$?   0
   b. For what value of n is b_n within .001 of the limit?   14

■ **REPRESENTATIONS** *Objective G*
In 10 and 11, graph the first six terms of the sequence and find its limit as $n \to \infty$.

10. $a_n = \frac{2n^2 + 1}{n^2}$

11. $b_n = 3 + \frac{(-1)^n}{n}$

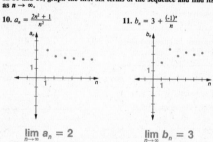

$\lim_{n \to \infty} a_n = 2$

$\lim_{n \to \infty} b_n = 3$

Precalculus and Discrete Mathematics © Scott, Foresman and Company

LESSON MASTER 2-5
QUESTIONS ON **SPUR** OBJECTIVES

■ **PROPERTIES** *Objective D (See pages 146–150 for objectives.)*

1. Consider the function $f(x) = \frac{x}{x+2}$.

a. Complete the table below to give decimal approximations for function values as x becomes large.

x	10	100	1,000	10,000
$\frac{x}{x+2}$	.8333	.9804	.9980	.9998

b. What is $\lim_{x \to \infty} f(x)$? ___1___

c. Write an equation of the horizontal asymptote of f. $y = 1$

2. a. Let $g(x) = \frac{\sin x}{x}$. Find $\lim_{x \to \infty} g(x)$ and $\lim_{x \to -\infty} g(x)$. $0;\ 0$

b. For what values of x is $g(x)$ within .001 of the limit? $x < -1,000 \text{ or } x > 1,000$

c. Is g even, odd, or neither? even

3. If h is an even function and $\lim_{x \to \infty} h(x) = -3$, find $\lim_{x \to -\infty} h(x)$. -3

4. Describe the end behavior of $y = -6x^3$. $\lim_{x \to \infty}(-6x^3) = -\infty,\ \lim_{x \to -\infty}(-6x^3) = \infty$

■ **REPRESENTATIONS** *Objective G*

5. The function f is graphed at the right.

a. Is f even, odd, or neither? even

b. Describe its end behavior. $\lim_{x \to -\infty} f(x) = 2,\ \lim_{x \to \infty} f(x) = 2$

c. Write the equation of the horizontal asymptote. $y = 2$

6. Sketch the graph of an odd function f that has a relative maximum at $x = -2$ such that $\lim_{x \to \infty} f(x) = -1$.

sample:

LESSON MASTER 2-6
QUESTIONS ON **SPUR** OBJECTIVES

■ **PROPERTIES** *Objective D (See pages 146–150 for objectives.)*

1. Contrast the end behavior of $f(x) = 5^x$ with that of $g(x) = 5^{-x}$.
$\lim_{x \to \infty} f(x) = \infty = \lim_{x \to -\infty} g(x),\ \lim_{x \to -\infty} f(x) = 0 = \lim_{x \to \infty} g(x)$

■ **USES** *Objective E*

2. A lake has been polluted by a certain chemical. To have the water safe for use, the concentration of that chemical must be one-tenth of its present level. If the chemical naturally dissipates so that 4% of it is lost each year, about how many years will it take for the lake water to become usable? **about 56.4 years**

3. $5,000 is invested in an oil drilling company that promises to pay 17% interest compounded continuously. At that rate, about how long will it take the investment to double? **about 4.08 years**

4. The table below lists the number of Americans in thousands traveling to foreign countries other than Mexico and Canada.

Year	1970	1975	1980	1985
Number of Travelers	5,260	6,354	8,163	12,766

a. Use the Continuous Change Model to write a formula for the number $n(t)$ of American travelers t years after 1970, assuming an annual growth rate of 5.7%. $n(t) = 5,260e^{.057t}$

b. Use your formula to predict how many Americans will travel abroad in the year 2010. **51,425,000**

c. Use your formula to calculate $n(10)$. Does this figure agree with the information in the chart? **9,301; no, it is off by 1,138.**

■ **REPRESENTATIONS** *Objective G*

5. Under what conditions is $f(x) = b^x$ an increasing function? **when $b > 1$**

Lesson MASTER 2-6 (page 2)

6. Graph both $f(x) = 2e^x$ and $g(x) = e^{2x}$ on the axes at the right. What qualities do these two functions have in common? (Consider the attributes given at the beginning of Lesson 2–6.)
Domain of both is set of reals, range of both is set of positive reals. Both are increasing functions. Both approach 0 as $x \to -\infty$ and both approach ∞ as $x \to \infty$. Neither have any relative minima or maxima, and both have the exponential function $y = e^x$ as their parent.

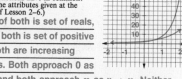

7. Use an automatic grapher to graph $h(x) = e^{x^2}$. Sketch the graph in the space at the right. Then analyze the function from the graph.
domain: set of all reals; range: $\{y : y \geq 0\}$; decreasing on $x < 0$; increasing on $x > 1$; minimum of 1 at $x = 0$; $\lim_{x \to -\infty} h(x) = \infty,\ \lim_{x \to \infty} h(x) = \infty$; even function

---

LESSON MASTER 2-7
QUESTIONS ON **SPUR** OBJECTIVES

■ **SKILLS** *Objective B (See pages 146–150 for objectives.)*
In 1–3, evaluate each expression.

1. $\log_2 8^2$ ___6___

2. $\log_b \sqrt[3]{b}$ $\frac{1}{3}$

3. $\log_{10} \sqrt{1,000}$ $\frac{3}{2}$

4. Express $\log_b \frac{n^3}{2w^4}$ in terms of $\log_b n$ and $\log_b w$. $3\log_b n - (\log_b 2 + 4\log_b w)$

5. Let $\log_k 2 = .231$ and $\log_k 3 = .367$.

a. Use properties of logarithms to find $\log_k 6$. .598

b. Find the value of k and use it to check your answer to part a. $k \approx 20;\ 20^{.598} \approx 6$

6. Solve: $\log_3 x = 6$ 729

■ **PROPERTIES** *Objective D*

7. Explain why $\lim_{x \to \infty} \log_b x = 0$ is false for any $b > 0$ with $b \neq 1$.
$\log_b x$ is undefined for $x < 0$, so the limit is also undefined.

■ **USES** *Objective E*

8. The sales of a certain new product increase over time according to $s(t) = 105 + 200\log(5t + 1)$ where $s(t)$ is the annual sales (in thousands of dollars) after t years. About how many years does it take for the annual sales to reach $500,000? ≈ 18.7 years

9. One formula that relates the average weight w in pounds of girls to their average height h in inches is

$$\log w = -2.86625 + 2.72158 \log h.$$

a. Predict the weight of a girl who is 63 inches tall. _____ 107.3 lb

b. Assume that a child's weight is normal if it is in a range of ±5% of the average. Give the range of normal weights for a girl who is 63 inches tall.

$$101.9 \le w \le 112.7$$

■**REPRESENTATIONS**   *Objective G*

10. a. Graph the function $g(x) = \log_2 x$.

b. Give the domain and range of g.

domain: $\{x : x > 0\}$,

range: set of all reals

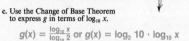

c. Use the Change of Base Theorem to express g in terms of $\log_{10} x$.

$$g(x) = \frac{\log_{10} x}{\log_{10} 2} \text{ or } g(x) = \log_2 10 \cdot \log_{10} x$$

d. Compare the graph of g to the graph of $f(x) = \log_{10} x$.

The height of the graph of g is $\log_2 10 \approx 3.3$

times the height of f; that is, the graph of g

results from the scale change $S_{1,\log_2 10}$ applied

to the graph of f.

■**PROPERTIES**   *Objective D* (See pages 146–150 for objectives.)

1. a. Graph $f(x) = 1 - \cos(.01x^2 - 1)^2$ on an automatic grapher using the viewing window $-10 \le x \le 10$, $-1 \le y \le 1$. Sketch the graph on the axes at the right.

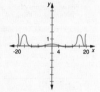

b. Describe the end behavior of f, based on your graph from part **a.**

It appears that $\lim\limits_{x \to -\infty} f(x) = 0$ and $\lim\limits_{x \to \infty} f(x) = 0$.

c. Graph f using the window $-20 \le x \le 20$, $-5 \le y \le 5$. Sketch the graph on the axes at the right.

d. Does your graph from part **c** agree with your answer to part **b**? Explain why or why not.

No, although the graph approaches the x-axis

near $x = \pm 8$, it then moves away from it past

$x = \pm 12$ and oscillates indefinitely.

■**USES**   *Objective E*

2. An office building is topped by a radio antenna. An observer on the ground 300 feet from the building finds that the angle α to the top of the antenna is 56°. The angle β to the top of the building is 52°. About how tall is the antenna?

$$\approx 60.8 \text{ ft}$$

---

3. The motion of a point P on a Ferris wheel is approximated by $f(t) = 50 \sin(1.5\pi t) + 58$, where t is the time in minutes and $f(t)$ is the height in feet.

a. Graph f.

b. What is the diameter of the Ferris wheel? _____ 100 ft

c. The lowest point on the wheel is how many feet above the ground? _____ 8 ft

d. How long does it take for the Ferris wheel to make one revolution? _____ $\frac{4}{3}$ min

■**REPRESENTATIONS**   *Objective G*

In 4–6, tell whether each function is odd, even, or neither.

4. $f(x) = \sin x$ **5.** $g(x) = |\sin x|$ **6.** $h(x) = \sin|x|$
   odd   even   even

7. Consider the function $f(x) = -\cos x$ on the interval $0 \le x \le 2\pi$.

a. Over what interval is f decreasing? _____ $\pi \le x \le 2\pi$

b. Where do any maximum and minimum values occur?

maximum at $x = \pi$, minimum at $x = 0$ and $x = 2\pi$

■**SKILLS**   *Objective A* (See pages 217–220 for objectives.)

In 1–8, find all real solutions.

1. $\sqrt[3]{x^2 - 13} = 3$ **2.** $\sqrt{y + 5} = y - 7$

   $x = \pm 16$ $y = 11$

3. $\sqrt{x - 3} + 2 = \sqrt{2x + 1}$ **4.** $\frac{1}{z^2 + 2z} = \frac{1}{5z}$

   $x = 4$ or 12 $z = 3$

5. $5^{3a - 3} = 25^a$ (Hint: $25 = 5^2$)   **6.** $e^{2x^2 - 6x} = e^{4x - 12}$

   $a = 3$ $x = 2$ or 3

7. $\ln(t^2 - 10) = \ln(3t + 30)$ **8.** $\ln(y^2 - 14) = \ln(6y + 13)$

   $t = 8$ or -5 $y = 9$

■**PROPERTIES**   *Objective F*

In 9–11, tell whether the step is always reversible.

9. taking the square root of both sides _____ no

10. subtracting a variable from both sides _____ yes

11. dividing both sides by a variable _____ no

■**USES**   *Objective J*

12. A baseball is thrown straight up with an initial velocity of 44 feet per second. After how many seconds is it 33 feet above the ground? (Hint: Use $h = -\frac{1}{2}gt^2 + v_0 t$, where h is the height in feet, t is the time in seconds, g is the acceleration due to gravity in feet/second², 9.8 ft/s², and v_0 is the initial velocity in feet/second.)

It never reaches 33 ft.

LESSON MASTER 3-2

QUESTIONS ON **SPUR** OBJECTIVES

■ **SKILLS** *Objective A (See pages 217–220 for objectives.)*
In 1–4, solve each equation.

1. $e^x = 280$
$$x = \ln 280 \approx 5.63$$

2. $y^{2/5} = 16$
$$y = 1024$$

3. $(\sqrt{2t+5})^3 = 27$
$$t = 2$$

4. $8 + \log_5 m = 133$
$$m = 5^{125}$$

■ **SKILLS** *Objective B*
5. Let $f(x) = 5x + 2$, $g(x) = x^2$, and $h(x) = \frac{1}{x}$. Give a simplified formula for each function.

a. $f \circ g$
$$5x^2 + 2$$

b. $g \circ f$
$$25x^2 + 20x + 4$$

c. $h \circ f$
$$\frac{1}{5x+2}$$

d. Does $g \circ h = h \circ g$?
yes

6. If r and s are real functions such that $r(x) = \sqrt{x}$ and $s(x) = \log x$, give the domains of $r \circ s$ and $s \circ r$.
domain of $r \circ s$ is $\{x : x \geq 1\}$; domain of $s \circ r$ is $\{x : x > 0\}$

■ **PROPERTIES** *Objective G*
7. If $f(x) = \frac{x-5}{7}$, give a formula for f^{-1}.
$$f^{-1}(x) = 7x + 5$$

8. Prove that $g(x) = \sqrt[3]{x+5}$ and $h(x) = x^3 - 5$ are inverses.
$(g \circ h)(x) = g(x^3 - 5) = \sqrt[3]{(x^3 - 5) + 5} = \sqrt[3]{x^3} = x$; $(h \circ g)(x) = h(\sqrt[3]{x+5}) = (\sqrt[3]{x+5})^3 - 5 = x + 5 - 5 = x$

■ **REPRESENTATIONS** *Objective M*
9. Given the graph of f at the right, graph the inverse of f on the same grid.

LESSON MASTER 3-3

QUESTIONS ON **SPUR** OBJECTIVES

■ **SKILLS** *Objective B (See pages 217–220 for objectives.)*
For 1 and 2, formulas for f and g are given. Write simplified formulas for a. $f + g$, b. $f \circ g$, and c. $\frac{f}{g}$.

1. $f(x) = e^x$ and $g(x) = e^{x+2}$
a. $(f+g)(x) = e^x + e^{x+2} = (1 + e^2)e^x$
b. $(f \circ g)(x) = e^{e^{x+2}}$
c. $\frac{f}{g}(x) = \frac{1}{e^2}$

2. $f(x) = x^3 - 5x$ and $g(x) = \frac{1}{x}$
a. $(f+g)(x) = x^3 - 5x + \frac{1}{x}$
b. $(f \circ g)(x) = \frac{1}{x^3} - \frac{5}{x}$
c. $\frac{f}{g}(x) = x^4 - 5x^2$

3. Using the formulas given in Question 2, give the domains of $\frac{f}{g}$ and $\frac{g}{f}$.
$\{x : x \neq 0\}$; $\{x : x \neq 0, x \neq \sqrt{5}, \text{ and } x \neq -\sqrt{5}\}$

■ **USES** *Objective K*
4. Working at its slowest speed, a machine can produce 250 magnetic disks per hour with a 98% efficiency rate (2% are defective). For each step up in speed, the machine can produce 10 more disks per hour, but its efficiency rate drops .5%.

a. Write a formula for n, where $n(x)$ is the total number of disks produced hourly when the speed is increased x steps.
$$n(x) = 250 + 10x$$

b. Write a formula for $e(x)$, the efficiency rate when the speed is raised x steps.
$$e(x) = .98 - .005x$$

c. Let $w(x)$ be the number of nondefective disks produced per hour when the speed is raised x steps. How are w, n, and e related?
$$w(x) = n(x)e(x)$$

d. Write a formula for $w(x)$ in terms of x.
$$w(x) = 245 + 8.55x - .05x^2$$

e. Graph the function w on the grid at the right.

---

f. At how many steps above the slowest speed should the machine be set to produce the maximum number of nondefective disks per hour?
85 or 86

g. What is the maximum number of nondefective disks that the machine can produce per hour?
610

■ **REPRESENTATIONS** *Objective M*
5. The functions f and g are graphed at the right. On the grids below, sketch the graphs of

a. $f + g$.   **b.** $f \cdot g$.

a.

b.

6. The graphs of two functions f and $f + g$ are shown at the right. Tell if $g(x)$ is positive, negative, or zero when

a. $x = a$.
negative

b. $x = b$.
zero

c. $x = c$.
positive

d. $x = d$.
zero

LESSON MASTER 3-4

QUESTIONS ON **SPUR** OBJECTIVES

■ **SKILLS** *Objective C (See pages 217–220 for objectives.)*
1. Consider the equation $(\log_7 (x + 4))^2 - 8 \log_7 (x + 4) + 15 = 0$.

a. Write the equation resulting from the substitution $u = \log_7 (x + 4)$.
$$u^2 - 8u + 15 = 0$$

b. Solve the equation you found in part **a**.
$$u = 3 \text{ or } u = 5$$

c. Substitute $u = \log_7 (x + 4)$ back into your results from part **b** and solve for x.
$$x = 339 \text{ or } x = 16{,}803$$

In 2 and 3, find the zeros of the function.

2. $g(x) = x^2 - 36$
$$x = \pm 6$$

3. $h(x) = x^3 - 7x^2 - 8x$
$$x = 0 \text{ or } x = 8 \text{ or } x = -1$$

In 4 and 5, find all solutions.

4. $(3k + 8)^3 - 2 = 3k + 6$
$$k = -3 \text{ or } k = -\frac{7}{3} \text{ or } k = -\frac{8}{3}$$

5. $0 = x^4 - 7x^2 + 12$
$$x = \pm 2 \text{ or } x = \pm\sqrt{3}$$

6. Give exact values of the zeros of $f(x) = 2 \sin^2 x + \sin x - 1$ on $0 \leq x \leq 2\pi$.
$$x = \frac{\pi}{6} \text{ or } x = \frac{5\pi}{6} \text{ or } x = \frac{3\pi}{2}$$

7. Approximate the solutions of $5^{2x} + 18 = 9 \cdot 5^x$ to the nearest tenth.
$$x \approx .7 \text{ or } x \approx 1.1$$

8. a. Multiply $(n^2 + 7n + 30)$ by $(n - 4)$.
$$n^3 + 3n^2 + 2n - 120$$

b. When spheres are stacked in a triangular pyramid with n layers, $s(n) = \frac{1}{6}n^3 + \frac{1}{2}n^2 + \frac{1}{3}n$ gives the number of spheres used. Use part **a** to help you find the number of layers that can be made with 20 spheres.
4

LESSON MASTER 3-5
QUESTIONS ON **SPUR** OBJECTIVES

■ **SKILLS** *Objective D (See pages 217–220 for objectives.)*
1. The function f is continuous on the interval $-3 \le x \le 3$. The chart below gives some values of f.

x	-3	-2	-1	0	1	2	3
$f(x)$	5	3	1	-.5	-2	1	9

Find consecutive integers a and b such that

a. $\exists\, x_1$ such that $a < x_1 < b$ and x_1 is a zero of f.   **$a = -1, b = 0$ or $a = 1, b = 2$**

b. $\exists\, x_2$ such that $a < x_2 < b$ and $f(x_2) = -1$.   **$a = 0, b = 1$ or $a = 1, b = 2$**

2. Consider the equation $\cos x = \frac{3}{2^x}$. Use the Intermediate Value Theorem to

a. find an interval of length 1 that contains a solution.   **sample: $7 < x < 8$**

b. find an interval of length .1 that contains a solution.   **sample: $7.8 < x < 7.9$**

■ **PROPERTIES** *Objective H*
3. Use the diagram at the right to fill in the blanks.

According to the Intermediate Value Theorem, if it is known that g is a continuous function and y_0 is between **$g(k)$** and **$g(j)$**, then $\exists$ **x_0 between j and k)** such that **$g(x_0) = y_0$**.

In 4–6, determine whether the function is continuous on the interval $0 \le x \le \pi$. If not, tell where the function is discontinuous.

4. $f(x) = x$ **yes**

5. $g(x) = \frac{1}{x-2}$ **no; discontinuous at $x = 2$**

6. $h(x) = \frac{1}{\cos x}$ **no; discontinuous at $x = \frac{\pi}{2}$**

---

7. *Multiple choice.* A function is graphed at the right. On which interval is the function *not* continuous?

(a) $b \le x \le c$
(b) $0 \le x \le c$
(c) $0 \le x \le d$
(d) $c \le x \le d$ **(a)**

■ **USES** *Objective J*
8. For some cardiac tests, a dye is injected into a vein. The concentration of the dye can be approximated by $f(x) = -.003x^4 + .07x^3 - .026x^2 + .8x$, where $f(x)$ is the percent of dye in the bloodstream after x seconds. After about how many seconds does half the dye remain in the bloodstream?   **about 22 sec**

■ **REPRESENTATIONS** *Objective O*
9. Refer to the graphs of $f(x) = e^x$ and $g(x) = -x^2 + 2x + 4$ below.

a. Write an equation for which c is a solution.   **$e^x = -x^2 + 2x + 4$**

b. Write a formula for a function h for which c is a zero.   **$h(x) = e^x + x^2 - 2x - 4$**

c. Find an interval of length .1 that contains c.   **$1.5 < c < 1.6$**

LESSON MASTER 3-6
QUESTIONS ON **SPUR** OBJECTIVES

■ **SKILLS** *Objective E (See pages 217–220 for objectives.)*
In 1–6, solve each inequality.

1. $4^x < 1024$ **$x < 5$**

2. $\frac{1}{y-5} \ge 3.2$ **$5 < y \le 5.3125$**

3. $(a + 10)(a - 3) < 0$ **$-10 < a < 3$**

4. $3b^2 + 10b \le b^2 - b - 5$ **$-5 \le b \le -\frac{1}{2}$**

5. $2x^2 - 2 \ge -x^2 - x$ **$x \le -1$ or $x \ge -\frac{2}{3}$**

6. $\log(2x - 8) > \log(6x + 9)$ **no solution**

7. When can the cube of a number be greater than twice its square?   **when the number is greater than 2**

8. Find all solutions to $\cos x < \frac{1}{2}$ on the interval $0 \le x \le 2\pi$.   **$\frac{\pi}{3} < x < \frac{5\pi}{3}$**

■ **PROPERTIES** *Objective F*
9. Since $f : x \to x^{35}$ is an increasing function, if $\sqrt[5]{x - 3} < \sqrt[7]{2 - x}$, what can you conclude?   **$(x-3)^7 < (2-x)^5$**

■ **USES** *Objective L*
10. The formula $R = e^{21.4b}$ relates the percent risk R of an automobile accident to the percent b of the blood alcohol level of the driver. At what value of b does a driver have at least a 50% chance of having an accident?   **when the blood alcohol level is over .1828%**

LESSON MASTER 3-7
QUESTIONS ON **SPUR** OBJECTIVES

■ **SKILLS** *Objective E (See pages 217–220 for objectives.)*
In 1–4, describe the solutions to the given inequality.

1. $3x^2 + 17x + 10 > 0$ **$x < -5$ or $x > -\frac{2}{3}$**

2. $x^2 - 4x < 77$ **$-7 < x < 11$**

3. $(x + 5)(x + 3)(2x - 1) > 0$ **$x > \frac{1}{2}$ or $-5 < x < -3$**

4. $x^3 + 2x^2 + x < 0$ **$x < 0$ and $x \ne -1$**

■ **USES** *Objective L*
5. Midville School has 3,700 students but is decreasing in enrollment by about 3% per year. Westville has 2,100 students but is gaining about 50 students per year. If these trends continue, when will Westville have a larger enrollment?   **in about 11 years**

6. When a particular baseball is hit, its height y in feet after traveling x feet horizontally is given by $y = -.04x^2 + 1.4x + 3$. At the same time the baseball is hit, a football is kicked. Its path is described by $y = -.02x^2 + 1.1x$. For how many feet horizontally is the baseball higher than the football?   **for about 21.9 ft**

■ **REPRESENTATIONS** *Objective O*
7. Let f and g be the functions graphed at the right.

a. For which values of x is $f(x) > g(x)$?   **$-3 < x < -1, 2 < x < 4$**

b. When is $g(x) > f(x)$?   **$-4 < x < -3, -1 < x < 2$**

8. Use a graph to determine when $\sin x > (x - 1)^2$ on the interval $0 \le x \le \pi$.   **$.38 < x < 1.96$**

LESSON MASTER 3-8
QUESTIONS ON SPUR OBJECTIVES

■ SKILLS   *Objective A (See pages 217–220 for objectives.)*
1. Interpret $|t - 15| = 9$ in terms of distance.
   The distance between t and 15 is 9.

In 2–5, solve the equation.

2. $|7 + 2q| = 19$
   $q = 6$ or $q = -13$

3. $|5 - x| = -6$
   no solution

4. $|2b - 3| = 17$
   $b = 10$ or $b = -7$

5. $|4m + 21| = 2m + 7$
   no solution

■ SKILLS   *Objective E*
In 6 and 7, write an absolute value inequality to describe each interval.

6.
   $|x| \le 6$

7.
   $|x - 25| < 3$

8. *Multiple choice.* Which of the following is equivalent
   to the inequality $|3x - 25| < 10$?   (c)

   (a) $3x - 25 < -10$ and $3x - 25 < 10$
   (b) $3x - 25 < -10$ or $3x - 25 < 10$
   (c) $3x - 25 > -10$ and $3x - 25 < 10$
   (d) $3x - 25 > -10$ or $3x - 25 < 10$

In 9 and 10, solve the inequality.

9. $|z - 12| > 2$
   $z < 10$ or $z > 14$

10. $|10y - 17| \le 13$
   $.4 \le y \le 3$

■ USES   *Objective L*
11. A contractor estimates that a construction job will cost \$27,500.
   Suppose the actual cost is within \$1,500 of the estimate. Describe
   this situation

   a. with absolute value.
   $|c - 27,500| \le 1,500$

   b. with a double inequality.
   $26,000 \le c \le 29,000$

LESSON MASTER 3-9
QUESTIONS ON SPUR OBJECTIVES

■ PROPERTIES   *Objective I (See pages 217–220 for objectives.)*
1. How is the graph of $y = \sin 4x$ related to the graph of $y = \sin x$?
   It is the image of $y = \sin x$ under $S_{\frac{1}{4}, 1}$.

In 2 and 3, give a. the amplitude, b. the period, and c. the phase shift.

2. $y = -5 \cos \left(2 \left(x - \frac{\pi}{2}\right)\right)$
   a. 5
   b. π
   c. $\frac{\pi}{2}$

3. $y = 3 \sin (4x + \pi)$
   a. 3
   b. $\frac{\pi}{2}$
   c. $\frac{-\pi}{4}$

4. Consider the graph at the right.
   a. Give the amplitude. 2
   b. Give the period. π
   c. Write the equation as an
      offspring of $y = \cos x$. $y = 2 \cos 2x$
   d. Write the equation as an
      offspring of $y = \sin x$. $y = 2 \sin \left(2x + \frac{\pi}{2}\right)$

■ REPRESENTATIONS   *Objective N*
5. Write the equation of the result when
   the graph of $y = |x|$ is transformed by
   $S_{5, 1}$ and then $T_{-4, 0}$. $y = \left|\dfrac{x + 4}{5}\right|$

6. a. Write an equation for the ellipse graphed at
      the right.
      $\dfrac{(x - 5)^2}{4} + \dfrac{(y - 4)^2}{16} = 1$

   b. If the graph is the result of applying $S_{a, b}$ and
      then $T_{c, d}$ to the unit circle, what are the
      values of a, b, c, and d?
      $a = 2, b = 4, c = 5, d = 4$

LESSON MASTER 4-1
QUESTIONS ON SPUR OBJECTIVES

■ SKILLS   *Objective E (See pages 283–286 for objectives.)*
1. Show that $x + 5$ is a factor of $x^2 + x - 20$.
   $x^2 + x - 20 = (x + 5)(x + 4)$

2. If $5x^2 - 8x - 21 = (x - 3) \cdot p(x)$, what is $p(x)$? $5x + 7$

■ PROPERTIES   *Objective F*
In 3–5, determine whether the statement is *true* or *false* and explain your
answer.

3. -6 is a factor of 720.
   True, because $720 = -6(-120)$ and -120 is an integer.

4. 21 is a factor of 98.
   False, because $\exists$ no integer k such that $98 = 21k$.

5. $2x + 7y$ is a factor of $4x^2 - 49y^2$.
   True, because $4x^2 - 49y^2 = (2x + 7y)(2x - 7y)$.

6. Prove: *If a, b, and c are integers such that a is a factor of b and b² is a
   factor of c, then a is a factor of c.*
   If a is a factor of b and b^2 is a factor of c, then $\exists$
   integers k and m such that $b = ak$ and $c = b^2 m$.
   Thus, by substitution, $c = b^2 m = (ak)^2 m = a(ak^2 m)$.
   Since $ak^2 m$ is an integer, a is a factor of m.

7. Prove: *If a(x), b(x), and c(x) are polynomials such that a(x) is a factor
   of b(x) and a factor of c(x), then a(x) is a factor of b(x) − c(x).*
   If $a(x)$ is a factor of $b(x)$ and of $c(x)$, then $\exists$ polynomials
   $k(x)$ and $m(x)$ such that $b(x) = a(x)k(x)$ and $c(x) =$
   $a(x)m(x)$. Thus, $b(x) - c(x) = a(x)k(x) - a(x)m(x) =$
   $a(x)[k(x) - m(x)]$. Since $k(x) - m(x)$ is a polynomial, $a(x)$
   is a factor of $b(x) - c(x)$.

8. Consider the conjecture *If a and b are integers and a is a factor of b,
   then a is a factor of (b + 1)² − 1.*

   a. Find values for a and b to illustrate this conjecture.   sample:
   $a = 3, b = 6$; then $(b + 1)^2 - 1 = 48$, and 3 is a factor of 48.

   b. Prove the conjecture.   If a is a factor of b, then $\exists$ an
      integer k such that $b = ak$. Then $(b + 1)^2 - 1 =$
      $b^2 + 2b = (ak)^2 + 2(ak) = a(ak^2 + 2k)$. Since $ak^2 + 2k$
      is an integer, a is a factor of $(b + 1)^2 - 1$.

LESSON MASTER 4-2
QUESTIONS ON SPUR OBJECTIVES

■ SKILLS   *Objective A (See pages 283–286 for objectives.)*
In 1–4, values for n and d are given. Find values for q and r as defined in
the Quotient-Remainder Theorem.

1. $n = 138, d = 23$ $q = 6, r = 0$
2. $n = 15; d = 40$ $q = 0, r = 15$
3. $n = -72; d = 13$ $q = -6, r = 6$
4. $n = 247,291; d = 718$ $q = 344, r = 299$

In 5–7, when n is divided by d, the quotient is 11 and the remainder is 5.

5. Can d be 4? Explain your answer.   No, because the
   remainder must be less than d.

6. If $n = 93$, find the value of d. 8
7. If $d = 10$, find the value of n. 115

In 8–10, suppose n is an integer and n is divided by 9.

8. How many different remainders are possible? 9

9. Give two positive values of n for which
   $r = 7$.   sample: $n = 16, 25$

10. Give two negative values of n for which
   $r = 7$.   sample: $n = -2, -11$

11. Explain why every integer m can be written in exactly one of the
   following forms (where k is an integer):
   $m = 6k$, $m = 6k + 1$, $m = 6k + 2$, $m = 6k + 3$, $m = 6k + 4$,
   $m = 6k + 5$
   Let $d = 6$ in the Quotient-Remainder
   Theorem. Then $\exists$ integers k and r such
   that $m = 6k + r$ where $0 \le r < 6$. Thus, r is
   one of the following: 0, 1, 2, 3, 4, 5. That is,
   exactly one of the following is true: $m = 6k$,
   $m = 6k + 1$, $m = 6k + 2$, ..., $m = 6k + 5$.

■ USES *Objective K*

12. A particular brand of pen is sold in three ways: individually (for \$4 each), in boxes of 12 (for \$45 per box), and in cases of 100 pens (for \$320 per case). Suppose n pens are bought using c cases, b boxes, and i individual pens, in such a way that the total cost is minimized.

  a. What are the values of c, b, and i if $n = 88$? **c = 0, b = 7, i = 4**

  b. What are the values of c, b, and i if $n = 362$? **c = 3, b = 5, i = 2**

  c. Are your answers to parts **a** and **b** unique? Why or why not?

  Yes, if a case (or box) is replaced by boxes or individual pens, the cost will be greater, and therefore not minimized.

■ SKILLS *Objective D* (See pages 283–286 for objectives.)

1. Name three elements in each of the congruence classes modulo 4.

  sample: R0 = {0, 4, 8}, R1 = {1, 5, 9},
  R2 = {2, 6, 10}, R3 = {3, 7, 11}

In 2–5, give the smallest positive integer that makes the congruence true.

2. $a \equiv 79 \pmod 3$ **a = 1**   3. $b \equiv 2013 \pmod{23}$ **b = 12**

4. $d \equiv 0 \pmod{13}$ **d = 13**   5. $e \equiv -7 \pmod{17}$ **e = 10**

6. *True or false?* An integer can belong to more than one congruence class for a given modulus.   **false**

7. Consider the congruence classes modulo 7: $R0, R1, \ldots, R6$. The product of an element of $R3$ and an element of $R6$ is in ____.   **R4**

■ PROPERTIES *Objective G*

8. Rewrite x can be expressed as $7k + 3$ for some integer k using congruence notation.   **x ≡ 3 (mod 7)**

9. If a leap year is defined as a year evenly divisible by 4 but not evenly divisible by 100, express leap year, y, as a solution to congruence sentences.

  y ≡ 0 (mod 4) and y ≢ 0 (mod 100)

10. If $m \equiv 4 \pmod{13}$ and $n \equiv 10 \pmod{13}$, write a congruence statement for

  a. $m + n$.   **m + n ≡ 1 (mod 13)**   b. $m - n$.   **m − n ≡ 7 (mod 13)**

  c. mn.   **mn ≡ 1 (mod 13)**

■ USES *Objective L*

11. Find the last three digits of 13^{13}.   **253**

In 12 and 13, fill in the missing digit in the ISBN number.

12. 0-466298-77-___   **3**   13. 2-470132-5___-X   **5**

■ SKILLS *Objective A* (See pages 283–286 for objectives.)

1. If $p(x) = q(x)d(x) + r(x)$, $p(x) = 3x^3 - 2x$, and $d(x) = x^2 - 3$, find $q(x)$ and $r(x)$.

  $q(x) =$ **3x** $r(x) =$ **7x**

2. a. Write an equation in the form $p(x) = q(x)d(x) + r(x)$ based on the long division at the right.

$$
3x^2 + 5x \overline{\smash{)}\ 6x^3 - 2x^2 + 0x + 3}
$$
quotient: $2x - 4$

  $6x^3 - 2x^2 + 3 =$
  (2x − 4)(3x² + 5x) + (20x + 3)

  working shown:
  $6x^3 + 10x^2$
  $-12x^2 + 0x$
  $-12x^2 - 20x$
  $20x + 3$

  b. Simplify the expression on the right side of the equation from part **a** to show that it in fact equals the left side.

  6x³ + 10x² − 12x² − 20x + 20x + 3 = 6x³ − 2x² + 3

3. Find k and m so that $-12x^2 + mx - 5 = (4x - 1)(kx + 2) - 3$ ∀ real numbers x.

  $k =$ **−3** $m =$ **11**

■ SKILLS *Objective C*

In 4–8, find the quotient $q(x)$ and the remainder $r(x)$ when the polynomial $p(x)$ is divided by the polynomial $d(x)$.

4. $p(x) = 4x^3 + 7x - 4$
   $d(x) = 2x + 1$

  $q(x) =$ **2x² − x + 4**
  $r(x) =$ **−8**

5. $p(x) = x^5 - x^3 + 2$
   $d(x) = x - 1$

  $q(x) =$ **x⁴ + x³**
  $r(x) =$ **2**

---

6. $p(x) = 18x^3 - 13x^2 - 4x + 1$
   $d(x) = 9x - 2$

  $q(x) =$ **$2x^2 - x - \frac{2}{3}$**
  $r(x) =$ **$-\frac{1}{3}$**

7. $p(x) = 4x^4 - 6x^3 + 6x^2 + 4$
   $d(x) = 2x^2 + x + 1$

  $q(x) =$ **2x² − 4x + 4**
  $r(x) =$ **0**

8. $p(x) = x^5 + 5x^4 - 7x^3 - 15x^2 - 16x + 44$
   $d(x) = x^2 + 4x - 11$

  $q(x) =$ **x³ + x² − 4**
  $r(x) =$ **0**

9. What is the length of a rectangle whose width is $x + 4$ units and whose area is $2x^3 + 10x^2 + 9x + 4$ square units?   **2x² + 2x + 1 units**

■ PROPERTIES *Objective H*

10. Suppose that polynomials $m(x)$ and $n(x)$ have degrees 6 and 2, respectively. If $m(x)$ is divided by $n(x)$, what do you know about the degrees of the quotient and remainder polynomials?

  The degree of the quotient polynomial is 4, and the degree of the remainder polynomial is 0 or 1, or the remainder is 0.

11. Suppose that a polynomial $p(x)$ is divided by a polynomial $d(x)$, and that the quotient polynomial has degree 4 while the remainder polynomial has degree 2. What do you know about the degrees of polynomials $d(x)$ and $p(x)$?

  The degree of polynomial d(x) is at least 3, and the degree of polynomial p(x) is at least 7.

LESSON MASTER 4-5
QUESTIONS ON SPUR OBJECTIVES

■ SKILLS *Objective B (See pages 283–286 for objectives.)*
In 1–4, use synthetic substitution to find $p(c)$ for the given polynomial and value of c.

1. $p(x) = 5x^3 - x^2 + 9$; $c = 3$

$p(c) = \underline{135}$

2. $p(x) = 4x^3 + 6x - 11$; $c = 0.5$

$p(c) = \underline{-7.5}$

3. $p(x) = 3x^4 - x^3 + 6x$; $c = 2.1$

$p(c) = \underline{61.6833}$

4. $p(x) = x^5 + x^4 - x^3$; $c = -0.2$

$p(c) = \underline{0.00928}$

5. *Multiple choice.* Which is not a zero of $x^3 - 5x^2 - 12x + 36$?
(a) 6   (b) 2   (c) -3   (d) 3 $\underline{(d)}$

6. What is the value of b if $p(x) = x^4 - 5x^2 - 7x + b$ and $p(-2) = 5$?

$b = \underline{-5}$

■ SKILLS *Objective C*
In 7–10, use synthetic division to find the quotient $q(x)$ and the remainder $r(x)$ when the given polynomial $p(x)$ is divided by the polynomial $d(x)$.

7. $p(x) = 3x^3 + 2x^2 + x$
$d(x) = x + 1$

$q(x) = \underline{3x^2 - x + 2}$
$r(x) = \underline{-2}$

8. $p(x) = x^5 - 1$
$d(x) = x - 1$

$q(x) = \underline{x^4 + x^3 + x^2 + x + 1}$
$r(x) = \underline{0}$

9. $p(x) = x^4 + 3x^3 - 2x + 60$
$d(x) = x + 4$

$q(x) = \underline{x^3 - x^2 + 4x - 18}$
$r(x) = \underline{132}$

10. $p(x) = 2x^3 + 5x^2 + 2x$
$d(x) = 2x + 1$

$q(x) = \underline{x^2 + 2x}$
$r(x) = \underline{0}$

LESSON MASTER 4-6
QUESTIONS ON SPUR OBJECTIVES

■ PROPERTIES *Objective H (See pages 283–286 for objectives.)*
1. If $x^2 - 4$ is a factor of a given polynomial $p(x)$, find the value(s) of c for which $p(c) = 0$. $\underline{-2, 2}$

2. If 3, 7, and -2 are the zeros of a cubic polynomial $c(x)$, give a possible formula for $c(x)$.

$\underline{(x - 3)(x - 7)(x + 2) = x^3 - 8x^2 + x + 42,}$
$\underline{\text{or a multiple thereof}}$

3. Suppose $p(t) = t^4 - 3t^2 - t + 14$. Find $p(3)$ by dividing $p(t)$ by $d(t) = t - 3$.

$p(3) = \underline{65}$

4. If -1 is a zero of $p(x) = x^3 - 5x^2 + 2x + 8$, find the remaining zeros of $p(x)$.

$\underline{2, 4}$

5. *Multiple choice.* If the graph of a polynomial $p(x)$ crosses the x-axis exactly two times, then $\underline{(c)}$
(a) $p(x)$ is of degree 2
(b) $p(x)$ is of degree greater than 2
(c) $p(x)$ is of degree 2 or more
(d) $p(x)$ may have more than two real zeros

6. *True or false?* If $t(c) = 0$ and $p(x) = q(x)t(x)$, then $p(c) = 0$. $\underline{\text{true}}$

7. If $p(x)$ and $q(x)$ are polynomials such that $p(x) = q(x)(x + 3) - 2$,
then you can conclude that $p(\underline{-3}) = \underline{-2}$

LESSON MASTER 4-7
QUESTIONS ON SPUR OBJECTIVES

■ REPRESENTATIONS *Objective M (See pages 283–286 for objectives.)*
In 1 and 2, find the base-2 representation of the number.

1. 40 $\underline{101000_2}$

2. 129 $\underline{10000001_2}$

In 3 and 4, find the base-10 representation of the number.

3. 110110_2 $\underline{54}$

4. 1000001_2 $\underline{65}$

In 5 and 6, perform the following steps:
a. Find the binary representation of r.
b. Find the binary representation of t.
c. Use your answers to parts a and b to find the base-2 representation of $r + t$.
d. Convert your answer from part c into base 10.

5. $r = 23$, $t = 24$
a. $\underline{10111_2}$
b. $\underline{11000_2}$
c. $\underline{101111_2}$
d. $\underline{47}$

6. $r = 62$, $t = 7$
a. $\underline{111110_2}$
b. $\underline{111_2}$
c. $\underline{1000101_2}$
d. $\underline{69}$

7. Express 94 in base n where

a. $n = 2$.
$\underline{1011110_2}$

b. $n = 8$.
$\underline{136_8}$

c. $n = 4$.
$\underline{1132_4}$

LESSON MASTER 4-8
QUESTIONS ON SPUR OBJECTIVES

■ SKILLS *Objective E (See pages 283–286 for objectives.)*
In 1–6, factor into prime factors over the real numbers.

1. $6y^2 + 17y + 5$

2. $25n^4 - 30n^2 + 9$

$\underline{(2y + 5)(3y + 1)}$ $\underline{(5n^2 - 3)^2}$

3. $x^4 - 2x^2 - 8$

4. $7x^2 - 49x + 42$

$\underline{(x - 2)(x + 2)(x^2 + 2)}$ $\underline{7(x - 6)(x - 1)}$

5. $p(x) = 2x^3 + 7x^2 - 14x + 5$, given that $x - 1$ is a factor of $p(x)$

$\underline{(2x - 1)(x - 1)(x + 5)}$

6. $(x^2 + xy)(3x^2 + y^2) - (x^2 + xy)(2x^2 + 2y^2)$

$\underline{x(x - y)(x + y)^2}$

■ PROPERTIES *Objective I*
7. *True or false?* In a proof by contradiction, the assumption which begins the proof is proved to be true. $\underline{\text{false}}$

Precalculus and Discrete Mathematics © Scott, Foresman and Company

8. Consider the statement *There is no largest real number less than one.*

a. To write a proof by contradiction, with what assumption would you start?

   Suppose ∃ a largest real number less than 1.

b. Complete the proof.

   Let that largest real number be r. Let s be the real number halfway between r and 1, that is, $s = \frac{r+1}{2}$. Then $r < s < 1$, so that s is a real number less than 1. But s is larger than r, contradicting the statement that r is the largest such number. Thus, the assumption must be false, so there is no largest real number less than 1.

c. What does this tell you about the number $0.\overline{9}$? Justify your answer.

   $0.\overline{9} = 1$, because if $0.\overline{9} < 1$, then $0.\overline{9}$ would be the largest real number less than 1.

■ **PROPERTIES** *Objective J*

9. a. List the numbers that must be tested as factors to determine whether 907 is prime.

   2, 3, 5, 7, 11, 13, 17, 19, 23, 29

b. Is 907 prime? _____ yes

10. a. *Multiple choice.* Which prime factorization is not equivalent to the others?

   (a) $2 \cdot 2 \cdot 2 \cdot 3 \cdot 11 \cdot 19$ (b) $2^3 \cdot 2 \cdot 3 \cdot 19 \cdot 11$
   (c) $19 \cdot 2^3 \cdot 3 \cdot 11$ (d) $2^3 \cdot 3 \cdot 11 \cdot 19$ (b)

b. Which of the above represents a standard prime factorization?   (d)

In 11 and 12, give the standard prime factorization of the number.

11. 360 $2^3 \cdot 3^2 \cdot 5$ 12. 1938 $2 \cdot 3 \cdot 17 \cdot 19$

13. *True or false?* In the context of the Fundamental Theorem of Arithmetic, $3 \cdot 5 \cdot 7$ and $7 \cdot 5 \cdot 3$ would be considered distinct factorizations.   false

---

■ **SKILLS** *Objective A* (See pages 341–344 for objectives.)
In 1–6, a. simplify and b. state any restrictions on the variables.

1. $\frac{3}{p^2 + 6p + 5} - \frac{4}{p^2 + 2p - 15}$

   a. $\dfrac{-p - 13}{(p-3)(p+1)(p+5)}$

   b. $p \neq -5, -1, 3$

2. $\frac{2r-3}{2r+3} + \frac{7}{r}$

   a. $\dfrac{2r^2 + 11r + 21}{r(2r+3)}$

   b. $r \neq 0, -\frac{3}{2}$

3. $\frac{4x^2 - 13x - 12}{2x^2 + 3x - 2} \div \frac{x-4}{2x^2 - 5x + 2}$

   a. $\dfrac{4x^2 - 5x - 6}{x + 2}$

   b. $x \neq -2, \frac{1}{2}, 2, 4$

4. $\dfrac{\frac{1}{x} + \frac{3}{x^2}}{\frac{9}{x^2} - 1}$

   a. $\dfrac{1}{3 - x}$

   b. $x \neq 0, -3, 3$

5. $\frac{4}{y^2 - 4} + \frac{6}{2y^2 - 7y + 6}$

   a. $\dfrac{14y}{(y+2)(y-2)(2y-3)}$

   b. $y \neq -2, 2, \frac{3}{2}$

6. $\frac{5}{n^2 + n - 12} - \frac{2}{n^2 + 6n + 8}$

   a. $\dfrac{3n + 16}{(n-3)(n+2)(n+4)}$

   b. $n \neq -4, -2, 3$

7. a. Prove that the equation $\frac{4x}{4x-3} + \frac{3}{3-4x} = 1$ is an identity.

   $\dfrac{4x}{4x-3} + \dfrac{3}{3-4x} = \dfrac{4x}{4x-3} + \dfrac{-3}{4x-3} = \dfrac{4x-3}{4x-3} = 1$

b. What is the domain of the identity?

   all real numbers except $\frac{3}{4}$

■ **SKILLS** *Objective B*
In 8–11, show that the given number is rational by expressing it as a ratio of two integers.

8. $\sqrt{\frac{1}{4}}$ $\frac{1}{2}$

9. $0.4\overline{18}$ $\frac{414}{990}$

10. 3.232 $\frac{3232}{1000}$

11. $3.2\overline{32}$ $\frac{2909}{900}$

■ **PROPERTIES** *Objective F*

12. *Prove:* If a rational number is divided by a nonzero rational number, the result is a rational number.

Suppose r and s are rational, $s \neq 0$. Then ∃ integers a, b, c, d with $b, c, d \neq 0$, such that $r = \frac{a}{b}$, $s = \frac{c}{d}$. So $\frac{r}{s} = \frac{\frac{a}{b}}{\frac{c}{d}} = \frac{a}{b} \cdot \frac{d}{c} = \frac{ad}{bc}$. Since ad and bc are integers, and neither b nor c is 0, $\frac{r}{s}$ is rational.

In 13 and 14, determine whether the statement is *true* or *false*. Justify your answer.

13. All whole numbers are rational numbers.

   True; any whole number n can be written as $\frac{n}{1}$, and n and 1 are integers.

14. The reciprocal of any nonzero rational number is rational.

   True; the rational number $\frac{a}{b}$ (where a, b are nonzero integers) has reciprocal $\frac{b}{a}$ which is rational.

■ **USES** *Objective I*

15. It takes 100 experienced construction workers N days to construct a large office building. It will take 80 novice workers $2N - 30$ days to construct the same building.

a. Write an expression for the fraction of work done on a single day by the 100 experienced workers. $\frac{1}{N}$

b. Write an expression for the fraction of work done on a single day by the 80 novice workers. $\frac{1}{2N - 30}$

c. Write and simplify a rational expression that represents the fraction of work done on a single day by both groups of workers working together. $\frac{3N - 30}{2N^2 - 30N}$

d. What restrictions must be placed on N? $N \neq 0, 15$

■ **SKILLS** *Objective B* (See pages 341–344 for objectives.)

1. If a real number is irrational, then its decimal representation is either ____terminating____ or ____repeating____.

In 2–5, identify each number as rational or irrational. Justify your answer.

2. $\frac{1}{2 - \sqrt{3}}$

   irrat.; since $\sqrt{3}$ is irrational.

3. $\sqrt{841}$

   rational; $\sqrt{841} = 29$

4. $2.1212212221\ldots$

   irrat.; neither repeating nor terminating

5. $-5.1\overline{37}$

   rational; it is a repeating decimal

■ **SKILLS** *Objective C*
In 6–8, rationalize the denominator.

6. $\frac{11\sqrt{2}}{1 - \sqrt{2}}$

   $-22 - 11\sqrt{2}$

7. $\frac{-5\sqrt{3}}{\sqrt{7} - \sqrt{3}}$

   $\dfrac{-5\sqrt{21} + 15}{4}$

8. $\frac{\sqrt{a} - \sqrt{b}}{\sqrt{a} + \sqrt{b}}$

   $\dfrac{a + b - 2\sqrt{ab}}{a - b}$

9. Rationalize the *numerator* in the expression $\frac{\sqrt{3} + \sqrt{2}}{2}$. $\dfrac{1}{2(\sqrt{3} - \sqrt{2})}$

■ **PROPERTIES** *Objective F*

10. Prove that $\sqrt{17}$ is irrational. Assume $\sqrt{17}$ is rational, then ∃ integers a, b ($b \neq 0$) with $\sqrt{17} = \frac{a}{b}$ in lowest terms. Thus, $17 = \frac{a^2}{b^2}$ and $17b^2 = a^2$. So 17 is a factor of a^2 and thus of a. Then $a = 17k$ and $17b^2 = (17k)^2 = 289k^2$, and $b^2 = 17k^2$. Therefore, 17 is a factor of b^2 and thus of b, contradicting the assumption that $\frac{a}{b}$ is in lowest terms. Therefore, $\sqrt{17}$ is irrational.

11. a. *True* or *false*? The quotient of two irrational numbers is irrational.　　　**false**

b. If true, prove the statement. Otherwise give a counterexample.

$\sqrt{2}$ and $\sqrt{8}$ are irrational, but $\frac{\sqrt{2}}{\sqrt{8}} = \frac{\sqrt{2}}{2\sqrt{2}} = \frac{1}{2}$, which is rational.

12. Prove that if a and b are integers and a is not a perfect square, then $\sqrt{a} + b$ is irrational.

Suppose $\sqrt{a} + b$ is rational. Then since $-b$ is rational (since b is), $(\sqrt{a} + b) + (-b) = \sqrt{a}$ is rational, contradicting the fact that $\sqrt{a}$ is irrational (since a is not a perfect square). Thus, $\sqrt{a} + b$ must be irrational.

■ **PROPERTIES** *Objective G* (See pages 341–344 for objectives.)

1. Refer to the graph of f at the right.

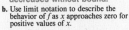

a. Explain in words what happens to $f(x)$ as x approaches zero.
As x approaches zero from the right or left, f(x) decreases without bound.

b. Use limit notation to describe the behavior of f as x approaches zero for positive values of x.　　$\lim\limits_{x \to 0^+} f(x) = -\infty$

c. Use limit notation to describe the behavior of f as x approaches zero for negative values of x.　　$\lim\limits_{x \to 0^-} f(x) = -\infty$

d. Describe, in words, the end behavior of f.
As x increases or decreases without bound, f(x) approaches zero.

e. Describe, using limit notation, the end behavior of f.
$\lim\limits_{x \to -\infty} f(x) = \lim\limits_{x \to \infty} f(x) = 0$

2. Consider the functions g and h where $g(x) = \frac{2}{x-3}$ and $h(x) = \frac{2}{x}$.

a. What transformation maps the graph of h to the graph of g?　　$T_{3,0}$

b. Describe, using limit notation, the behavior of g near any vertical asymptotes.
$\lim\limits_{x \to 3^+} g(x) = \infty, \ \lim\limits_{x \to 3^-} g(x) = -\infty$

c. Describe, using limit notation, the end behavior of g.
$\lim\limits_{x \to -\infty} g(x) = \lim\limits_{x \to \infty} g(x) = 0$

■ **REPRESENTATIONS** *Objective J*

3. Let f be the function $f(x) = \frac{1}{x+1}$.

a. Graph f.

b. Write an equation for the vertical asymptote to the graph of f.
$x = -1$

---

4. a. Graph the function g where $g(x) = \frac{-1}{x^4}$.

b. Use limit notation to describe the end behavior of g.
$\lim\limits_{x \to -\infty} g(x) = \lim\limits_{x \to +\infty} g(x) = 0$

c. Use limit notation to describe the behavior of g near any vertical asymptotes.
$\lim\limits_{x \to 0^-} g(x) = \lim\limits_{x \to 0^+} g(x) = -\infty$

5. Describe, in words, the difference between the graphs of $f(x) = \frac{1}{x^{2k}}$ and $g(x) = \frac{1}{x^{2k+1}}$, for positive integers k.

The graph of f lies above the x-axis and is symmetric with respect to the y-axis, while the graph of g lies in Quadrants 1 and 3 and is symmetric with respect to the origin. Both graphs have the x-axis as a horizontal asymptote, f approaching it from above and g from below.

■ **REPRESENTATIONS** *Objective K*

In 6 and 7, **a.** write an equation for the graph's vertical asymptote and **b.** use limit notation to describe the behavior of the function near the vertical asymptote.

6.

a. $x = 2$
b. $\lim\limits_{x \to 2^-} f(x) = \lim\limits_{x \to 2^+} f(x) = \infty$

7.

a. $x = 0$
b. $\lim\limits_{x \to 0^-} f(x) = \lim\limits_{x \to 0^+} f(x) = -\infty$

8. Let f be the function defined by $f(x) = \frac{1}{x^n}$ such that $\lim\limits_{x \to -\infty} f(x) = \infty$.

a. Sketch a possible graph of f.

b. Is n even or odd?　　even

c. Find $\lim\limits_{x \to 0^+} f(x)$.　　∞

■ **PROPERTIES** *Objective G* (See pages 341–344 for objectives.)

1. Consider the function g defined by $g(y) = \frac{-2y}{4y^2 - 9}$.

a. Identify the vertical asymptotes of the graph of g.　　$y = -\frac{3}{2}, \ y = \frac{3}{2}$

b. Use limit notation to describe the behavior of g near the asymptotes.
$\lim\limits_{y \to -\frac{3}{2}^-} g(y) = \infty, \ \lim\limits_{y \to -\frac{3}{2}^+} g(y) = -\infty,$
$\lim\limits_{y \to \frac{3}{2}^-} g(y) = \infty, \ \lim\limits_{y \to \frac{3}{2}^+} g(y) = -\infty,$

c. Use limit notation to describe the end behavior of g.
$\lim\limits_{y \to -\infty} g(y) = \lim\limits_{y \to \infty} g(y) = 0$

2. Given $f(x) = \frac{x+4}{x^2 + 2x - 8}$, find

a. $\lim\limits_{x \to -4^-} f(x)$.　　$-\frac{1}{6}$
b. $\lim\limits_{x \to -4^+} f(x)$.　　$-\frac{1}{6}$
c. $\lim\limits_{x \to 2^-} f(x)$.　　$-\infty$
d. $\lim\limits_{x \to 2^+} f(x)$.　　∞

■ **PROPERTIES** *Objective H*

3. Given $f(x) = \frac{x+2}{x^2 - x - 6}$, f has a(n) __removable__ discontinuity at $x = -2$ and a(n) __essential__ discontinuity at $x = 3$.

In 4 and 5, classify any discontinuities as essential or removable, and at each removable discontinuity, redefine the function to make it continuous.

4. $f(a) = \frac{2a^2 + a - 3}{a + 1}$
essential at $a = -1$

5. $f(b) = \frac{2b^2 + b - 3}{b - 1}$
removable at $b = 1$; redefine $f(1) = 5$

6. Find a rule for a function that has a removable discontinuity at $x = -2$ and no essential discontinuities.

sample: $f(x) = \frac{(x+1)(x+2)}{x+2} = \frac{x^2 + 3x + 2}{x + 2}$

Precalculus and Discrete Mathematics © Scott, Foresman and Company

■ REPRESENTATIONS Objective J

In 7–10, sketch a graph of the function, indicating holes at the removable discontinuities and dashed lines for any asymptotes.

7. $g(x) = \dfrac{2x^2 + 7x}{x + 3}$

8. $f(x) = \dfrac{x^2 + 2x}{x^3 - 4x}$

9. $h(x) = \dfrac{x^2 + 5x - 6}{x + 6}$

10. $f(x) = \dfrac{x - 2}{x^2 - 4}$

■ REPRESENTATIONS Objective K

In 11 and 12, a. find equations for any vertical asymptotes, b. use limit notation to describe the behavior of the function near any asymptote, and c. use limit notation to describe the behavior of the function near any removable discontinuity.

11. the function in Question 8

b. $\lim\limits_{x\to-3^-} f(x) = -\infty,\ \lim\limits_{x\to-3^+} f(x) = \infty$

a. $x = 2$

c. $\lim\limits_{x\to-2} f(x) = -\frac{1}{4},\ \lim\limits_{x\to 0} f(x) = -\frac{1}{2}$

12. the function graphed at the right

a. $x = -3,\ x = 4$

b. $\lim\limits_{x\to-3^-} f(x) = \infty,\ \lim\limits_{x\to-3^+} f(x) = -\infty$

$\lim\limits_{x\to 4^-} f(x) = \infty,\ \lim\limits_{x\to 4^+} f(x) = \infty$

c. $\lim\limits_{x\to 1} f(x) = 2$

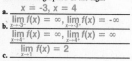

■ PROPERTIES Objective G (See pages 341–344 for objectives.)

In 1–4, a. find a constant function, linear function, power function, or reciprocal of a power function whose end behavior resembles that of the given function, b. use limit notation to describe the end behavior, and c. use limit notation to describe the behavior near any vertical asymptotes.

1. $f(x) = \dfrac{3x^2 + 2x + 1}{5x - 2x^3}$

a. $y = -\dfrac{3}{2x}$

b. $\lim\limits_{x\to-\infty} f(x) = 0,\ \lim\limits_{x\to\infty} f(x) = 0$

c. $\lim\limits_{x\to-\sqrt{\frac{5}{2}}^-} f(x) = \lim\limits_{x\to 0^+} f(x) = \lim\limits_{x\to\sqrt{\frac{5}{2}}^-} f(x) = \infty$,
$\lim\limits_{x\to-\sqrt{\frac{5}{2}}^+} f(x) = \lim\limits_{x\to 0^-} f(x) = \lim\limits_{x\to\sqrt{\frac{5}{2}}^+} f(x) = -\infty$

2. $g(x) = \dfrac{2x^2 - 5}{5x^2 + 2}$

a. $y = \dfrac{2}{5}$

b. $\lim\limits_{x\to-\infty} g(x) = \lim\limits_{x\to\infty} g(x) = \dfrac{2}{5}$

c. no vertical asymptotes

3. $h(x) = \dfrac{x^2 + x - 1}{x - 1}$

a. $y = x + 2$

b. $\lim\limits_{x\to-\infty} h(x) = -\infty,\ \lim\limits_{x\to\infty} h(x) = \infty$

c. $\lim\limits_{x\to 1^-} h(x) = -\infty,\ \lim\limits_{x\to 1^+} h(x) = \infty$

4. $f(t) = t^5 + 12t^3 - 4t - \dfrac{2}{t}$

a. $y = x^5$

b. $\lim\limits_{t\to-\infty} f(t) = -\infty,\ \lim\limits_{t\to\infty} f(t) = \infty$

c. no vertical asymptotes

■ REPRESENTATIONS Objective J

In 5–7, a. find the x- and y-intercepts of the graph of the function and b. sketch the graph.

5. the function in Question 1

a. no x- or y-intercepts

b.

6. the function in Question 2

a. x-int.: $\pm\sqrt{\frac{5}{2}}$; y-int.: $-\frac{5}{2}$

b.

---

7. the function in Question 3

a. x-intercepts: $\approx -1.5,\ \approx 0.7$

y-intercept: 1

b.

■ REPRESENTATIONS Objective K

In 8–10, find an equation for each asymptote of the graph of the function and state whether the asymptote is vertical, horizontal, or oblique.

8. the function in Question 2

$y = \frac{2}{5}$, horizontal

9. the function in Question 3

$x = 1$, vertical

$y = x + 2$, oblique

10. the function graphed at the right

$x = -2$, vertical; $x = 2$, vertical;

$y = \frac{1}{2}x + 1$, oblique

11. Sketch the graph of a function with asymptotes $y = -x + 4$ and $x = 3$, $\lim\limits_{x\to 3^-} f(x) = -\infty$, and $\lim\limits_{x\to 3^+} f(x) = \infty$.

■ SKILLS Objective D (See pages 341–344 for objectives.)

1. If $\sin x = \frac{-\sqrt{3}}{2}$ and $\cos x = -\frac{1}{2}$, find the value of $\tan x$, $\sec x$, $\cot x$, and $\csc x$.

$\sqrt{3}$ -2 $\dfrac{\sqrt{3}}{3}$ $-\dfrac{2\sqrt{3}}{3}$

In 2–7, find the indicated value.

2. $\cot \frac{7\pi}{6}$ $\sqrt{3}$

3. $\sec -\frac{3\pi}{2}$ undefined

4. $\csc \frac{\pi}{2}$ 1

5. $\tan \pi$ 0

6. $\sec \frac{3\pi}{4}$ $-\sqrt{2}$

7. $\tan -\frac{\pi}{4}$ -1

■ PROPERTIES Objective H

8. Consider the cotangent function $f: x \to \cot x$. For what values of x does this function have essential discontinuities?

$x = n\pi$, where n is an integer

9. What transformation can be applied to the graph of the function $\csc x$ so that the image has essential discontinuities at $x = \frac{n\pi}{2}\ \forall$ integers n?

$S_{\frac{1}{2}, 1}$

■ REPRESENTATIONS Objective J

10. a. Sketch a graph of $y = \cot x$ for $-2\pi < x < 2\pi$.

b. On the same axes, sketch a graph of $y = \csc x$.

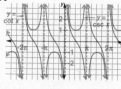

c. For which values of x is $\cot x > \csc x$?

$(2n - 1)\pi < x < 2n\pi$, where n is an integer

■ REPRESENTATIONS Objective L

In 11–14, use the right triangle below to find the indicated value.

11. $\cot \theta$ $\dfrac{\sqrt{2}}{2}$

12. $\csc \phi$ $\sqrt{3}$

13. $\sec \theta$ $\sqrt{3}$

14. $\tan \phi$ $\dfrac{\sqrt{2}}{2}$

LESSON MASTER 5-7
QUESTIONS ON SPUR OBJECTIVES

■SKILLS *Objective E* (See pages 341–344 for objectives.)
In 1–6, solve each equation.

1. $\frac{1}{y-3} = \frac{y}{y+4} + \frac{7y}{(y+4)(y-3)}$

$\underline{\quad y = 1 \quad}$

2. $\frac{8}{t+3} + \frac{t}{t-3} = \frac{-2}{t^2-9}$

$\underline{\quad t = \frac{-11 \pm \sqrt{209}}{2} \quad}$

3. $\frac{r}{r-1} + \frac{r-1}{r} = 1$

$\underline{\quad r = \frac{1 \pm i\sqrt{3}}{2} \quad}$

4. $2 + \frac{20}{s^2-s-6} = \frac{-3}{s-3}$

$\underline{\quad s = \frac{-1 \pm i\sqrt{111}}{4} \quad}$

5. $\frac{z+3}{z-6} + \frac{z}{3z-4} = \frac{2z^2-3}{3z^2-22z+24}$

$\underline{\quad z = \frac{1 \pm \sqrt{73}}{4} \quad}$

6. $\frac{x}{2x-1} = \frac{6}{5x+7} + \frac{x^2-x+1}{10x^2+9x-7}$

$\underline{\quad x = \frac{1}{2} \pm i \quad}$

■USES *Objective I*

7. A tired swimmer takes 30 minutes longer to return to shore from a pier as it took to swim from shore to the pier. The pier is 1 km from shore and the swimmer's average speed returning is 3 km/h less than the swimmer's average speed going out to the pier. What is the swimmer's average speed going out to the pier?

$\underline{\quad \text{about 4.4 km/h} \quad}$

8. In an electrical circuit, if two resistors with resistances R_1 and R_2 are connected in parallel, then the equivalent resistance, R, is found using the equation $\frac{1}{R} = \frac{1}{R_1} + \frac{1}{R_2}$. If R_1 is 5 ohms less than R_2 and R is one-third of R_2, what are the values of R_1, R_2, and R?

$\underline{\quad R_1 = 5 \text{ ohms}, R_2 = 10 \text{ ohms}, R = \frac{10}{3} \text{ ohms} \quad}$

LESSON MASTER 6-1
QUESTIONS ON SPUR OBJECTIVES

■REPRESENTATIONS *Objective G* (See pages 396–398 for objectives.)
In 1–6, use an automatic grapher to determine whether the equation appears to be an identity. If so, conjure the domain of the identity. If not, give a counterexample.

1. $1 + \cos^2 x = 2\sin^2\left(x + \frac{\pi}{2}\right)$

$\underline{\quad \text{no; sample: } x = \frac{3\pi}{2} \quad}$

2. $\tan y = \cot\left(\frac{\pi}{2} - y\right)$

$\underline{\quad \text{yes; } \{x: x \neq \frac{(2k+1)\pi}{2} \text{ where } k \text{ is an integer}\} \quad}$

3. $\sin x \cdot \tan x = \sec x + \cos x$

$\underline{\quad \text{no; sample: } x = 0 \quad}$

4. $\sin x \cdot \tan x = \sec x - \cos x$

$\underline{\quad \text{yes; } \{x: x \neq \frac{(2k+1)\pi}{2} \text{ where } k \text{ is an integer}\} \quad}$

5. $\sin 3z = 3\sin z \cos z$

$\underline{\quad \text{no; sample: } z = \frac{\pi}{2} \quad}$

6. $\csc u = -\csc(\pi + u)$

$\underline{\quad \text{yes; } \{u: u \neq k\pi \text{ where } k \text{ is an integer}\} \quad}$

7. Use an automatic grapher to decide whether $\tan(\alpha + \beta) = \tan \alpha + \tan \beta$, for $\alpha = \frac{\pi}{4}$, $\alpha = \frac{\pi}{2}$, and a value of your choice for α.

$\underline{\quad \text{no, no, no} \quad}$

8. *True* or *false*? Identities can be proved using an automatic grapher.

$\underline{\quad \text{false} \quad}$

LESSON MASTER 6-2
QUESTIONS ON SPUR OBJECTIVES

■SKILLS *Objective A* (See pages 396–398 for objectives.)

1. Suppose x is in the interval $\frac{\pi}{2} < x < \pi$ and $\sin x = \frac{\sqrt{2}}{\sqrt{3}}$. Use trigonometric identities to find each value.

a. $\sec x$ $\underline{\quad -\sqrt{3} \quad}$ b. $\tan x$ $\underline{\quad -\sqrt{2} \quad}$

c. $\cos x$ $\underline{\quad \frac{-\sqrt{2}}{2} \quad}$ d. $\csc x$ $\underline{\quad \frac{\sqrt{3}}{\sqrt{2}} \quad}$

2. If $\sin \alpha = -.8$ and $\tan \alpha = 2.1$, find $\sec \alpha$. $\underline{\quad \approx -2.63 \quad}$

■PROPERTIES *Objective D*
In 3–5, prove the identity and specify its domain.

3. $\sec x \cdot \cos x = \sin x \csc x$

$\sec x \cos x$	$\sin x \csc x$
$\left(\frac{1}{\cos x}\right)\cos x$	$\sin x\left(\frac{1}{\sin x}\right)$
$1 = 1$	

$\{x: x \neq \frac{k\pi}{2}, k \text{ is an integer}\}$

4. $\frac{1}{1+\cos x} + \frac{1}{1-\cos x} = 2\csc^2 x$

L.S. $= \frac{(1-\cos x) + (1+\cos x)}{1 - \cos^2 x}$
$= \frac{2}{\sin^2 x}$
$= 2\csc^2 x$
$\{x: x \neq k\pi, k \text{ is an integer}\}$

5. $\cot x \cdot \sin x \cdot \sec x = \cos^2 x + \sin^2 x$

$\cot x \sin x \sec x$	$\cos^2 x + \sin^2 x$
$\left(\frac{\cos x}{\sin x}\right)\sin x\left(\frac{1}{\cos x}\right)$	1
$1 = 1$	

$\{x: x \neq \frac{k\pi}{2} \text{ where } k \text{ is an integer}\}$

6. Fill in the blank to make an identity: $\cos x \cdot \cot x + \sin x = $ $\underline{\quad \csc x \quad}$

■REPRESENTATIONS *Objective G*
In 7 and 8, use an automatic grapher to conjecture whether the equation is an identity. If so, prove it and identify its domain. If not, give a counterexample.

7. $\cot 2x + \cot x = \cot 3x$

no; sample: $x = \frac{\pi}{4}$

8. $\frac{\cos x \cot x}{1 - \sin x} = 1 + \csc x$ yes;

$\frac{\cos x \cot x}{1 - \sin x}$	$1 + \csc x$
$\frac{\cos^2 x}{(1 - \sin x)\sin x}$	$1 + \frac{1}{\sin x}$
$\frac{1 - \sin^2 x}{(1 - \sin x)\sin x}$	$\frac{\sin x + 1}{\sin x}$
$\frac{1 + \sin x}{\sin x}$	

$\{x: x \neq k\pi \text{ and } x \neq \frac{(4k+1)\pi}{2} \text{ where } k \text{ is an integer}\}$

LESSON MASTER 6-3
QUESTIONS ON SPUR OBJECTIVES

■SKILLS *Objective A* (See pages 396–398 for objectives.)

1. Suppose $0 < \alpha < \frac{\pi}{2} < \beta < \pi$, $\cos \alpha = .75$, and $\sin \beta = .3$. Find the following values.

a. $\sin \alpha$ $\underline{\quad .66 \quad}$ b. $\cos \beta$ $\underline{\quad -.95 \quad}$

c. $\cos(\alpha + \beta)$ $\underline{\quad -.91 \quad}$ d. $\cos(\alpha - \beta)$ $\underline{\quad -.52 \quad}$

In 2–4, express the following in terms of rational numbers and radicals.

2. $\cos\left(\frac{\pi}{4} + \frac{\pi}{6}\right)$

$\underline{\quad \frac{\sqrt{6} - \sqrt{2}}{4} \quad}$

3. $\cos \frac{11\pi}{12}$

$\underline{\quad \frac{-\sqrt{2} - \sqrt{6}}{4} \quad}$

4. $\cos \frac{\pi}{9}\cos \frac{2\pi}{9} - \sin \frac{\pi}{9}\sin \frac{2\pi}{9}$

$\underline{\quad \frac{1}{2} \quad}$

5. Find the cosine of $\frac{\pi}{12}$:

a. by writing $\frac{\pi}{12}$ as $\frac{\pi}{4} - \frac{\pi}{6}$.

$\underline{\quad \frac{\sqrt{6} + \sqrt{2}}{4} \quad}$

b. by writing $\frac{\pi}{12}$ as $\frac{\pi}{3} - \frac{\pi}{4}$.

$\underline{\quad \frac{\sqrt{6} + \sqrt{2}}{4} \quad}$

6. Simplify $\cos\left(\frac{\pi}{2} + x\right) + \cos\left(\frac{\pi}{2} - x\right)$. $\underline{\quad 0 \quad}$

■ **PROPERTIES** *Objective D*
In 7–9, prove the identity and specify the domain.

7. $-2 \sin x \sin y = \cos(x+y) - \cos(x-y)$
Right side $= \cos x \cos y - \sin x \sin y -$
$\qquad (\cos x \cos y + \sin x \sin y)$
$\qquad = -2 \sin x \sin y$
{all real numbers}

8. $\cos(\pi - x) = -\cos x$
Left side $= \cos \pi \cos x + \sin \pi \sin x$
$\qquad = (-1) \cos x + (0) \sin x$
$\qquad = -\cos x$
{all real numbers}

9. $\sin x = \cos\left(x + \frac{3\pi}{2}\right)$
Right side $= \cos x \cos \frac{3\pi}{2} - \sin x \sin \frac{3\pi}{2}$
$\qquad = (\cos x)(0) - (\sin x)(-1)$
$\qquad = \sin x$
{all real numbers}

LESSON MASTER 6–4
QUESTIONS ON **SPUR** OBJECTIVES

■ **SKILLS** *Objective A (See pages 396–398 for objectives.)*
In 1–4, express the following in terms of rational numbers and radicals.

1. $\sin\left(\frac{2\pi}{3} - \frac{\pi}{4}\right)$ — $\frac{\sqrt{6}+\sqrt{2}}{4}$

2. $\tan \frac{7\pi}{12}$ — $\frac{1+\sqrt{3}}{1-\sqrt{3}}$

3. $\frac{\tan\frac{3\pi}{16} + \tan\frac{\pi}{16}}{1 - \tan\frac{3\pi}{16}\tan\frac{\pi}{16}}$ — 1

4. $\sin \frac{13\pi}{12}$ — $\frac{\sqrt{2}-\sqrt{6}}{4}$

5. Given that $\sin \alpha = \frac{2}{3}$, find $\sin(\pi - \alpha)$. — $\frac{2}{3}$

In 6–9, suppose r is in the interval $0 < r < \frac{\pi}{2}$ with $\cos r = \frac{3}{5}$ and s is in the interval $\pi < s < \frac{3\pi}{2}$ with $\sin s = -\frac{1}{4}$. Use this information to find each value.

6. $\sin(s-r)$ — $\frac{4\sqrt{15}-3}{20}$

7. $\tan(r+s)$ — $\frac{4\sqrt{15}+3}{3\sqrt{15}-4}$

8. $\sin(\pi + s - r)$ — $\frac{3-4\sqrt{15}}{20}$

9. $\tan(\pi + s - r)$ — $\frac{3-4\sqrt{15}}{3\sqrt{15}+4}$

■ **PROPERTIES** *Objective D*
In 10–13, prove the identity and specify its domain.

10. $\sin\left(\frac{3\pi}{2} + x\right) = -\cos x$
Left side $= \sin \frac{3\pi}{2} \cos x + \cos \frac{3\pi}{2} \sin x$
$\qquad = (-1) \cos x + (0) \sin x$
$\qquad = -\cos x$
{all real numbers}

11. $\tan x = -\tan(\pi - x)$
Right side $= -\left(\frac{\tan \pi - \tan x}{1 + \tan \pi \tan x}\right)$
$\qquad = -\frac{0 - \tan x}{1 + (0)\tan x}$
$\qquad = \tan x$
$\left\{x: x \neq \frac{(2k+1)\pi}{2} \text{ where } k \text{ is an integer}\right\}$

12. $\sin(x+y)\cos(x-y) = \sin x \cos x + \sin y \cos y$
Left side $= (\sin x \cos y + \cos x \sin y)(\cos x \cos y + \sin x \sin y)$
$\qquad = \sin x \cos x \cos^2 y + \sin^2 x \sin y \cos y + \cos^2 x \sin y \cos y + \cos x \sin x \sin^2 y$
$\qquad = \sin x \cos x (\cos^2 y + \sin^2 y) + (\sin^2 x + \cos^2 x)\sin y \cos y$
$\qquad = \sin x \cos x + \sin y \cos y$
{all real numbers}

13. $\sin(x+y) + \cos(x-y) = (\sin x + \cos x)(\sin y + \cos y)$
(Compare this identity to the one in Question 12.)
Left side $= \sin x \cos y + \cos x \sin y + \cos x \cos y + \sin x \sin y$
$\qquad = \sin x (\cos y + \sin y) + \cos x (\sin y + \cos y)$
$\qquad = (\sin x + \cos x)(\cos y + \sin y)$
{all real numbers}
(Note that replacing multiplication with addition in the identity in Question 12 (except for in $(x+y)$) yields the identity in Question 13!)

LESSON MASTER 6–5
QUESTIONS ON **SPUR** OBJECTIVES

■ **SKILLS** *Objective A (See pages 396–398 for objectives.)*
1. Given $0 < x < \frac{\pi}{2}$ and $\cos x = \frac{8}{17}$, find $\sin 2x$ and $\sin \frac{x}{2}$. — $\frac{240}{289}$; $\frac{3}{\sqrt{34}}$

In 2 and 3, express the following in terms of rational numbers and radicals.

2. $\cos \frac{\pi}{8}$ — $\frac{\sqrt{\sqrt{2}+2}}{2}$

3. $\sin \frac{\pi}{12}$ — $\frac{\sqrt{2-\sqrt{3}}}{2}$

4. a. Use the identity for $\cos(\alpha - \beta)$ to find $\cos \frac{7\pi}{12}$. — $\frac{\sqrt{2}-\sqrt{6}}{2}$

b. Use the identity $\cos 2\alpha = 2\cos^2 \alpha - 1$ to find $\cos \frac{7\pi}{12}$. — $\frac{-\sqrt{2-\sqrt{3}}}{2}$

c. Show that your answers to parts a and b are equal.

$\left(\frac{\sqrt{2}-\sqrt{6}}{4}\right)^2 = \frac{2+6-2\sqrt{12}}{16} = \frac{1}{2} - \frac{\sqrt{3}}{4}$

$\left(\frac{-\sqrt{2-\sqrt{3}}}{2}\right)^2 = \frac{2-\sqrt{3}}{4} = \frac{1}{2} - \frac{\sqrt{3}}{4}$

Since both answers are negative and their squares are equal, they are equal.

■ **PROPERTIES**   *Objective D*

5. *Multiple choice.* Which expression equals $\cos 2x$ for all x? ___(d)___

(a) $1 - 2\cos^2 x$ (b) $\sin^2 x - \cos^2 x$
(c) $2\sin^2 x - 1$ (d) $2\cos^2 x - 1$

In 6–9, prove the identity and specify its domain.

6. $(\sin x + \cos x)^2 = \sin 2x + 1$

Left side = $\sin^2 x + \cos^2 x + 2\sin x \cos x$
$= 1 + \sin x$
{all real numbers}

7. $1 - \tan^2 \theta = \frac{2 \tan \theta}{\tan 2\theta}$

Right side = $\dfrac{2 \tan \theta}{\dfrac{2 \tan \theta}{1 - \tan^2 \theta}}$

$= 2 \tan \theta \cdot \dfrac{1 - \tan^2 \theta}{2 \tan \theta}$

$= 1 - \tan^2 \theta$

$\left\{\theta : \theta \neq \dfrac{k\pi}{4} \text{ where } k \text{ is an integer}\right\}$

8. $4\sin^2 \alpha \cos^2 \alpha + (\cos^2 \alpha - \sin^2 \alpha)^2 = 1$

Left side = $(2 \sin \alpha \cos \alpha)^2 + (\cos 2\alpha)^2$
$= (\sin 2\alpha)^2 + (\cos 2\alpha)^2$
$= 1$
{all real numbers}

9. $2 \sin \beta \csc 2\beta = \sec \beta$

Left side = $2 \sin \beta \left(\dfrac{1}{\sin 2\beta}\right)$

$= 2 \sin \beta \left(\dfrac{1}{2 \sin \beta \cos \beta}\right)$

$= \dfrac{1}{\cos \beta}$

$= \sec \beta$

$\left\{\beta : \beta \neq \dfrac{k\pi}{2} \text{ where } k \text{ is an integer}\right\}$

■ **SKILLS**   *Objective B* (See pages 396–398 for objectives.)

1. Let $f(x) = \tan^{-1}(x)$.

a. Within what interval must x lie?   _x can be any real number._

b. Within what interval must $f(x)$ lie? $-\dfrac{\pi}{2} < f(x) < \dfrac{\pi}{2}$

In 2–5, compute without using a calculator.

2. $\sin^{-1}\left(\dfrac{-\sqrt{3}}{2}\right)$ $-\dfrac{\pi}{3}$

3. $\tan(\tan^{-1} 0)$ 0

4. $\cos(\sin^{-1} 1)$ 0

5. $\sin\left(\tan^{-1}\left(\tan \dfrac{\pi}{6}\right)\right)$ $\dfrac{1}{2}$

In 6 and 7, use $\triangle ABC$ to evaluate the expression.

6. $\sin\left(\tan^{-1}\left(\dfrac{a}{b}\right)\right)$ $\dfrac{a}{c}$

7. $\cos^{-1}\left(\dfrac{a}{c}\right)$ ϕ

■ **USES**   *Objective E*

8. Snell's Law of Refraction states that when a light ray passes from one medium into a second one, its path bends so that the angles α and β (shown in the diagram) obey $\dfrac{\sin \alpha}{\sin \beta} = C$, where C is a constant called the *index of refraction*. If the index of refraction is 1.24, and a ray of light strikes the liquid at an angle of incidence of $\alpha = 65°$, find the angle of refraction β.   _about 47.0°_

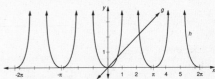

9. Suppose that the sun, Earth, and Jupiter are positioned as shown in the diagram at the right.

a. If Jupiter is x km from the sun and Earth is 150 million km from the sun, give an expression for the angle θ formed by the sight lines from Earth to the other two bodies.
$\theta = \tan^{-1}\left(\dfrac{x}{1.5 \cdot 10^8}\right)$

b. If $x = 7.8 \cdot 10^8$ km, find θ.   _about 79.1°_

■ **SKILLS**   *Objective C* (See pages 396–398 for objectives.)
In 1–4, solve without a calculator over the interval $0 \leq x \leq 2\pi$.

1. $\csc x = \dfrac{2\sqrt{3}}{3}$

2. $\tan x \leq -\sqrt{3}$

$x = \dfrac{\pi}{3}$ or $\dfrac{2\pi}{3}$

$\dfrac{\pi}{2} < x \leq \dfrac{2\pi}{3}$ or
$\dfrac{3\pi}{2} < x \leq \dfrac{5\pi}{3}$

3. $\sec 2x = 2$

4. $(\sin x)(2 \sin x - 1) < 0$

$x = \dfrac{\pi}{6}, \dfrac{5\pi}{6}, \dfrac{7\pi}{6},$ or $\dfrac{11\pi}{6}$

$0 < x < \dfrac{\pi}{6}$ or
$\dfrac{5\pi}{6} < x < \pi$

In 5 and 6, solve over the reals using a calculator or automatic grapher, if necessary.

5. $\sec^2 x + \csc^2 x = \sec^2 x \csc^2 x$

$\left\{x : x \neq \dfrac{k\pi}{2} \text{ where } k \text{ is an integer}\right\}$

6. $7 \sin^2 \phi + 10 \sin \phi + 3 = 0$

$\sin \phi = -1$ or $-\dfrac{3}{7}$
Therefore,
$\phi = \dfrac{3\pi}{2} + 2k\pi$ or
$\phi = -.44 + 2k\pi$ or
$\phi = 3.58 + 2k\pi$
where k is an integer

■ **USES**   *Objective F*

7. Two jugglers toss bowling pins to each other with an initial velocity v_0 of 35 ft/s. The horizontal distance R that the bowling pins travel is approximated by the equation $R = \dfrac{v_0^2}{32} \sin 2\theta$. At what angle should the pins be thrown if the jugglers are standing 30 ft apart?

   about 25.8°

■ **REPRESENTATIONS**   *Objective H*

8. Use an automatic grapher to approximate to the nearest tenth all solutions to $\tan x + \sin x = 1.7$ over the interval $0 \leq x \leq 2\pi$.

   $x \approx 0.8$ or ≈ 4.3

9. Refer to the graph below of $g(x) = x$ and $h(x) = \tan^2 x$.

a. Solve $\tan^2 x = x$ over the interval $-\pi \leq x \leq \pi$.

   $x = 0$ or $x \approx .7$ or $x \approx 2.2$

b. Solve $\tan^2 x < x$ over the interval $-\pi \leq x \leq \pi$.

   $0 < x < .7$ or $2.2 < x \leq \pi$

Precalculus and Discrete Mathematics © Scott, Foresman and Company

LESSON MASTER 7-1
QUESTIONS ON SPUR OBJECTIVES

■ SKILLS *Objective A (See pages 462–464 for objectives.)*
In 1–6, write the first five terms of the sequence defined by the given formula.

1. $d_n = n^3 + 4n^2 - 3n + 1$

2. $\begin{cases} a_1 = 4 \\ a_{k+1} = -3a_k - 7 \ \forall \ k \geq 1 \end{cases}$

3, 19, 55, 117, 211   4, -19, 50, -157, 464

3. $a_n = 2\left\lceil \frac{n}{3} \right\rceil$

4. $b_n = (-1)^n \cdot \frac{n(n+1)}{2}$

2, 2, 2, 4, 4   -1, 3, -6, 10, -15

5. $f_n = \begin{cases} \cos n\pi, \ n \text{ even} \\ \sin n\pi, \ n \text{ odd} \end{cases}$

6. $c_n = 3\left\lfloor \frac{n}{3} \right\rfloor$

0, 1, 0, 1, 0   0, 0, 3, 3, 3

7. Let a be the sequence defined by $a_n = (-2)^{n+1}$.

  a. Which term is greater: a_7 or a_8? a_7

  b. Given two consecutive integers, how can one tell which will yield the greater term of the sequence?

    The odd integer will yield the greater term.

8. Let b be the sequence defined by
$\begin{cases} b_1 = 2 \\ b_{k+1} = 3b_k - 2 \ \forall \ k \geq 1 \end{cases}$. Find b_6.   244

9. Which of the sequences in Questions 1–7 are defined recursively?   Questions 2, 7

10. If 5, a, b, c, d, 14 are consecutive terms of an arithmetic sequence, find a, b, c, and d.   6.8, 8.6, 10.4, 12.2

■ USES *Objective H*

10. A leading brand of soap advertises that it is $99\frac{44}{100}\%$ pure. Suppose that in the manufacturing process, the soap is initially 80% pure, and is then put through a series of chemical processes to purify it further, each step removing 40% of the existing impurities. Let A_n represent the percent of impurities present after the nth step.

  a. Write a recursive definition for the sequence A. $\begin{cases} A_1 = .12 \\ A_{k+1} = .6A_k \ \forall \ k \geq 1 \end{cases}$

  b. Find A_3.   .0432

  c. Find n so that the soap is at least $99\frac{44}{100}\%$ pure.   7

11. A phone company suggests that you call two friends, with instructions for each of them to call two of their friends. If this process is continued, how many friends will receive a call as the seventeenth in the line of calls?   131,072

12. Suppose an economist suggests that the government adopt an income tax system consisting of income brackets of equal size, and in which the tax rate increases by a constant amount from one bracket to the next. A possible tax table for this system is given below.

Income Bracket	Annual Income (in dollars)	Tax Rate (in percent)
1	0 – 20,000	12
2	20,001 – 40,000	16.5
3	40,001 – 60,000	21
4	60,001 – 80,000	25.5

  a. If the tax rate in the nth income bracket is R_n, write a recursive definition for R_n. $\begin{cases} R_1 = .12 \\ R_{k+1} = R_k + .045 \ \forall \ k \geq 1 \end{cases}$

  b. Find R_8.   .435

  c. If the maximum tax rate were 48 percent, what level of income would be taxed at this rate?   Bracket 9: $160,001 and above

  d. Suppose the tax rates change so that the lowest rate is 9 percent, with an increase of 5.1 percent from one bracket to the next. At what rate would someone who earned $136,000 annually be taxed? Is this more or less than under the originally proposed system?   39.6%, more

---

LESSON MASTER 7-2
QUESTIONS ON SPUR OBJECTIVES

■ SKILLS *Objective B (See pages 462–464 for objectives.)*
In 1–4, a. write the first five terms of the sequence and b. determine an explicit formula that is suggested by the pattern of numbers in part a.

1. $\begin{cases} a_1 = 2 \\ a_{k+1} = 3a_k \ \forall \ k \geq 1 \end{cases}$ **a.** 2, 6, 18, 54, 162   **b.** $a_n = 2 \cdot 3^{n-1}$

2. $\begin{cases} d_1 = -1 \\ d_{k+1} = d_k + 5 \ \forall \ k \geq 1 \end{cases}$ **a.** -1, 4, 9, 14, 19   **b.** $d_n = 5n - 6$

3. $\begin{cases} a_1 = 1 \\ a_{k+1} = (k+1)a_k \ \forall \ k \geq 1 \end{cases}$ **a.** 1, 2, 6, 24, 120   **b.** $a_n = n!$

4. $\begin{cases} x_1 = 3 \\ x_2 = 5 \\ x_{k+1} = x_k + 2x_{k-1} - 2 \ \forall \ k \geq 1 \end{cases}$ **a.** 3, 5, 9, 17, 33   **b.** $x_n = 2^n + 1$
(Hint: Subtract 1 from each term to see the pattern.)

5. Conjecture an explicit formula for S_n, the sum of the first n positive odd integers. $S_n = n^2$

■ REPRESENTATIONS *Objective J*

6. a. List the terms generated by the program at the right.
    0, 10, 30, 60, 100, 150, 210

```
10 FOR N=0 TO 6
20   C=5N*(N+1)
30   PRINT C
40 NEXT N
```

  b. Does the program use a recursive or explicit formula? What is this formula?
    explicit; $c_n = 5n(n + 1)$

7. Complete the program at the right so it uses a recursive formula to generate the first seven terms of the sequence defined by $a_n = \frac{n}{2} + 3$ $\forall \ n \geq 1$.

```
10 TERM = 3.5
20 PRINT TERM
30 FOR K = 2 TO 7
40   TERM = TERM+.5
50   PRINT TERM
60 NEXT K
```

LESSON MASTER 7-3
QUESTIONS ON SPUR OBJECTIVES

■ SKILLS *Objective C (See pages 462–464 for objectives.)*

1. If $n = 3$, find $\sum_{k=-1}^{n} k^2 + 3k$.   30

In 2 and 3, write using summation notation.

2. $7 + 14 + 21 + 28 + 35 + 42$ $\sum_{j=1}^{6} 7j$

3. $-\frac{2}{(k+1)^2} - \frac{1}{(k+1)} + 0 + (k+1) + 2(k+1)^2$ $\sum_{j=-2}^{2} j(k+1)^j$

4. a. Rewrite the equation $1^3 + 2^3 + 3^3 + 4^3 + \ldots + n^3 = (1 + 2 + 3 + 4 + \ldots + n)^2$ using summation notation.
    $\sum_{j=1}^{n} j^3 = \left(\sum_{j=1}^{n} j \right)^2$

  b. Show that the equation is true for $n = 5$.   Both sides yield 225.

■ SKILLS *Objective D*

5. a. Express $\sum_{j=0}^{11} (j^4 - j)$ in terms of $\sum_{j=0}^{10} (j^4 - j)$. $\sum_{j=0}^{10} (j^4 - j) + (11^4 - 11)$

  b. Given that $\sum_{j=0}^{10} (j^4 - j) = 25,278$, find $\sum_{j=0}^{11} (j^4 - j)$.   39,908

6. Let $S(k)$ be the statement: $\sum_{j=1}^{k} j^3 = \frac{1}{4}k^2(k + 1)^2$.

  a. Find $\sum_{j=1}^{5} j^3$ and show that $S(5)$ is true.
    $\sum_{j=1}^{5} j^3 = 225$; $\frac{1}{4}(5^2)(5+1)^2 = 225$; thus, $S(5)$ is true.

  b. Rewrite $\sum_{j=1}^{k+1} j^3$ in terms of $\sum_{j=1}^{k} j^3$. $\sum_{j=1}^{k} j^3 + (k + 1)^3$

  c. Use your answers to parts **a** and **b** to find $\sum_{j=1}^{6} j^3$. $225 + 6^3 = 441$

  d. Use the answer to part **c** to determine if $S(6)$ is true.
    $\frac{1}{4}(6^2)(6 + 1)^2 = 441 = \sum_{j=1}^{6} j^3$, so $S(6)$ is true.

■ **PROPERTIES** *Objective F*

7. Prove that the sequence defined by $\begin{cases} a_1 = \frac{1}{2} \\ a_{k+1} = \frac{a_k}{k+2} \end{cases} \forall\, k \ge 1$

has explicit formula $a_n = \frac{1}{(n+1)!}$.

$a_1 = \frac{1}{(1+1)!} = \frac{1}{2!} = \frac{1}{2}$; $a_{k+1} = \frac{1}{(k+1+1)!} =$

$\frac{1}{(k+2)!} = \frac{1}{(k+2)(k+1)!} = \frac{1}{k+2} \cdot \frac{1}{(k+1)!} =$

$\frac{1}{k+2} \cdot a_k = \frac{a_k}{k+2}$

8. Prove that the sequence defined by $\begin{cases} x_1 = 3 \\ x_{k+1} = \frac{x_k}{4} \end{cases} \forall\, k \ge 1$

has explicit formula $x_n = \frac{3}{4^{n-1}}$.

$x_1 = \frac{3}{4^{1-1}} = 3$; $x_{k+1} = \frac{3}{4^{k+1-1}} = \frac{3}{4^k} = \frac{3}{4 \cdot 4^{k-1}} =$

$\frac{1}{4} \cdot \frac{3}{4^{k-1}} = \frac{x_k}{4}$

■ **REPRESENTATIONS** *Objective J*

9. Consider the computer program below.

```
10  INPUT N
20  SUM = 0
30  FOR K = 4 TO N
40      TERM = K/(K + 1)
50      SUM = SUM + TERM
60  NEXT K
70  PRINT SUM
```

a. Use summation notation to express the sum computed by this program. $\displaystyle\sum_{k=4}^{n} \frac{k}{k+1}$

b. If 7 is input for N, what output is generated?   3.36547619

10. How would you change the program in Question 9 so it would

compute $\displaystyle\sum_{k=n}^{15} \frac{n-k}{k}$?   30 FOR K = N TO 15
40   TERM = (N − K)/K

LESSON **MASTER 7-4**
QUESTIONS ON **SPUR** OBJECTIVES

■ **PROPERTIES** *Objective F (See pages 462–464 for objectives.)*

1. Prove that the sequence defined by $\begin{cases} a_1 = 2 \\ a_{k+1} = a_k + k + 1 \end{cases} \forall\, k \ge 1$

has explicit formula $a_n = \frac{n^2}{2} + \frac{n}{2} + 1$.

Let $S(n)$: $a_n = \frac{n^2}{2} + \frac{n}{2} + 1$. Show $S(1)$ is true:

$a_1 = \frac{1^2}{2} + \frac{1}{2} + 1 = 2$, so $S(1)$ is true. Assume $S(k)$

is true $\left(a_k = \frac{k^2}{2} + \frac{k}{2} + 1\right)$ for a positive integer k.

Show $S(k + 1)$ is true:

$a_{k+1} = a_k + k + 1 = \frac{k^2}{2} + \frac{k}{2} + 1 + k + 1$

$= \frac{k^2 + k + 2 + 2k + 2}{2}$

$= \frac{k^2 + 2k + 1 + k + 1 + 2}{2} = \frac{(k+1)^2}{2} + \frac{k+1}{2} + 1$

So $S(k + 1)$ is true. Therefore, by induction, $S(n)$ is true $\forall$ positive integers n.

2. Identify the basis step and the inductive step in your proof for Question 1.

basis: _The verification that $S(1)$ is true_

inductive: _Proving that $S(k)$ is true $\Rightarrow S(k + 1)$ is true_

3. Find an explicit formula for the sequence defined by $\begin{cases} a_1 = 2 \\ a_{k+1} = 3a_k \end{cases} \forall\, k \ge 1$. Use mathematical induction to prove that your formula is correct.

$a_n = \frac{2}{3} \cdot 3^n$ $\forall$ positive integers n. Proof: Let $S(k)$:

$a_k = \frac{2}{3} \cdot 3^k$. Show $S(1)$ is true: $a_1 = \frac{2}{3} \cdot 3^1 = 2$, so

$S(1)$ is true. Assume $S(k)$ is true for a positive

integer k; that is, $a_k = \frac{2}{3} \cdot 3^k$. Show $S(k + 1)$ is true:

$a_{k+1} = \frac{2}{3} \cdot 3^{k+1} = \frac{2}{3}(3^k \cdot 3) = 3\left(\frac{2}{3} \cdot 3^k\right) = 3a_k$

So $S(k + 1)$ is true. Therefore, by induction, $S(n)$ is true $\forall$ positive integers n.

■ **PROPERTIES** *Objective G*

In 4–6, use mathematical induction to prove that $S(n)$ is true for all positive integers n, or find a counterexample.

4. $S(n)$: $3 + 9 + 15 + \ldots + (6n - 3) = 3n^2$

Show $S(1)$ is true: $3 = 3 \cdot 1^2$. Assume $S(k)$ is true for a positive integer k: $3 + 9 + 15 + \ldots +$ $(6k - 3) = 3k^2$. Show $S(k + 1)$ is true:

$3 + 9 + 15 + \ldots + (6(k + 1) - 3)$
$\quad = 3 + 9 + 15 + \ldots + (6k - 3) +$
$\quad\quad (6(k + 1) - 3)$
$\quad = 3k^2 + 6k + 3$
$\quad = 3(k^2 + 2k + 1)$
$\quad = 3(k + 1)^2$

So $S(k + 1)$ is true. Therefore, by induction, $S(n)$ is true $\forall$ positive integers n.

5. $S(n)$: $\displaystyle\sum_{i=0}^{n} 2^i = 2^{n+1} - 1$

Show $S(1)$ is true: $\displaystyle\sum_{i=0}^{1} 2^i = 1 + 2 = 3 = 2^{1+1} - 1$.

Assume $S(k)$ is true for a positive integer k:

$\displaystyle\sum_{i=0}^{k} 2^i = 2^{k+1} - 1$. Show $S(k + 1)$ is true:

$\displaystyle\sum_{i=0}^{k+1} 2^i = \sum_{i=0}^{k} 2^i + 2^{k+1} = 2^{k+1} - 1 + 2^{k+1}$
$\quad = 2 \cdot 2^{k+1} - 1 = 2^{(k+1)+1} - 1$

So $S(k + 1)$ is true. Therefore, by induction, $S(n)$ is true $\forall$ positive integers n.

6. $S(n)$: $(a + b)^n = a^n + b^n$

False; sample: Let $a = b = n = 2$. Then $(a + b)^n = (2 + 2)^2 = 16$, but $a^n + b^n = 2^2 + 2^2 = 8$.

LESSON **MASTER 7-5**
QUESTIONS ON **SPUR** OBJECTIVES

■ **PROPERTIES** *Objective G (See pages 462–464 for objectives.)*

1. Let $P(n)$ be a statement in n. What can be concluded in each of the following instances?

a. $P(1)$ is true and $P(k) \Rightarrow P(k + 1)$.
   $P(n)$ is true $\forall$ positive integers n.

b. $P(1)$ is true and $P(k)$ does not imply $P(k + 1)$.
   $P(1)$ is true.

c. $P(6)$ is true and $P(k) \Rightarrow P(k + 1)$.
   $P(n)$ is true $\forall$ integers $n \ge 6$.

In 2 and 3, use mathematical induction to prove that the statement is true.

2. 4 is a factor of $5^n - 1$ $\forall$ positive integers n.

Let $S(n)$: 4 is a factor of $5^n - 1$. Show $S(1)$ is true: $5^1 - 1 = 4$ which has 4 as a factor. Assume $S(k)$ is true for a positive integer k: 4 is a factor of $5^k - 1$. Show $S(k + 1)$ is true:

$5^{k+1} - 1 = 5(5^k) - 1 = 5(5^k - 1 + 1) - 1$
$\quad = 5(5^k - 1) + 5 \cdot 1 - 1 = 5(5^k - 1) + 4$

Since 4 is a factor of $5^k - 1$ and of 4, 4 is a factor of $5(5^k - 1) + 4$, and $S(k + 1)$ is true. Therefore, by induction, $S(n)$ is true $\forall$ positive integers n.

3. 3 is a factor of $n^3 + 8n$ $\forall$ positive integers n.

Let $S(n)$: 3 is a factor of $n^3 + 8n$. Show $S(1)$ is true: $1^3 + 8(1) = 9$ which has 3 as a factor. Assume $S(k)$ is true for a positive integer k: 3 is a factor of $k^3 + 8k$. Show $S(k + 1)$ is true:

$(k + 1)^3 + 8(k + 1) = k^3 + 3k^2 + 3k + 1 + 8k + 8$
$\quad = (k^3 + 8k) + 3(k^2 + k + 3)$

Since 3 is a factor of $k^3 + 8k$ and of $3(k^2 + k + 3)$, 3 is a factor of their sum, so $S(k + 1)$ is true. Therefore, by induction, $S(n)$ is true $\forall$ positive integers n.

---

4. a. Show that $x + y$ is a factor of $x^3 + y^3$.

$x^3 + y^3 = (x + y)(x^2 - xy + y^2)$, therefore $x + y$ is a factor of $x^3 + y^3$.

b. Use mathematical induction to prove that $x + y$ is a factor of $x^{2n-1} + y^{2n-1}$ ∀ positive integers n. (Hint: In the inductive step, add and subtract $x^2 y^{2k-1}$.)

Let $S(n)$: $x + y$ is a factor of $x^{2n-1} + y^{2n-1}$. Show $S(1)$ is true: $x^{2 \cdot 1 - 1} + y^{2 \cdot 1 - 1} = x + y$, and $x + y$ is a factor of itself. Assume $S(k)$ is true for a positive integer k: $x + y$ is a factor of $x^{2k-1} + y^{2k-1}$. Show $S(k + 1)$ is true:

$x^{2(k+1)-1} + y^{2(k+1)-1} = x^{2k+1} + y^{2k+1}$

$= x^{2k+1} + x^2 y^{2k-1} - x^2 y^{2k-1} + y^{2k+1}$

$= x^2(x^{2k-1} + y^{2k-1}) - y^{2k-1}(x^2 - y^2)$

Since $x + y$ is a factor of $x^{2k-1} + y^{2k-1}$ and of $x^2 - y^2$, it is a factor of $x^2(x^{2k-1} + y^{2k-1}) - y^{2k-1}(x^2 - y^2)$, so $S(k + 1)$ is true. Therefore, by induction, $S(n)$ is true ∀ positive integers n.

LESSON **MASTER 7–6**
QUESTIONS ON **SPUR** OBJECTIVES

■**SKILLS** *Objective E (See pages 462–464 for objectives.)*
In 1–3, **a.** find the value of the series for $n = 4$ and **b.** find the limit of the series as $n \to \infty$.

1. $\sum_{k=0}^{n} \frac{2}{7^k}$ **2.** $\sum_{k=1}^{n} 4^k$ **3.** $\sum_{k=1}^{n} c(.9)^k$

a. __2.333__   **a.** __340__   **a.** __3.095c__

b. __$2\frac{1}{3}$__   **b.** __∞__   **b.** __9c__

4. Let b be the sequence defined by $\begin{cases} b_1 = 2 \\ b_{k+1} = \frac{3}{4}b_k \ \forall \ k \geq 1. \end{cases}$
Let S_n be the nth partial sum of the sequence.
a. Find a formula for S_n. $S_n = 8\left[1 - \left(\frac{3}{4}\right)^n\right]$

b. Find S_6.   __6.576__

c. Find $\lim_{n \to \infty} S_n$.   __8__

5. Give an example of a series which converges and whose seventh term is greater than $\frac{1}{2}$.   sample: $\sum_{j=1}^{\infty} (.95)^j$

6. Consider the finite geometric series
$a + 2a + 4a + \ldots + 512a$.
a. Use sigma notation to express the series. $\sum_{n=0}^{9} 2^n a$

b. If the value of the series is 613.8, find a.   __.6__

■**REPRESENTATIONS** *Objective J*
7. Consider the computer program below.

```
10   TERM = 3
20   PRINT TERM
30   SUM = TERM
40   FOR K = 2 TO 15
50      TERM = 2 * (TERM)/3
60      PRINT TERM
70      SUM = SUM + TERM
80   NEXT K
90   PRINT SUM
```

a. Use summation notation to write the sum that is calculated by the program.   sample: $\sum_{n=1}^{15} 3\left(\frac{2}{3}\right)^{n-1}$

b. Use the formula for the sum of the terms of a finite geometric series to find the sum in part **a.** ≈ 8.98

c. What would the sum approach if the 15 in line 40 were changed to a larger and larger number?   9

8. What changes would have to be made to the program in Question 7 to compute the partial sums of the sequence defined by $a_n = 2(.3)^n$?

sample: 10   TERM = .6
         50   TERM = 3 * (TERM)/10

LESSON **MASTER 7–7**
QUESTIONS ON **SPUR** OBJECTIVES

■**PROPERTIES** *Objective G (See pages 462–464 for objectives.)*
1. The Strong Form of Mathematical Induction differs from the original form only in the ___inductive___ step.

In 2–4, use the Strong Form of Mathematical Induction.

2. Consider the sequence defined recursively by
$\begin{cases} a_1 = 3 \\ a_2 = -12 \\ a_{k+1} = a_k - 4a_{k-1} \ \forall \text{ integers } k \geq 2. \end{cases}$
Prove that every term of the sequence is a multiple of 3.

Let $S(n)$: a_n is a multiple of 3. Show $S(1)$ and $S(2)$ are true: $a_1 = 3$ and $a_2 = -12$ are both multiples of 3. Assume $S(1), S(2), \ldots, S(k)$ are all true for a positive integer k. Show $S(k + 1)$ is true: $a_{k+1} = a_k - 4a_{k-1}$. Since $S(k)$ and $S(k-1)$ are true, a_k and a_{k-1} are multiples of 3. Therefore, $a_k - 4a_{k-1}$ is a multiple of 3. Thus, $S(k + 1)$ is true. Therefore, by strong induction, $S(n)$ is true ∀ positive integers n.

3. Consider the sequence defined recursively by
$\begin{cases} a_1 = 2 \\ a_2 = 4 \\ a_{k+1} = 2a_k - 3a_{k-1} \ \forall \text{ integers } k \geq 2. \end{cases}$
Prove that every term of the sequence is an even integer.

Let $S(n)$: a_n is even. Show $S(1)$ and $S(2)$ are true: $a_1 = 2$ and $a_2 = 4$ are both even. Assume $S(1), S(2), \ldots, S(k)$ are all true for a positive integer k. Show $S(k + 1)$ is true: $a_{k+1} = 2a_k - 3a_{k-1}$. Since $S(k)$ and $S(k-1)$ are true, a_k and a_{k-1} are even. Therefore, $2a_k - 3a_{k-1}$ is even. Thus, $S(k + 1)$ is true. Therefore, by strong induction, $S(n)$ is true ∀ positive integers n.

4. Let c be a fixed integer. Prove that every term of the sequence defined by
$$\begin{cases} b_1 = c \\ b_2 = 2c \\ b_{k+1} = 2b_k + b_{k-1} \ \forall \text{ integers } k \geq 2 \end{cases}$$
is divisible by c.

Let $S(n)$: b_n is divisible by c. Show $S(1)$ and $S(2)$ are true: b_1 and b_2 are divisible by c since $b_1 = c$ and $b_2 = 2c$. Assume $S(1)$, $S(2)$, $\ldots$, $S(k)$ are all true for a positive integer k. Show $S(k + 1)$ is true: $b_{k+1} = 2b_k + b_{k-1}$. Since $S(k)$ and $S(k-1)$ are true, b_k and b_{k-1} are divisible by c. Therefore, $2b_k + b_{k-1}$ is divisible by c. Thus, $S(k + 1)$ is true. Therefore, by strong induction, $S(n)$ is true $\forall$ positive integers n.

LESSON **MASTER 7–8**
QUESTIONS ON **SPUR** OBJECTIVES

■**USES** *Objective I (See pages 462–464 for objectives.)*
In 1–5, use the specified algorithm to arrange the given list in increasing order. Show all intermediate steps.

1. -7, 3, 0, 1 (Bubblesort)

```
1        3
0   →    1
3        0
-7       -7
```

2. 9, 4, -2, 10, 8 (Quicksort)

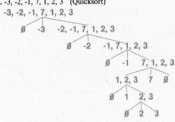

-2, 4, 8, 9, 10

3. 2, -3, .5, -7, -6 (Quicksort)

```
        2, -3, .5, -7, -6
     -3, .5, -7, -6   2   Ø
   -7, -6   -3   .5
  Ø  -7  -6
```

-7, -6, -3, .5, 2

4. 1, 3, 5, 7, 2, 4, 6 (Bubblesort)

```
6    7        7    7
4    6        6    6
2    4        5    5
7 →  2   →    4 →  4
5    5        2    3
3    3        3    2
1    1        1    1
```

5. -3, -2, -1, 7, 1, 2, 3 (Quicksort)

```
-3, -2, -1, 7, 1, 2, 3
Ø  -3   -2, -1, 7, 1, 2, 3
       Ø  -2   -1, 7, 1, 2, 3
              Ø  -1   7, 1, 2, 3
                     1, 2, 3  7  Ø
                  Ø  1   2, 3
                        Ø  2   3
```

-3, -2, -1, 1, 2, 3, 7

6. For a list of four numbers, what is the maximum number of passes needed for the Bubblesort algorithm to arrange them in increasing order? **3**

7. Is the Quicksort algorithm recursive or iterative? **recursive**

LESSON **MASTER 8–1**
QUESTIONS ON **SPUR** OBJECTIVES

■**SKILLS** *Objective A (See pages 534–536 for objectives.)*
In 1 and 2, rewrite the complex number as an ordered pair.

1. $3 + 5i$ **(3, 5)**   2. $-i - 2$ **(-2, -1)**

In 3 and 4, rewrite the complex number in $a + bi$ form.

3. $(-5, 0)$ **$-5 + 0i$**   4. $(\frac{1}{4}, -1)$ **$\frac{1}{4} - i$**

5. If the real part and the imaginary part of a complex number are 7 and 15, respectively, write the number in $a + bi$ form.   **$7 + 15i$**

■**SKILLS** *Objective B*
In 6–10, perform the indicated operation. Write the result in $a + bi$ form.

6. $\sqrt{-4} \cdot \sqrt{-81}$ **-18**   7. $\frac{6 - 2\sqrt{9}}{3}$ **0**

8. $(12 - 3i) - i(5 + 7i)$
    $19 - 8i$

9. $\frac{5i}{1 - i} + 3 - 4i$
    $\frac{1}{2} - \frac{3}{2}i$

10. $(5 - 8i)(2 + 7i)$ **$66 + 19i$**

In 11 and 12, express the solutions in $a + bi$ form.

11. $z^2 = -45$ **$\pm 3\sqrt{5}i$**   12. $-3 + 2i + w = 8 - 9i$ **$11 - 11i$**

■**PROPERTIES** *Objective F*
13. Let $z = 6 - 2i$. Verify that $z \cdot \bar{z}$ is a real number.

$(6 - 2i)(6 + 2i) = 36 + 4 = 40$

14. Let $z = a + bi$. Prove that $\bar{\bar{z}} = z$.

$\bar{z} = a - bi$, so $\bar{\bar{z}} = a - (-bi) = a - bi = z$

---

15. Prove that for all complex numbers u, v, and w, $(u + w)v = uv + wv$.

Let $u = a + bi$, $v = c + di$, and $w = e + fi$. Then $(u + w)v = [(a + e) + (b + f)i](c + di) = (ac + ec - bd - fd) + (ad + ed + bc + fc)i$. Also, $uv + wv = [(ac - bd) + (bc + ad)i] + [(ce - df) + (cf + de)i] = (ac - bd + ce - df) + (bc + ad + cf + de)i$. Therefore, $(u + w)v = uv + wv$

■**USES** *Objective H*
16. If the voltage in an AC circuit is 120V and the current is $6 + 3i$ amps, find the impedance.   **$16 - 8i$ ohms**

17. Two AC circuits with impedances of $9 + 16i$ ohms and $-6 + 8i$ ohms are connected in series.

a. Find the total impedance.   **$3 + 24i$ ohms**

b. If the total voltage is 10 volts, find the current.   **$\frac{2}{39} - \frac{16}{39}i$ amps**

■**REPRESENTATIONS** *Objective I*
In 18 and 19, let $A = 0$, $B = -2i$, and $C = -4 + 2i$.

18. a. Graph A, B, and C on the same complex plane.

b. Find the area of $\triangle ABC$.   **4**

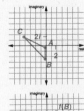

19. Let f be the function defined by $f(z) = (-2 + i)z$. Graph the points $f(A)$, $f(B)$, and $f(C)$ in the same complex plane.

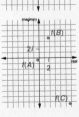

LESSON MASTER 8-2
QUESTIONS ON SPUR OBJECTIVES

■ SKILLS *Objective C* *(See pages 534–536 for objectives.)*
In 1 and 2, give one pair of polar coordinates for each (x, y) pair.

1. $(1, \sqrt{3})$ **[2, 60°]** 2. $(-5, -12)$ **[13, 247°]**

3. If $P = [r, \frac{7\pi}{4}] = (5, y)$, $r = $ **$5\sqrt{2}$** and $y = $ **-5**.

4. Suppose $P = [10, \frac{\pi}{4}]$. Give another polar coordinate representation for P:

 a. with $r < 0$; sample: $[-10, \frac{5\pi}{4}]$

 b. with $r > 0$, $\theta < 0$. sample: $[10, -\frac{7\pi}{4}]$

In 5 and 6, find the rectangular coordinates for the point P whose polar coordinates are given.

5. $[5\sqrt{2}, 225°]$ **(-5, -5)** 6. $[-4, -\frac{\pi}{3}]$ **(-2, 2$\sqrt{3}$)**

■ REPRESENTATIONS *Objective I*
7. Plot the following points on the polar grid at the right.

 a. $[1, 45°]$ **b.** $[-4, -\frac{\pi}{2}]$

 c. $[0, -\frac{3\pi}{2}]$ **d.** $[-3, -\frac{2\pi}{3}]$

8. On the polar grid, sketch all solutions to the equation $r = 3$.

9. Give two polar representations of the point P graphed below.
 sample: $[3, -60°]$, $[3, 300°]$

LESSON MASTER 8-3
QUESTIONS ON SPUR OBJECTIVES

■ SKILLS *Objective A* *(See pages 534–536 for objectives.)*
In 1–4, the complex number is written in either binomial, rectangular, polar, or trigonometric form. Write it in the other three forms.

1. 10
 (10, 0)
 [10, 0°]
 10(cos 0° + i sin 0°)

2. $[-3, \frac{3\pi}{2}]$
 $3i$
 (0, 3)
 $-3(\cos \frac{3\pi}{2} + i \sin \frac{3\pi}{2})$

3. $(7\sqrt{3}, -7)$
 $7\sqrt{3} - 7i$
 [14, 330°]
 14(cos 330° + i sin 330°)

4. 4 [cos (-120°) + i sin (-120°)]
 $-2 - 2\sqrt{3}i$
 (-2, -2$\sqrt{3}$)
 [4, -120°]

In 5 and 6, find the modulus and the argument θ ($0 \le \theta < 2\pi$) of the complex number.

5. $15 - 4i$
 modulus: ≈ 15.5
 $\theta \approx 6.02$

6. $a - ai$ where $a > 0$
 modulus: $a\sqrt{2}$
 $\theta = \frac{7\pi}{4}$

■ SKILLS *Objective B*
7. Let $z = \sqrt{3}(\cos 25° + i \sin 25°)$ and $w = \sqrt{2}(\cos 60° + i \sin 60°)$.

 a. Find z^2.
 $3(\cos 50° + i \sin 50°)$

 b. Find $z \cdot w$.
 $\sqrt{6}(\cos 85° + i \sin 85°)$

In 8 and 9, solve for z, writing the answer in polar form.

8. $z = [3, 115°] \cdot [4, 290°]$
 [12, 45°]

9. $[8, 50°] \cdot z = [6, 172°]$
 $[\frac{3}{4}, 122°]$

■ PROPERTIES *Objective F*
10. Let z be a complex number with argument θ. Show that $z \cdot [1, -2\theta] = \bar{z}$.
 Let $z = [r, \theta]$. Then $z \cdot [1, -2\theta] = [r, \theta] \cdot [1, -2\theta] = [r, -\theta] = \bar{z}$.

---

11. What does multiplying a complex number by a real number do to its polar representation?
 Let r be the real number. If $r > 0$, the argument remains the same. If $r < 0$, the argument increases by π. In each case, the modulus is multiplied by $|r|$.

■ REPRESENTATIONS *Objective I*
12. Let $G = 0$, $H = -2 - 3i$, $I = 3 - i$, and $J = H + I$.

 a. Sketch quadrilateral $GHJI$ in the complex plane.

 b. What kind of figure is $GHJI$? **parallelogram**

 c. Prove your answer to part **b**.
 Slope of $\overline{GH} = \frac{3}{2}$ = slope of $\overline{IJ}$, so $\overline{GH} \parallel \overline{IJ}$. Slope of $\overline{GI} = -\frac{1}{3}$ = slope of $\overline{HJ}$, so $\overline{GI} \parallel \overline{HJ}$. Therefore, $GHJI$ is a parallelogram.

13. Illustrate the multiplication of $z = 2(\cos 75° + i \sin 75°)$ by $w = 4(\cos 45° + i \sin 45°)$ with a diagram showing the appropriate size transformation and rotation.

14. **a.** Graph $\triangle ABC$ in the complex plane where $A = 0$, $B = 3 - 4i$, and $C = -2 - i$.

 b. Let A', B', and C' be the images of A, B, and C under the transformation $f: z \rightarrow (-1 + i)z$. Graph $\triangle A'B'C'$.

 c. Find the ratio of similitude of $\triangle A'B'C'$ to $\triangle ABC$ and relate it to the Geometric Multiplication Theorem.
 $-1 + i = [\sqrt{2}, \frac{3\pi}{4}]$; Multiplication by $-1 + i$ multiplies the modulus by $\sqrt{2}$. The ratio of similitude is $\sqrt{2}$.

 d. How does the argument of C' compare to that of C? Use the Geometric Multiplication Theorem.
 Multiplying by $[\sqrt{2}, \frac{3\pi}{4}]$ increases the argument by $\frac{3\pi}{4}$.

LESSON MASTER 8-4
QUESTIONS ON SPUR OBJECTIVES

■ REPRESENTATIONS *Objective J* *(See pages 534–536 for objectives.)*
In 1–6, sketch the graph of the polar equation and identify the type of curve obtained.

1. $r = 5$ _____ **circle**

2. $\theta = 60°$ _____ **line**

3. $r \sin \theta = -3$ _____ **line**

4. $r = 2 + 2 \cos \theta$ _____ **cardioid**

---

5. a. Sketch the rectangular graph of the equation $r = 1 + 3 \sin \theta$.

b. Use the rectangular graph in part **a** to sketch its polar graph.

c. Identify the type of curve that results in part **b.** ___limaçon___

6. a. Sketch the graph of $r = 5 \cos \theta$.

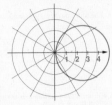

b. Prove that the graph is a circle and find its center.

$$\sqrt{x^2 + y^2} = 5 \cdot \frac{x}{\sqrt{x^2 + y^2}}$$
$$x^2 + y^2 = 5x$$
$$x^2 - 5x + y^2 = 0$$
$$x^2 - 5x + \frac{25}{4} + y^2 = \frac{25}{4}$$
$$\left(x - \frac{5}{2}\right)^2 + y^2 = \left(\frac{5}{2}\right)^2$$
center: $\left(\frac{5}{2}, 0\right)$

■ **REPRESENTATIONS**   *Objective J (See pages 534–536 for objectives.)*
In 1–3, sketch the graph of the polar equation and identify the type of curve obtained.

1. $r = 5 \cos 2\theta$ ___rose curve___

2. $r = \frac{3}{2}\theta + 2$ ___spiral of Archimedes___

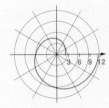

3. $r = 5^\theta$ ___logarithmic spiral___

---

4. a. Graph the three-leafed rose curve $r = 6 \sin 3\theta$.

b. Does it have any reflection symmetries? Prove that your answer is correct.

Reflection-symmetric over the line $\theta = \frac{\pi}{2}$; If $[r, \theta]$ is on the graph, then $r = 6 \sin 3\theta$.
$6 \sin 3(\pi - \theta) =$
$6 \sin (3\pi - 3\theta) =$
$6 \sin (\pi - 3\theta) = -6 \sin (3\theta - \pi) = 6 \sin (3\theta)$;
Therefore, $[r, \pi - \theta]$ is on the graph.

5. a. Write an equation for a five-leafed rose with leaves of length 2.5 which is reflection-symmetric over the polar axis. $r = 2.5 \cos 5\theta$

b. Graph this curve.

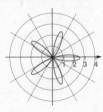

■ **SKILLS**   *Objective D (See pages 534–536 for objectives.)*
In 1–3, use DeMoivre's Theorem to compute the power. Write your answer in the same form as the base.

1. $(3 + 3i)^5$ ___$-972 - 972i$___

2. $\left[\sqrt{2}\left(\cos \frac{3\pi}{4} + i \sin \frac{3\pi}{4}\right)\right]^4$ ___$4(\cos \pi + i \sin \pi)$___

3. $\left[2, \frac{\pi}{2}\right]^{10}$ ___$[1024, \pi]$___

4. A sixth root of a certain complex number z is $2(\cos 30° + i \sin 30°)$. Write z in $a + bi$ form.   ___$-64 + 0i$___

■ **PROPERTIES**   *Objective F*

5. Let $z = [3, -12°]$.

a. Write a polar representation of z^5.   ___$[243, -60°]$___

b. Use your answer to part **a** to find a polar representation for $(z^5)^4$.   ___$[243^4, -240°]$___

c. Verify that $(z^5)^4 = z^{20}$.

$z^{20} = [3, -12°]^{20} = [3^{20}, -240°] = [(3^5)^4, -240°]$
$= [243^4, -240°] = (z^5)^4$

6. Let $z = [r, \theta]$ and $w = [s, \phi]$, and let n be a positive integer.

a. Write polar representations for z^n, w^n, and $z \cdot w$.
$[r^n, n\theta], \ [s^n, n\phi], \ [rs, \theta + \phi]$

b. Use your answer to part **a** to prove that $z^n \cdot w^n = (z \cdot w)^n$.
$z^n \cdot w^n = [r^n, n\theta] \cdot [s^n, n\phi] = [r^n s^n, n\theta + n\phi]$
$= [(rs)^n, n(\theta + \phi)]; (z \cdot w)^n = [rs, \theta + \phi]^n$
$= [(rs)^n, n(\theta + \phi)]; $ Therefore, $z^n \cdot w^n = (z \cdot w)^n$.

Precalculus and Discrete Mathematics © Scott, Foresman and Company

171

■ **REPRESENTATIONS** *Objective K*

7. a. Graph z^1, z^2, z^3, z^4, z^5, and z^6 when $z = \frac{3}{2}(\cos\frac{\pi}{3} + i\sin\frac{\pi}{3})$.

b. Is the sequence of points getting closer to or farther from the origin?

___closer___

8. Give the polar coordinates of the points w^1, w^2, w^3, w^4, and w^5 where the first four are graphed below.

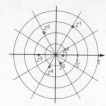

$w^1 = $ $\left[2, \frac{\pi}{4}\right]$

$w^2 = $ $\left[4, \frac{\pi}{2}\right]$

$w^3 = $ $\left[8, \frac{3\pi}{4}\right]$

$w^4 = $ $[16, \pi]$

$w^5 = $ $\left[32, \frac{5\pi}{4}\right]$

LESSON **MASTER 8–7**
QUESTIONS ON **SPUR** OBJECTIVES

■ **SKILLS** *Objective D (See pages 534–536 for objectives.)*
In 1 and 2, find the roots. Express them in the same form as the given number.

1. cube roots of $[125, \pi]$

$$\left[5, \frac{\pi}{3}\right], [5, \pi], \left[5, \frac{5\pi}{3}\right]$$

2. seventh roots of $128(\cos\frac{\pi}{3} + i\sin\frac{\pi}{3})$

$$2\left(\cos\frac{\pi}{21} + i\sin\frac{\pi}{21}\right), 2\left(\cos\frac{7\pi}{21}, + i\sin\frac{7\pi}{21}\right),$$
$$2\left(\cos\frac{13\pi}{21} + i\sin\frac{13\pi}{21}\right), 2\left(\cos\frac{19\pi}{21} + i\sin\frac{19\pi}{21}\right),$$
$$2\left(\cos\frac{25\pi}{21} + i\sin\frac{25\pi}{21}\right), 2\left(\cos\frac{31\pi}{21} + i\sin\frac{31\pi}{21}\right),$$
$$2\left(\cos\frac{37\pi}{21} + i\sin\frac{37\pi}{21}\right)$$

3. The fifth power of some complex number z is 243. Find all possible values of z.

$$[3, 0°], [3, 72°], [3, 144°], [3, 216°], [3, 288°]$$

In 4–6, solve the equation over the set of complex numbers. Express the solutions in $a + bi$ form.

4. $x^6 = -1$

$$\pm i, \frac{\pm\sqrt{3}\pm i}{2}$$

5. $z^8 = 16$

$$\pm\sqrt{2}, \pm\sqrt{2}i, \pm 1 \pm i$$

6. $(z-1)^8 = 16$ (Hint: Use your answer to Question 5.)

$$1 \pm \sqrt{2}, 1 \pm \sqrt{2}i, 2 \pm i, \pm i$$

---

7. A sixth root of a certain complex number is $\sqrt{2}(\cos 108° + i\sin 108°)$. Find the complex number and its other sixth roots.

___The number is $8(\cos 288° + i\sin 288°)$. The other___
___roots are: $\sqrt{2}(\cos 48° + i\sin 48°)$, $\sqrt{2}(\cos 168° +$___
___$i\sin 168°)$, $\sqrt{2}(\cos 228° + i\sin 228°)$, $\sqrt{2}(\cos 288°$___
___$+ i\sin 288°)$, and $\sqrt{2}(\cos 348° + i\sin 348°)$.___

■ **REPRESENTATIONS** *Objective K*

8. Graph the sixth roots of -1 on a complex plane. (Refer to Question 4.)

9. a. The seventh roots of $128(\cos\frac{\pi}{3} + i\sin\frac{\pi}{3})$ form the vertices of what figure? (Refer to Question 2.)

___regular heptagon___

b. Graph the figure.

LESSON **MASTER 8–8**
QUESTIONS ON **SPUR** OBJECTIVES

■ **SKILLS** *Objective E (See pages 534–536 for objectives.)*
In 1–3, find all zeros and their multiplicities for the given polynomial.

1. $f(x) = 2x^5 + x^4 - 3x^3$
zeros: $0, 1, -\frac{3}{2}$
mult.: 3, 1, 1

2. $g(x) = (x-1)^4(x+3)^2(x^2+1)^5$
zeros: $1, 3, i, -i$
mult.: 4, 2, 5, 5

3. $p(r) = r^3 + 3r^2 - 9r + 5$ given that 1 is a zero of $p(r)$
zeros: 1, -5; mult.: 1, 1

4. Give a polynomial of degree 3 that has the zeros 3, i, and -i.
$$p(x) = (x-3)(x^2+1)$$

■ **PROPERTIES** *Objective G*

5. A polynomial $g(x)$ has the following zeros: 2, 1, i, -i, and $\frac{1}{2}$. The 1 has multiplicity 3, and the other zeros have multiplicity 1.

a. What is the degree of $g(x)$? ___7___

b. Write a possible formula for $g(x)$ in factored form.
sample: $g(x) = (x-2)(x-1)^3(x^2+1)(2x-1)$

6. According to the Fundamental Theorem of Algebra,
$p(x) = 6x^{12} - x^4 + 10x^3 + 5$ has exactly ___12___ complex zeros, counting multiplicities.

7. Suppose $p(x)$ and $g(x)$ are polynomials such that $\frac{p(x)}{q(x)}$ is a polynomial with 5 zeros (counting multiplicities), and $p(x) + q(x)$ has 7 zeros (counting multiplicities).

a. What is the degree of $p(x)$? ___7___

b. What is the degree of $q(x)$? ___2___

c. How many zeros does $p(x)q(x)$ have (counting multiplicities)? ___9___

NAME _____

LESSON MASTER 8–9
QUESTIONS ON SPUR OBJECTIVES

■ SKILLS *Objective E (See pages 534–536 for objectives.)*
1. **a.** Find the zeros and corresponding multiplicities of
$p(x) = (2x^2 + ix - 5)^2$.

$\frac{-i \pm \sqrt{39}}{4}$, each with multiplicity 2

b. Does your answer to part **a** contradict the Conjugate Zeros Theorem? Explain.

No; Although the zeros are not in conjugate pairs, the coefficients of $p(x)$ are not all real.

2. If $-i$ is a zero of $p(x) = x^4 - 5x^3 + 5x^2 - 5x + 4$, find the remaining zeros.   *i, 4, 1*

3. Two of the zeros of the polynomial $f(t) = t^4 - 4t^3 + 9t^2 - 16t + 20$ are $2 - i$ and $2i$. Find the remaining zeros of $f(t)$.   *2 + i, -2i*

■ PROPERTIES *Objective G*
4. Does there exist a polynomial $p(x)$ with real coefficients which has exactly five zeros: $2i, -2i, 3 + i, 3 - i$, and $11i$? Justify your answer.
No, by the Conjugate Zeros Theorem, $-11i$ must also be a zero.

5. What is the smallest possible degree of a polynomial $p(x)$ with real coefficients if $1 + 2i, 7 - 5i$, and 2 are zeros of $p(x)$?   5

6. Use the Conjugate Zeros Theorem to prove: Every polynomial of odd degree with real coefficients has at least one real zero.
By the Conjugate Zeros Theorem, nonreal zeros must always come in conjugate pairs, so there must be an even number of nonreal zeros. Thus, if a polynomial has odd degree, it must have an odd number of zeros, so at least one must be real.

7. Find a polynomial of smallest degree with real coefficients that has zeros $2 - 3i$ and 0.
$p(x) = (x - 2 + 3i)(x - 2 - 3i)x = x^3 - 4x^2 + 13x$

8. Suppose $p(x)$ is a polynomial with real coefficients such that $p(x) = (x + 2 + i)q(x)$ where $q(x)$ is a polynomial. Give a factor of $q(x)$. $(x + 2 - i)$

Precalculus and Discrete Mathematics © Scott, Foresman and Company   **101**

NAME _____

LESSON MASTER 9–1
QUESTIONS ON SPUR OBJECTIVES

■ SKILLS *Objective A (See pages 581–584 for objectives.)*
1. Find the average rate of change in $f(x) = 2x^3 + 5x - 4$ from $x = -2$ to $x = 5$.   43

2. Find the average rate of change in $h(x) = x^2 + 25$ over the interval $-3 \le x \le 3$.   0

3. Let $g(x) = \frac{1}{2}t^2 + 6t$.
a. Find the average rate of change in g from t to $t + \Delta t$. $t + 6 + \frac{1}{2}\Delta t$

b. Use your answer to part **a** to find the average rate of change in g from 0 to 2.   7

■ USES *Objective D*
4. A ball is thrown upward from a height of 4.5 feet with an initial velocity of 21 feet per second. If only the effect of gravity is considered, then its height (in feet) after t seconds is given by the equation $u(t) = -16t^2 + 21t + 4.5$.
a. Find a formula for the average velocity from $t = \frac{1}{2}$ to $t = \frac{1}{2} + \Delta t$. $5 - 16\Delta t$

b. Use the formula from part **a** to find the average velocity from $t = \frac{1}{2}$ to $t = 4\frac{1}{2}$. Include appropriate units with your answer.   -59 ft/sec

■ REPRESENTATIONS *Objective G*
5. Refer to the graph of f at the right.
a. Find the average rate of change in f from A to C. $\frac{5}{2}$

b. Over what interval is the average rate of change in f zero? $1 \le x \le 7$

c. Over what interval is the average rate of change $\frac{2}{3}$? $4 \le x \le 7$

d. Find the average rate of change in f over the interval $0 \le x \le 8$. $\frac{1}{2}$

6. Suppose P and Q are points on the graph of the function g, with $P = (-4, b)$ and $Q = (6, 1)$. If the average rate of change in g from $x = -4$ to $x = 6$ is -2, find b. $b = 21$

102   *Precalculus and Discrete Mathematics © Scott, Foresman and Company*

NAME _____

LESSON MASTER 9–2
QUESTIONS ON SPUR OBJECTIVES

■ SKILLS *Objective B (See pages 581–584 for objectives.)*
In 1–3, find the derivative of the function at the given point.

1. $f(x) = 2x^2 - x + 5$; (0, 5)   -1

2. $g(x) = 20x + 17$; (.6, 29)   20

3. $h(y) = -15$; (18, -15)   0

4. Let $f(x) = -x^3 + 3x$. Use the definition of derivative to compute $f'(1)$ and $f'(\frac{3}{2})$. $f'(1) = 0$, $f'(\frac{3}{2}) = -\frac{15}{4}$

■ USES *Objective D*
5. Suppose that the profit (in cents per pound) a grocer makes in a day from selling hamburger at a price of s cents per pound is given by $P(s) = -s^2 + 320s - 5000$.
a. Find the derivative when $s = 120$.   80

b. What does your answer to part **a** mean?
sample: At the price of $1.20/lb, each increase of 1¢/lb in the price results in an increase of 80¢ in profit.

■ USES *Objective E*
6. Suppose the distance in meters that a car has travelled at time t (in seconds) is given by $s(t) = 4t^2 + 3t$. Find its instantaneous velocity at time $t = \frac{1}{4}$.   5

Precalculus and Discrete Mathematics © Scott, Foresman and Company   *Continued*   **103**

NAME _____
Lesson MASTER 9–2 (page 2)

7. A ball is dropped from the roof of a house 25 feet high. The height (in feet) of the ball above the ground at time t seconds is given by $h(t) = -16t^2 + 25$.
a. What is the instantaneous velocity of the ball at time $t = .5$ seconds?   -16 ft/sec

b. At what time t does the ball hit the ground? $t = 1.25$ sec

c. What is the instantaneous velocity of the ball at the moment it hits the ground?   -40 ft/sec

■ REPRESENTATIONS *Objective H*
8. Refer to the graph of f at the right. Estimate $f'(x)$ for each value of x given below.
a. $x = 0$ 0
b. $x = 2$ 2
c. $x = -3$ 0
d. $x = -4$ -2

104   *Precalculus and Discrete Mathematics © Scott, Foresman and Company*

Precalculus and Discrete Mathematics © Scott, Foresman and Company   **173**

LESSON MASTER 9-3
QUESTIONS ON SPUR OBJECTIVES

■ **SKILLS** *Objective B* (See pages 581–584 for objectives.)
In 1–4, find the derivative of the function whose formula is given.

1. $f(x) = -6x$
-6

2. $p(x) = 2x^2 - 6$
4x

3. $q(x) = \frac{1}{2}x^2 - 4x + 650$
x − 4

4. $g(x) = 620$
0

■ **USES** *Objective D*
5. If $500 is invested at an interest rate of 6% compounded continuously, the amount in the account after t years is $A(t) = 500e^{.06t}$ dollars. The derivative of A is $A'(t) = 30e^{.06t}$.

a. Find the amount in the account after 10 years.
$911

b. Find $A'(10)$.
$55

c. What does the answer to part **b** mean?
sample: After 10 years, the amount is increasing by $55 per year.

6. A piece of metal expands by heat so that the surface area at time t (in minutes) is $A(t) = \frac{\pi}{10}t^2 + \frac{1}{6}t + 3$.

a. Find the surface area at $t = 10$ minutes.
$4\frac{2}{3} + 10\pi$

b. Find the derivative of $A(t)$.
$A'(t) = \frac{\pi}{5}t + \frac{1}{6}$

c. Find the instantaneous rate of change of the surface area when $t = 10$ minutes.
$2\pi + \frac{1}{6}$

d. Calculate $A'(2)$.
$\frac{2}{5}\pi + \frac{1}{6}$

e. What is the initial rate of change of the surface area (that is, at $t = 0$)?
$\frac{1}{6}$

■ **USES** *Objective E*
7. A particle moves so that the distance s traveled in meters at time t seconds is given by $s(t) = t^2 + 3t - 2$.

a. Find the average velocity between 2 and 3 seconds.
8 m/sec

b. What is the instantaneous velocity of the particle at time $t = 6$?
15 m/sec

c. What is the initial velocity of the particle?
3 m/sec

■ **REPRESENTATIONS** *Objective H*
8. The function g is graphed at the right.

a. Estimate the values of $g'(x)$ when $x = -5, -4, -2, 0,$ and 2.
**$g'(-5) = -1, g'(-4) = 0,$
$g'(-2) = 1, g'(0) = 0,$
$g'(2) = -3$**

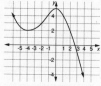

b. Use this information and the graph of g to sketch a graph of g'.

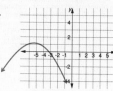

LESSON MASTER 9-4
QUESTIONS ON SPUR OBJECTIVES

■ **USES** *Objective D* (See pages 581–584 for objectives.)
1. A pot of water is being heated on a stove. The temperature (in degrees Fahrenheit) of the water after t minutes is given by $F(t) = 212 - 140e^{-.5t}$. For this function, $F'(t) = 70e^{-.5t}$ and $F''(t) = -35e^{-.5t}$.

a. What units should be used to measure $F''(t)$?
degrees/min

b. What units should be used to measure $F''(t)$?
degrees/min²

c. How fast is the temperature changing at time $t = 2$ minutes?
25.8 degrees/min

d. How fast is the rate of heating changing at time $t = 2$ minutes?
12.9 degrees/min²

e. How fast is the temperature changing at time $t = 3$ minutes?
15.6 degrees/min

■ **USES** *Objective E*
2. A kite which is 125 feet high is rising vertically. The height of the kite after t minutes is given by $h(t) = 2t^2 + 6t + 125$.

a. How fast is the string being played out when $t = 2$ minutes?
14 ft/min

b. What is the vertical acceleration of the kite at $t = 10$ minutes?
4 ft/min²

c. Is the velocity of the kite changing at a constant rate?
yes

3. A ball thrown directly upward with a speed of 96 ft/sec moves according to the equation $h(t) = 96t - 16t^2$, where h is the height of the ball in feet and t is the time in seconds after the ball is thrown.

a. Find the velocity of the ball 2 seconds after it is thrown.
32 ft/sec

b. For how many seconds does the ball rise?
3 sec

c. What is the highest height reached by the ball?
144 ft

d. Find its acceleration at time t.
-32 ft/sec²

4. If the position of a particle at time t is given by $s(t) = (2t + 3)^2$, find its velocity and acceleration at time $t = 0$.
$v(0) = 12, a(0) = 8$

LESSON MASTER 9-5
QUESTIONS ON SPUR OBJECTIVES

■ **PROPERTIES** *Objective C* (See pages 581–584 for objectives.)
1. Suppose f is a function such that $f(x) = \frac{1}{3}x^3 - \frac{1}{2}x^2 - 2x$. Then $f'(x) = x^2 - x - 2$. Use the first derivative to find

a. the interval(s) on which f is increasing,
$x < -1, x > 2$

b. the interval(s) on which f is decreasing,
$-1 < x < 2$

c. the points at which f may have a relative maximum or minimum.
$x = -1, 2$

2. Suppose $f(x) = 2x^3 + x - 620$. Then $f'(x) = 6x^2 + 1$. Is f increasing on the set of all real numbers? Justify your answer.
Yes; $f'(x) = 6x^2 + 1 > 0$ for all x. Therefore, f is an increasing function.

■ **USES** *Objective F*
3. What rectangle with the largest area can be formed using 80 ft of fencing?
20 ft × 20 ft square (area: 400 ft²)

■ **REPRESENTATIONS** *Objective I*
4. The derivative g' of a function g is graphed at the right.

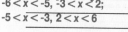

a. Where is g increasing? decreasing?
**$-6 < x < -5, -3 < x < 2;$
$-5 < x < -3, 2 < x < 6$**

b. Where may g have a relative maximum or minimum?
-5, -3, 2

5. Consider the function f graphed at right.

a. On what interval(s) is $f'(x)$ positive?
$-2 < x < 0, 2 < x < 6$

b. On what interval(s) is $f'(x)$ negative?
$-6 < x < -2, 0 < x < 2$

c. For what value(s) of x is $f'(x) = 0$?
$x = -2, 0, 2$

d. Is $f''(x)$ greater than or less than 0 on the interval $-4 < x < -2$?
$f''(x) > 0$

LESSON MASTER 10-1
QUESTIONS ON **SPUR** OBJECTIVES

■ **SKILLS** *Objective A (See pages 636–638 for objectives.)*
In 1–5, describe the essential features of the problem.

1. The coach of a volleyball team chooses six starting players from a group of nine people. How many different starting teams are possible?

unordered symbols, repetition not allowed

2. A department store offers a free monogramming service for customers who purchase a set of bath towels. If the monogram consists of three letters, how many different monograms are possible?

ordered symbols, repetition allowed

3. The winner of a contest held by a record store is allowed to pick a total of 10 free albums from any of five different musical categories: reggae, classical, country, jazz, and rock. How many different selections are possible?

unordered symbols, repetition allowed

4. Five married couples attend an opera performance together. If they wish to be seated in a row of 10 seats so that each person is sitting next to his or her spouse, how many different seating arrangements are possible?

ordered symbols, repetition not allowed

5. How many numbers between 100 and 999 have at least one digit that is a seven?

ordered symbols, repetition allowed

6. Ten Olympic swimmers compete for gold (1st place), silver (2nd place), and bronze (3rd place) medals in a 400-meter freestyle event. In how many different ways can the three medals be awarded?

ordered symbols, repetition not allowed

LESSON MASTER 10-2
QUESTIONS ON **SPUR** OBJECTIVES

■ **USES** *Objective F (See pages 636–638 for objectives.)*

1. At a pharmacy, toothbrushes are available in c different colors, three different firmnesses (hard, medium, and soft), and two different sizes (adult and youth). How many different kinds of toothbrushes are available?   6c

2. How many numbers between 1,000 and 9,999 inclusive have at least one digit that is a seven?   3,168

3. If Roger owns 12 shirts, 4 belts, and 10 pairs of pants, how many more shirts must he buy in order to have at least 600 different outfits?   3

4. How many 6-letter codewords can be made from the letters F, G, H, I, J, K, and L:

   a. if the letters can be repeated?   117,649

   b. if the letters cannot be repeated?   5,040

5. A mother, a father, and their seven children plan to have a family portrait taken. If one parent is to stand at each end of the row, in how many ways can the family members be arranged?   10,080

6. a. How many 3-digit numbers contain at least one six?   252

   b. What is the probability of choosing one of the numbers in part **a** which has exactly two sixes? $\frac{26}{252}$, or ≈ .103

7. How many lines of output are produced by the following computer program?   120

```
10    FOR I = 0 TO 7
20      FOR J = 1 TO 3
30        FOR K = 2 TO 6
40          PRINT I * J * K
50        NEXT K
60      NEXT J
70    NEXT I
```

■ **REPRESENTATIONS** *Objective I*

8. Draw a possibility tree to count the number of different 3-letter codewords that can be made from the letters A, B, and C if only the C may be repeated.   11

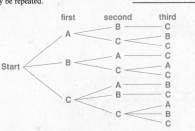

9. Jack, Patrice, Lydia, and Miguel are the finalists in a statewide science fair. First and second prizes will be awarded.

   a. Draw a possibility tree to determine all possible distributions of the awards.

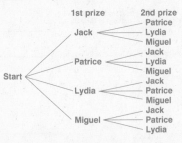

   b. In how many of these distributions does Patrice receive 2nd prize?   3

LESSON MASTER 10-3
QUESTIONS ON **SPUR** OBJECTIVES

■ **SKILLS** *Objective B (See pages 636–638 for objectives.)*
In 1 and 2, evaluate the expressions.

1. $P(18, 4)$ 73,440   2. $P(12, 3)$ 1,320

3. $P(7, 4) \cdot P(3, 1) = P(\underline{7}, \underline{5})$

4. Find n so that $P(13, n) = \frac{13!}{4!}$.   9

■ **PROPERTIES** *Objective D*

5. Verify that $P(7, 6) = P(7, 7)$ and generalize your result.

$P(7, 6) = \frac{7!}{(7 - 6)!} = \frac{7!}{1!} = \frac{7!}{1} = 7!$;

$P(7, 7) = \frac{7!}{(7 - 7)!} = \frac{7!}{0!} = \frac{7!}{1} = 7!$;

So $P(7, 6) = P(7, 7)$;

In general, $P(n, n - 1) = P(n, n)$, ∀ integers $n \geq 2$.

6. If $(n - 4)! = (n - 4) \cdot x!$, what is x? $n - 5$

■ **USES** *Objective F*

7. Each player of a certain board game must choose a different token to move around the board. If there are 8 tokens, in how many different ways can 5 players choose them?   6,720

8. Nine high school swim teams are competing in a 400-meter freestyle event. The pool contains 10 lanes. If the two swimmers from Lincoln High must swim in adjacent lanes and one swimmer from each of the other schools fill the remaining eight lanes, how many different arrangements of the swimmers are possible?   725,760

LESSON MASTER 10-4
QUESTIONS ON SPUR OBJECTIVES

■ SKILLS *Objective B* (See pages 636–638 for objectives.)
In 1 and 2, evaluate the expressions.

1. $C(12, 8)$ _____ 495

2. $\binom{11}{6}$ _____ 462

3. Find integers r and n such that $C(n, 2) = \frac{7!}{r! \cdot 2}$. ____ $r = 5$, $n = 7$

4. $C(7, 2) \cdot 2! = P($__7__ , __2__ $)$

■ PROPERTIES *Objective D*

5. Show that $\binom{10}{4} = \binom{10}{6}$.

$\binom{10}{4} = \frac{10!}{4!(10-4)!} = \frac{10!}{4!6!}$, $\binom{10}{6} = \frac{10!}{6!(10-6)!} = \frac{10!}{6!4!} = \frac{10!}{4!6!}$,

So, $\binom{10}{4} = \binom{10}{6}$.

6. Prove that ∀ positive integers n, $C(n, n) = 1$.
By the $C(n, r)$ Calculation Theorem,
$C(n, n) = \frac{n!}{n!(n-n)!} = \frac{n!}{n!0!} = \frac{n!}{n!(1)} = \frac{n!}{n!} = 1$

■ USES *Objective G*

7. Suppose there are seven points in a plane, with no three points collinear. How many distinct triangles can be formed which have these points as vertices? _____ 35

8. In a standard deck of 52 playing cards, how many different 4-card hands contain exactly one card from each of the four suits? _____ 28,561

9. A choir director is to assemble a choir consisting of 4 girls and 5 boys. If 9 girls and 12 boys audition, how many different choirs are possible? _____ 99,792

10. a. A questionnaire for a psychology experiment consists of 10 questions. Each one asks the subject to pick two words out of a group of five which he or she feels are most closely related. How many different responses are possible? _____ 1×10^{10}

  b. A second version of the questionnaire contains 15 questions, each with four words. Which version has a greater number of possible responses?

  version with 15 questions (4.7×10^{11})

LESSON MASTER 10-5
QUESTIONS ON SPUR OBJECTIVES

■ SKILLS *Objective C* (See pages 636–638 for objectives.)
In 1–3, expand using the Binomial Theorem.

1. $(y + z)^6$

  $y^6 + 6y^5z + 15y^4z^2 + 20y^3z^3 + 15y^2z^4 + 6yz^5 + z^6$

2. $(3a - 2b)^5$

  $243a^5 - 810a^4b + 1080a^3b^2 - 720a^2b^3 + 240ab^4 - 32b^5$

3. $(x + 2)^4$

  $x^4 + 8x^3 + 24x^2 + 32x + 16$

4. What is the coefficient of the x^3y^4 term in the expansion of $(2x - 4y)^7$? _____ 71,680

5. Find the tenth term of $(x - 3y)^{12}$. ____ $-4,330,260x^3y^9$

6. a. What combination is the coefficient of the $x^{12}y^8$ term in the expansion of $(x + y)^{20}$? ____ $\binom{20}{8}$ or $\binom{20}{12}$

  b. What is this coefficient? _____ 125,970

7. Express as the power of a binomial: $\sum_{k=0}^{9} \binom{9}{k} y^{9-k} 3^k$. ____ $(y + 3)^9$

8. The coefficients of which terms in the expansion of $(x + y)^8$ are equal?

  1st and 9th, 2nd and 8th, 3rd and 7th, 4th and 6th

LESSON MASTER 10-6
QUESTIONS ON SPUR OBJECTIVES

■ PROPERTIES *Objective E* (See pages 636–638 for objectives.)

1. The number of 4-element subsets that can be formed from a set with 7 elements is given by the combination ____ $\binom{7}{4}$

2. How is $_7C_5 + _7C_6 + _7C_7$ related to the number of subsets that can be formed from a set?

  It gives the number of subsets containing at least 5 elements that can be formed from a 7-element set.

■ USES *Objective G*

3. In how many ways is it possible to obtain at least five heads in 13 tosses of a coin? _____ 7,099

4. An "all-you-can-eat" buffet table contains 10 meat dishes. How many different combinations of meat dishes are possible, assuming that each customer chooses at least one? _____ 1,023

■ USES *Objective H*

5. If the "DON'T WALK" symbol on a pedestrian signal is lit for 40 seconds per minute, and the "WALK" symbol is lit for 20 seconds per minute, what is the probability that the signal will say "WALK" two out of six times that it is approached? _____ .329

6. A soft drink manufacturer gives away prizes by printing the name of the prize on the inside of some of the cans. If 6% of the cans produced result in a prize, what is the probability that in a 24-can case,

  a. exactly three cans result in a prize? _____ .119

  b. no more than one can results in a prize? _____ .573

LESSON MASTER 10-7
QUESTIONS ON SPUR OBJECTIVES

■ USES *Objective G* (See pages 636–638 for objectives.)

1. How many terms are there in the expansion of $(m + n + p)^{11}$? _____ 78

2. How many positive integers less than 10,000 have digits which add to 16? _____ 969

3. The spinner for a game consists of a circle with five sections, colored red, blue, yellow, purple, and green. If an outcome is defined as a certain number of occurrences of each color, how many different outcomes are possible in seven spins? _____ 330

4. a. How many integers from 1 to 999 have the property that the sum of their digits is 9? _____ 55

  b. How many of these have exactly one five? _____ 15

LESSON MASTER 11-1
QUESTIONS ON **SPUR** OBJECTIVES

■USES *Objective E* (See pages 694–698 for objectives.)
In 1–4, suppose that a reporter conducts a poll of voters regarding a plan to construct a new sports stadium using city funds. Of those polled, 77% are people who vote regularly, while 23% vote only occasionally. Of the regular voters, 42% are in favor of the plan to construct the stadium. Among the occasional voters, 54% favor its construction.

1. Draw a probability tree to represent this situation.

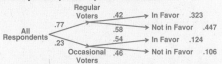

Regular Voters .42 → In Favor .323
All Respondents .77 .58 → Not in Favor .447
.23 .54 → In Favor .124
Occasional Voters .46 → Not in Favor .106

2. If 1,500 voters respond, how many are regular voters not in favor of the plan? **about 670**

3. Which category contains the largest percentage of respondents? **regular voters not in favor of the plan**

4. What is the probability that a randomly chosen voter who is not in favor of the plan is a regular voter? **.808**

5. Suppose the process of conducting an archaeological dig involves the following tasks:

Task	Description	Time Required (Days)	Prerequisite Tasks
A	choose a site	1	none
B	organize a team	3	none
C	travel to site	1	A, B
D	set up equipment	2	C
E	dig	8	D
F	keep journal of findings	9	D
G	write a report of findings	12	E, F

a. Sketch a directed graph to represent the situation.

A ① → C ① → D ② → ⑧ E → G ⑫
B ③ → ⑨ F

b. What is the minimal time required to conduct the entire dig? **27 days**

■USES *Objective G*
In 6 and 7, the vertices of the graph at the right represent traffic lights and the edges represent streets.

sample:

6. Draw a path that will allow a maintenance person to pass each light exactly once.

7. Suppose light 8 and the part of the street connecting it to light 7 are removed (so lights 4 and 11 are connected directly). Would a path satisfying Question 6 still be possible? **yes**

LESSON MASTER 11-2
QUESTIONS ON **SPUR** OBJECTIVES

■SKILLS *Objective A* (See pages 694–698 for objectives.)
In 1–3, draw a graph with the specified characteristics.

1. two vertices and three edges
sample:
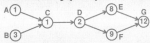

2. an isolated vertex, two loops, and three edges
sample:

3. two parallel edges, three vertices, and a loop
sample:

4. Draw the graph G defined as follows:
set of vertices: $\{v_1, v_2, v_3, v_4, v_5\}$;
set of edges: $\{e_1, e_2, e_3, e_4\}$

edge-endpoint function:

edge	endpoints
e_1	$\{v_1\}$
e_2	$\{v_2, v_4\}$
e_3	$\{v_3, v_5\}$
e_4	$\{v_1, v_3\}$

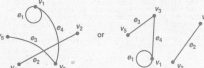

or

■PROPERTIES *Objective B*
5. A graph consists of a finite set of **vertices**, a finite set of **edges**, and a **function** that maps each **edge** to a set of either one or two **vertices**.

---

6. Use the graph at the right.

a. Identify any isolated vertices. **v_4**

b. Identify all edges adjacent to e_3. **e_1, e_2, e_4**

c. Identify any loops. **e_6**

d. Give the edge-endpoint function table for the graph.

edge	endpoints
e_1	$\{v_1, v_3\}$
e_2	$\{v_1, v_2\}$
e_3	$\{v_2, v_3\}$
e_4	$\{v_2, v_3\}$
e_5	$\{v_1, v_5\}$
e_6	$\{v_5\}$

■REPRESENTATIONS *Objective I*
7. Write the adjacency matrix for the directed graph below.

$$\begin{array}{c} \quad v_1\ v_2\ v_3\ v_4 \\ \begin{array}{c} v_1 \\ v_2 \\ v_3 \\ v_4 \end{array} \begin{bmatrix} 1 & 1 & 1 & 1 \\ 0 & 1 & 1 & 0 \\ 0 & 0 & 0 & 1 \\ 1 & 0 & 0 & 0 \end{bmatrix} \end{array}$$

8. What does the sum of the components of the matrix for a directed graph represent? **number of edges of the graph**

9. Draw an undirected graph with the following adjacency matrix.

$$\begin{array}{c} \quad v_1\ v_2\ v_3 \\ \begin{array}{c} v_1 \\ v_2 \\ v_3 \end{array} \begin{bmatrix} 0 & 0 & 1 \\ 0 & 2 & 0 \\ 1 & 0 & 2 \end{bmatrix} \end{array}$$

Top-left panel (page 121):

NAME _____

LESSON MASTER 11-3
QUESTIONS ON **SPUR** OBJECTIVES

■ **SKILLS**   *Objective A*   *(See pages 694–698 for objectives.)*

1. Draw a graph with four vertices of the following degrees: 1, 3, 3, and 5.

2. Draw a simple graph with three vertices of degrees 1, 2, and 1.

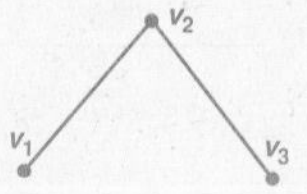

■ **PROPERTIES**   *Objective B*

3. *Fill in the blank with the word even or odd.* Every graph has an **even** number of vertices of **odd** degree.

4. A graph has four edges. What is its total degree?   **8**

5. Refer to the graph below.

   a. Give the degree of each vertex. v_1: 4; v_2: 4; v_3: 6; v_4: 0

   b. Give the total degree of the graph.   **14**

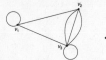

Precalculus and Discrete Mathematics © Scott, Foresman and Company   *Continued*   **121**

Top-right panel (page 122):

NAME _____

Lesson MASTER 11-3 (page 2)

■ **PROPERTIES**   *Objective C*

In 6 and 7, either draw a graph with the given properties or explain why no such graph exists.

6. a graph with five vertices of degrees 1, 2, 2, 3, and 5
   The graph is not possible since there would be an odd number of vertices of odd degree.

7. a graph with six vertices of degrees 1, 1, 2, 3, 4, and 5

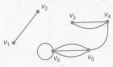

■ **USES**   *Objective F*

8. Thirty-three parents meet at a graduation ceremony. Is it possible for each parent to shake hands with exactly seven other parents? Explain.
   No; Represent the situation as a graph. The 33 vertices would each have degree 7, which contradicts the corollary that states every graph has an even number of vertices of odd degree.

9. The instructor of a Spanish class requests that each one of the 12 students in the class meet with three other students, one at a time, to practice speaking Spanish.

   a. Draw a graph to represent this situation.

   b. How many different pairings result?   **18**

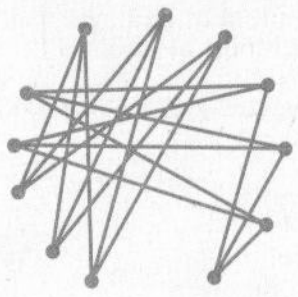

122   Precalculus and Discrete Mathematics © Scott, Foresman and Company

---

Bottom-left panel (page 123):

NAME _____

LESSON MASTER 11-4
QUESTIONS ON **SPUR** OBJECTIVES

■ **SKILLS**   *Objective A*   *(See pages 694–698 for objectives.)*

1. Draw a graph with 4 vertices, one loop, and 2 parallel edges, and which has an Euler circuit. Identify the circuit.
   sample: starting at v_1:
   $e_1\ e_6\ e_4\ e_5\ e_3\ e_2$

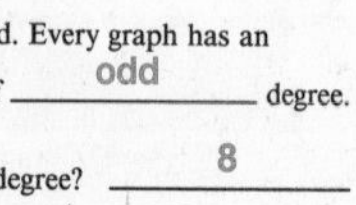

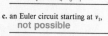

2. Consider the graph at the right below. Describe, if possible:

   a. a walk from v_1 to v_4,
      sample: $e_1\ e_5\ e_4$

   b. a path from v_4 to v_7,
      sample: $e_4\ e_6\ e_7$

   c. an Euler circuit starting at v_1,
      not possible

   d. a walk from v_1 to v_4 that is not a path.
      sample: $e_1\ e_8\ e_7\ e_6\ e_6\ e_5\ e_2\ e_3\ e_5\ e_4$

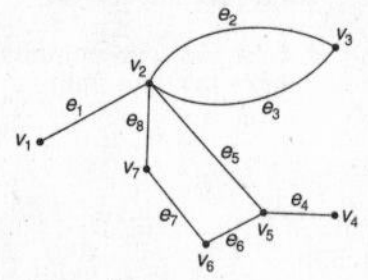

In 3–5, determine whether or not the graph is connected.

3. 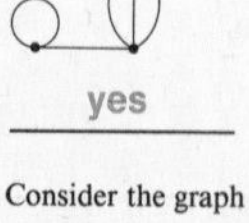   **yes**

4. 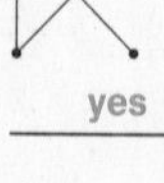   **yes**

5. 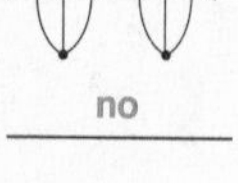   **no**

6. Consider the graph at the right.

   a. Give each edge whose removal (by itself) would keep the graph connected.
      $e_1,\ e_2,\ e_4,\ e_5,\ e_6,\ e_7,\ e_8$

   b. What is the maximum number of edges that can be removed simultaneously while keeping the graph connected?   **2**

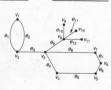

Precalculus and Discrete Mathematics © Scott, Foresman and Company   *Continued*   **123**

Bottom-right panel (page 124):

NAME _____

Lesson MASTER 11-4 (page 2)

■ **PROPERTIES**   *Objective D*

7. Consider the statement: *If every vertex of a graph has even degree, then the graph has an Euler circuit.*

   a. Write the converse of the statement.
      If a graph has an Euler circuit, then every vertex of the graph has even degree.

   b. Which is true, the statement or its converse?   **converse**

   c. What additional characteristic, if possessed by the graph, makes both statements true?   **connectedness**

In 8 and 9, determine whether or not the graph described has an Euler circuit. Justify your answer.

8.

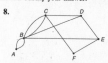

   No; Vertices D and E have odd degree.

9. the graph with adjacency matrix

$$\begin{array}{c c} & \begin{matrix} v_1 & v_2 & v_3 & v_4 \end{matrix} \\ \begin{matrix} v_1 \\ v_2 \\ v_3 \\ v_4 \end{matrix} & \begin{bmatrix} 2 & 0 & 0 & 4 \\ 0 & 2 & 1 & 0 \\ 0 & 1 & 2 & 0 \\ 4 & 0 & 0 & 2 \end{bmatrix} \end{array}$$

   No; Vertices v_2 and v_3 have odd degree.

■ **REPRESENTATIONS**   *Objective G*

10. Suppose a pirate finds a treasure map like the one below. If the treasure is at one end of the points marked, is it possible for the pirate to search at every point, starting and ending at the same point and using each edge only once? If so, draw arrows on the map to show a possible route. If not, draw arrows on the map to show a route which starts and ends at the same point and passes through as many other points as possible.

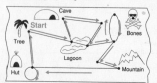

   Not possible; skip edge shown across lagoon

124   Precalculus and Discrete Mathematics © Scott, Foresman and Company

---

178

Precalculus and Discrete Mathematics © Scott, Foresman and Company

Top Left — Lesson Master 11-5

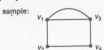

LESSON **MASTER 11-5**
QUESTIONS ON **SPUR** OBJECTIVES

■ **SKILLS** *Objective A (See pages 694–698 for objectives.)*
1. Draw a simple graph with four vertices and three walks of length 2 from v_1 to v_2.

sample:

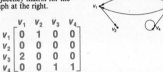

■ **PROPERTIES** *Objective B*
2. Refer to the graph at the right.

a. How many walks of length 3 are there from v_1 to v_2? **39**

b. List four of these walks.

samples: $e_1 e_4 e_5$, $e_1 e_5 e_4$, $e_1 e_2 e_3$, $e_3 e_2 e_1$

c. What is the length of the longest path from v_1 to v_2? **5**

■ **REPRESENTATIONS** *Objective J*
3. The adjacency matrix for an undirected graph is $\begin{bmatrix} 1 & 0 & 1 \\ 0 & 2 & 3 \\ 1 & 3 & 0 \end{bmatrix}$.

a. How many walks of length 2 go from v_1 to v_3? **1**

b. How many walks of length 2 start from v_2? **22**

4. a. Give the adjacency matrix for the directed graph at the right.

$\begin{array}{c} \\ v_1 \\ v_2 \\ v_3 \\ v_4 \end{array} \begin{array}{cccc} v_1 & v_2 & v_3 & v_4 \\ \begin{bmatrix} 0 & 1 & 0 & 0 \\ 0 & 0 & 0 & 0 \\ 2 & 0 & 0 & 0 \\ 0 & 0 & 1 & 1 \end{bmatrix} \end{array}$

b. How many walks of length 3 start at v_4? **6**

Top Right — Lesson Master 11-6

LESSON **MASTER 11-6**
QUESTIONS ON **SPUR** OBJECTIVES

■ **USES** *Objective H (See pages 694–698 for objectives.)*
1. In a chemical experiment, molecules of a liquid are changing phase in a flask. It is known that from one minute to the next, 80% of the molecules remain liquid, while 20% become gaseous. At the same time, 40% of the gaseous molecules become liquid. The rest remain gaseous.

a. Give T, the transition matrix.

$$T = \begin{array}{c} \\ L \\ G \end{array} \begin{array}{cc} L & G \\ \begin{bmatrix} .8 & .2 \\ .4 & .6 \end{bmatrix} \end{array}$$

liquid to gas 20%   gas to liquid 40%

b. After sufficient time, the substance will reach equilibrium so that the percent that is liquid and the percent that is gaseous become constant. Estimate these percents by calculating T^8.

$$T^8 \approx \begin{bmatrix} .6669 & .3331 \\ .6663 & .3337 \end{bmatrix}$$

c. Find the exact percents by solving a system of equations.

67% liquid, 33% gas

2. At a particular time, it was found that 25% of adults drank Kool Cola, 20% drank Klassic Cola, and 55% preferred Fizzy Cola. The Kool Cola Company's surveys showed that people switched brands each month according to the directed graph below.

a. Based on these data, what percent of the adults drank each brand one month after the initial data were gathered?

Kool: **33%**

Klassic: **21%**

Fizzy: **46%**

b. What percent would eventually drink each brand after a long period of time?

Kool: **44%**   Klassic: **24%**   Fizzy: **32%**

Bottom Left — Lesson Master 12-1

LESSON **MASTER 12-1**
QUESTIONS ON **SPUR** OBJECTIVES

■ **SKILLS** *Objective A (See pages 756–758 for objectives.)*
In 1 and 2, find the magnitude and direction of the given vector.

1. (2, -3) **$\sqrt{13}$, 303.7** 2. (-5, -12) **13, 247.4°**

3. Find a polar representation of the vector (12, 16). **[20, 53.1°]**

■ **USES** *Objective G*
4. A plane's velocity is represented by [550, 160°], where the magnitude is measured in miles per hour and the direction is in degrees counter-clockwise from due east.

a. Sketch the vector for the velocity.

b. Give the vector in component form.
(-517, 188)

c. Interpret the components.
Each hour the plane flies 517 miles to the west and 188 miles to the north.

5. A fish is caught at the end of a 15-meter fishline. Its angle with the horizontal is 37°. Assume the fishline is taut.

a. Write a polar representation for the fish's position, using the end of the fishing rod (point O) as the origin.
[15, 217°]

b. Compute a component representation. **(-12, -9)**

c. Interpret the components.
The fish is 9 meters below the tip of the fishing rod and 12 meters horizontally away from the tip.

Bottom Right — Lesson Master 12-1 (page 2)

■ **REPRESENTATIONS** *Objective I*
6. Suppose $A = (1, -2)$ and $B = (x, y)$ are points in a plane and $\vec{v}$ is the vector from A to B. If $\vec{v} = \left[6, \frac{\pi}{3} \right]$, find the coordinates of B. **$(4, 3\sqrt{3} - 2)$**

7. Find the component representation of [3, 210°] and sketch the vector.
$\left(-\frac{3}{2}\sqrt{3}, -\frac{3}{2} \right)$

8. a. Find the component representation of the vector shown at the right.
(-4, -5)

b. Sketch the vector in standard position.

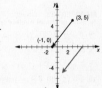

LESSON MASTER 12-2
QUESTIONS ON SPUR OBJECTIVES

■ **SKILLS** *Objective B* (See pages 756–758 for objectives.)
In 1–4, let $\vec{u} = (0, -5)$, $\vec{v} = (2, 3)$, and $\vec{w} = (-1, -6)$. Find the sum or difference.

1. $\vec{u} + \vec{v}$ _____ (2, -2)
2. $-\vec{w}$ _____ (1, 6)
3. $\vec{v} - \vec{w}$ _____ (3, 9)
4. $\vec{v} - \vec{u} + \vec{w}$ _____ (1, 2)

In 5 and 6, let $\vec{s} = [3, 15°]$ and $\vec{t} = [2, 160°]$. Compute and express the answer in its polar representation.

5. $\vec{s} + \vec{t}$ _____ [1.8, 55°]
6. $-\vec{s}$ _____ [3, 195°]

■ **PROPERTIES** *Objective E*
7. If $\vec{u} + \vec{v}$ is the zero vector, prove that $\vec{v}$ is the opposite of $\vec{u}$.
Let $\vec{u} = (u_1, u_2)$ and $\vec{v} = (v_1, v_2)$. Then $\vec{u} + \vec{v} =$
$(u_1 + v_1, u_2 + v_2) = (0, 0)$. Thus, $u_1 + v_1 = 0$ and
$u_2 + v_2 = 0$. So $u_1 = -v_1$ and $u_2 = -v_2$. Therefore,
$\vec{u} = (u_1, u_2) = (-v_1, -v_2)$, the opposite of $\vec{v}$.

8. Show that $\vec{v} = (2 \cos 215°, 2 \sin 215°)$ is the opposite of $\vec{u} = (2 \cos 35°, 2 \sin 35°)$.
$\vec{v} = (2 \cos 215°, 2 \sin 215°) = (-1.6, -1.1)$;
$\vec{u} = (2 \cos 35°, 2 \sin 35°) = (1.6, 1.1)$;
Thus, $\vec{u}$ and $\vec{v}$ are opposites.

■ **USES** *Objective H*
9. Two people push a disabled car with the forces shown at the right.

   a. Give the resultant force in polar form.
   _____ [4,162, 10°]

   b. Interpret your answer to part a.
   The total force applied is 4,162 lb in the
   direction 10° north of east.

   c. How much more forward force (to the right) is provided by the person exerting 2,500 lb of force than the person exerting 2,000 lb of force? _____ 233 lb

10. Relative to the water, a boat is moving with a speed of 20 mph in the direction 15° west of north. Due to the current which is moving in the direction 60° south of east, the boat is actually heading north relative to the land.

   a. Find the speed of the current. _____ 10.35 mph

   b. Find the speed of the boat moving north. _____ 10.35 mph

■ **REPRESENTATIONS** *Objective J*
11. The vectors $\vec{v}$ and $\vec{w}$ are shown at the right. Sketch the following.

   a. $\vec{v} + \vec{w}$

   b. $-\vec{w}$

   c. $\vec{w} - \vec{v}$

LESSON MASTER 12-3
QUESTIONS ON SPUR OBJECTIVES

■ **SKILLS** *Objective B* (See pages 756–758 for objectives.)
In 1–4, let $\vec{u} = (6, -2)$ and $\vec{v} = (-1, 5)$, and compute.

1. $\frac{1}{2}\vec{u}$ _____ (3, -1)
2. $2\vec{v}$ _____ (-2, 10)
3. $\frac{1}{2}\vec{u} + 2\vec{v}$ _____ (1, 9)
4. $2\vec{u} - 3\vec{v}$ _____ (15, -19)

■ **PROPERTIES** *Objective E*
5. Show that $\vec{v} = (3, 7)$ and $\vec{u} = (-18, -42)$ are parallel.
$\vec{u} = (-18, -42) = -6(3, 7) = -6\vec{v}$

6. Show that the line passing through (-1, 2) and (3, 4) is parallel to the vector $\vec{v} = (-2, -1)$.
$(3 - (-1), 4 - 2) = (4, 2) = -2(-2, -1) = -2\vec{v}$

■ **PROPERTIES** *Objective F*
In 7–10, determine whether or not $\vec{u}$ and $\vec{v}$ are parallel.

7. $\vec{u} = (2, -3)$, $\vec{v} = (4, 6)$ _____ not parallel
8. $\vec{u} = \left(-1, -\frac{1}{2}\right)$, $\vec{v} = (10, 5)$ _____ parallel
9. $\vec{u} = (7, 3)$, $\vec{v} = (7, 3)$ _____ parallel
10. $\vec{u} = [3, 20°]$, $\vec{v} = [5, 200°]$ _____ parallel

■ **REPRESENTATIONS** *Objective I*
11. Sketch $\vec{v} = (5, 1)$ and $-2\vec{v}$ on the same set of axes.

---

12. a. Give the endpoint of a vector $\vec{w}$ which has polar representation [2, 150°] and starts at the point (-1, 1).
   _____ $(-1 - \sqrt{3}, 2)$

   b. Give the endpoint of the vector $3\vec{w}$ if it starts at (-1, 1).
   _____ $(-1 - 3\sqrt{3}, 4)$

   c. Sketch both vectors.

■ **REPRESENTATIONS** *Objective J*
13. Given the vectors $\vec{u}$ and $\vec{v}$ shown at the right. Sketch the following.

   a. $2\vec{u}$

   b. $-3\vec{v}$

   c. $2\vec{u} - 3\vec{v}$

■ **REPRESENTATIONS** *Objective L*
14. a. Find parametric equations of the line through (-3, 5) that is parallel to the vector $\vec{v} = (3, 3)$.
   _____ $\begin{cases} x = -3 + 3t \\ y = 5 + 3t \end{cases}$

   b. Graph the line.

15. Write a vector equation for the line through $P = (-5, 2)$ that is parallel to $\vec{v} = 2, -1)$.
   _____ $(x + 5, y - 2) = t(2, -1)$

LESSON MASTER 12-4
QUESTIONS ON **SPUR** OBJECTIVES

■ SKILLS   *Objective B*   *(See pages 756–758 for objectives.)*
In 1–3, let $\vec{u} = (5, 10)$, $\vec{v} = (-1, 3)$, and $\vec{w} = (4, 7)$, and compute.

1. $\vec{u} \cdot \vec{v}$ ___**25**___   2. $(\vec{u} \cdot \vec{v})\vec{w}$ ___**(100, 175)**___

3. $(\vec{u} + \vec{v}) \cdot (\vec{v} - \vec{w})$ ___**-72**___

■ SKILLS   *Objective D*
In 4–6, find the measure of the angle between the two vectors.

4. $(-1, 1)$ and $(4, 2)$ ___**108°**___   5. $(0, 8)$ and $(-4, 0)$ ___**90°**___

6. $[18, 63°]$ and $[42, 172°]$ ___**109°**___

■ PROPERTIES   *Objective E*
7. Show that $\vec{v} = (20, 18)$ and $\vec{u} = (-6, 10)$ are not orthogonal.

$$\frac{\vec{u} \cdot \vec{v}}{|\vec{u}||\vec{v}|} = \frac{-120 + 180}{|\vec{u}||\vec{v}|} \neq 0$$

8. If $\vec{u}$ and $\vec{v}$ are vectors in a plane, prove that $(\vec{u} + \vec{v}) \cdot (\vec{u} - \vec{v}) = \vec{u} \cdot \vec{u} - \vec{v} \cdot \vec{v}$.

Let $\vec{u} = (x, y)$ and $\vec{v} = (z, w)$. Then
$$\begin{aligned}(\vec{u} + \vec{v}) \cdot (\vec{u} - \vec{v}) &= (x + z, y + w) \cdot (x - z, y - w) \\ &= (x + z)(x - z) + (y + w)(y - w) \\ &= x^2 - z^2 + y^2 - w^2 \\ &= x^2 + y^2 - (z^2 + w^2) \\ &= (x, y) \cdot (x, y) - (z, w) \cdot (z, w) \\ &= \vec{u} \cdot \vec{u} - \vec{v} \cdot \vec{v}\end{aligned}$$

■ PROPERTIES   *Objective F*
In 9–11, determine whether $\vec{u}$ and $\vec{v}$ are perpendicular, parallel, or neither.

9. $\vec{u} = (-2, 1)$, $\vec{v} = (10, -5)$ ___**parallel**___

10. $\vec{u} = (3, -4)$, $\vec{v} = (6, 2)$ ___**neither**___

11. $\vec{u} = (7, -3)$, $\vec{v} = (-6, -14)$ ___**perpendicular**___

■ REPRESENTATIONS   *Objective L*
In 12 and 13, let $\vec{v} = (4, -4)$. Write a vector equation for the line through $P = (-1, 8)$ that is

12. parallel to $\vec{v}$.   ___$(x + 1, y - 8) = t(4, -4) = 0$___

13. perpendicular to $\vec{v}$.   ___$(x + 1, y - 8) \cdot (4, -4) = 0$___

LESSON MASTER 12-5
QUESTIONS ON **SPUR** OBJECTIVES

■ REPRESENTATIONS   *Objective M*   *(See pages 756–758 for objectives.)*

1. Give an equation that describes the xy-plane. ___$z = 0$___

2. Write an equation for the sphere with radius 6 and center $(6, 0, -1)$.
   ___$(x - 6)^2 + y^2 + (z + 1)^2 = 36$___

3. Let M be the plane parallel to the xz-plane that is 2 units in the positive direction from the xz-plane. Give a system of two linear equations that describes the intersection of M and the yz-plane. $\begin{cases} x = 0 \\ y = 2 \end{cases}$

4. Find the center and radius of the sphere with equation $x^2 + y^2 + z^2 - 4x + 6z = 12$.
   ___$(2, 0, -3)$, $r = 5$___

5. a. Sketch $A(2, 8, 0)$ and $B(0, 1, 2)$ in three-dimensional space.

   b. Write an equation for the sphere with center A and radius $\overline{AB}$.
   ___$(x - 2)^2 + (y - 8)^2 + z^2 = 57$___

6. Write a system of two linear equations that describes the line parallel to the x-axis passing through the point $(9, -4, 7)$. $\begin{cases} y = -4 \\ z = 7 \end{cases}$

LESSON MASTER 12-6
QUESTIONS ON **SPUR** OBJECTIVES

■ SKILLS   *Objective C*   *(See pages 756–758 for objectives.)*
In 1–5, let $\vec{u} = (-1, 2, 5)$ and $\vec{v} = (3, -4, -6)$, and compute.

1. $\vec{u} + \vec{v}$ ___**(2, -2, -1)**___   2. $7\vec{u} - 2\vec{v}$ ___**(-13, 22, 47)**___

3. $|\vec{v}|$ ___$\sqrt{61}$___   4. $\vec{u} \cdot \vec{v}$ ___**-41**___

5. Find a vector orthogonal to both $\vec{u}$ and $\vec{v}$.   ___**(-8, -9, 2) or any nonzero scalar multiple thereof**___

■ SKILLS   *Objective D*
In 6–8, find the measure of the angle between the two vectors.

6. $\vec{u} = (2, 0, 3)$, $\vec{v} = (9, -5, -6)$ ___**90°**___

7. $\vec{u} = (-7, 1, -4)$, $\vec{v} = (14, -2, 8)$ ___**180°**___

8. $\vec{u} = (3, -1, -1)$, $\vec{v} = (4, 2, 5)$ ___**77°**___

■ PROPERTIES   *Objective E*
9. Prove that if $\vec{u}$, $\vec{v}$, and $\vec{w}$ are vectors in three-dimensional space, then $\vec{u} \cdot (\vec{v} + \vec{w}) = \vec{u} \cdot \vec{v} + \vec{u} \cdot \vec{w}$.

Let $\vec{u} = (u_1, u_2, u_3)$, $\vec{v} = (v_1, v_2, v_3)$, and $\vec{w} = (w_1, w_2, w_3)$.
Then $\begin{aligned}\vec{u} \cdot (\vec{v} + \vec{w}) &= (u_1, u_2, u_3) \cdot (v_1 + w_1, v_2 + w_2, v_3 + w_3) \\ &= (u_1(v_1 + w_1), u_2(v_2 + w_2), u_3(v_3 + w_3)) \\ &= (u_1v_1 + u_1w_1, u_2v_2 + u_2w_2, u_3v_3 + u_3w_3) \\ &= (u_1v_1, u_2v_2, u_3v_3) + (u_1w_1, u_2w_2, u_3w_3) \\ &= \vec{u} \cdot \vec{v} + \vec{u} \cdot \vec{w}\end{aligned}$

■ **PROPERTIES** *Objective F*
In 10 and 11, determine whether $\vec{u}$ and $\vec{v}$ are perpendicular, parallel, or neither.

10. $\vec{u} = (4, 1, 2)$ and $\vec{v} = (-1, 2, 1)$ — perpendicular

11. $\vec{u} = (-1, 3, -5)$ and $\vec{v} = (2, -6, 10)$ — parallel

12. Let $\vec{v} = (x, 4, 3)$ and $\vec{u} = (x - 4, 4, -4)$. If $\vec{u}$ and $\vec{v}$ are orthogonal, find x. — $x = 2$

■ **REPRESENTATIONS** *Objective K*
In 13 and 14, let $\vec{u} = (-1, 5, 3)$ and $\vec{v} = (2, 7, 0)$.

13. Sketch the vectors $\vec{u}$ and $\vec{v}$.

14. Find $\vec{u} - \vec{v}$ and sketch the vector $\vec{u} - \vec{v}$ in standard position on the same graph as vectors $\vec{u}$ and $\vec{v}$. — $(-3, -2, 3)$

LESSON **MASTER   12-7**
QUESTIONS ON **SPUR** OBJECTIVES

■ **REPRESENTATIONS** *Objective M* (See pages 756–758 for objectives.)
1. a. Find the intercepts of the plane defined by the equation $x + 4y + 2z = 8$.

$x = 8, \ y = 2, \ z = 4$

b. Sketch the plane.

2. Find a vector equation for the line through $(2, -1, 3)$ that is perpendicular to the plane given by $x - 4y + 2z = 8$.
$(x - 2, \ y + 1, \ z - 3) = t(1, -4, 2)$

3. Let l be a line passing through the two points $(7, 12, -8)$ and $(-4, 6, -9)$. Describe l with
a. a vector equation. $(x + 4, \ y - 6, \ z + 9) = t(11, 6, 1)$

b. parametric equations.
$$\begin{cases} x = -4 + 11t \\ y = 6 + 6t \\ z = -9 + t \end{cases}$$

4. Find a vector perpendicular to the plane defined by the equation $2x + 5y - 3z = 30$. — $(2, 5, -3)$

5. Find parametric equations for the line in 3-space through the point $(6, -3, 5)$ that is parallel to the vector $(-4, 12, -7)$.
$$\begin{cases} x = 6 - 4t \\ y = -3 + 12t \\ z = 5 - 7t \end{cases}$$

6. Find an equation for the plane that is perpendicular to $\vec{u} = (-3, -2, 14)$ and that contains the point $(7, 0, -1)$.
$-3(x - 7) - 2y + 14(z + 1) = 0$

---

7. Let N be the plane defined by the equation $4x - 3y - 6z = 12$.

a. Sketch N.

b. Show that $(3, 2, -1)$ is a point on the plane.
$4(3) - 3(2) - 6(-1) =$
$12 - 6 + 6 = 12$; since the point satisfies the equation, it is on the plane.

c. Show that the vector $\vec{u} = (-2, 1.5, 3)$ is perpendicular to N.
The vector $\vec{w} = (4, -3, -6)$ is perpendicular to N. Since $\vec{u} = (-2, 1.5, 3) = -\frac{1}{2}(4, -3, -6) = -\frac{1}{2}\vec{w}$, $\vec{u}$ is parallel to $\vec{w}$ and thus perpendicular to N.

d. Find an equation for the plane K that is parallel to N and passes through the point $(2, 3, -1)$.
$4(x - 2) - 3(y - 3) - 6(z + 1) = 0$

LESSON **MASTER   13-1**
QUESTIONS ON **SPUR** OBJECTIVES

■ **USES** *Objective D* (See pages 810–813 for objectives.)
1. What is the total distance traveled by a car which travels at a rate of 65 mph for 1.5 hours, 15 mph for 30 minutes, and 40 mph for 45 minutes? — 135 mi

2. Use summation notation to express the total distance traveled by an object whose rate-time graph is given at the right.
$$\sum_{i=1}^{5} r_i t_i$$

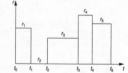

3. Suppose a space probe travels on a straight line with an initial speed of 100 m/sec and a constant acceleration of 9.8 m/sec². Then its velocity at time t seconds is given by $100 + 9.8t$. Find the distance it will have traveled in 10 seconds. — 1,490 m

■ **USES** *Objective F*
In 4 and 5, each rate-time graph depicts a runner competing in a track event. From the graph, estimate the distance of the race.
4. — ≈ 100 m
5. — $\approx 1,500$ m

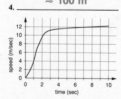

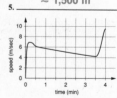

LESSON MASTER 13-2
QUESTIONS ON SPUR OBJECTIVES

■SKILLS *Objective A (See pages 810–813 for objectives.)*
1. For the function $f(x) = 3x^3 - 1$, calculate the Riemann sum over the interval $0 \le x \le 2$ for $\Delta x = .25$ when

   a. z_i = the left endpoint of the ith subinterval.   **7.19**

   b. z_i = the right endpoint of the ith subinterval.   **13.19**

2. **a.** For the function $g(x) = 2 \sin x$, evaluate
the Riemann sum $\sum_{i=1}^{n} g(z_i)\Delta x$ over the
interval from 0 to $\frac{\pi}{2}$ with $n = 4, 8,$ and 16.
Let z_i be the right endpoint of the ith
subinterval.
    2.367 ($n = 4$);
    2.190 ($n = 8$);
    2.097 ($n = 16$)

   b. Which value of n provides an answer that is nearest the area under the graph of g? Why?
   $n = 16$; By making the rectangles narrower,
   the amount of error is decreased.

   c. To what value might you expect the Reimann sum to converge as n grows larger and larger?   **2**

3. Use a computer or programmable calculator to evaluate the Reimann sum for the function $g(x) = x^2(\sin x - 2 \cos x)$ over the interval from 0 to $\frac{\pi}{2}$ with $n = 10, 50, 100,$ and 500. Choose z_i to be the right endpoint of the ith subinterval.
   .1472 ($n = 10$); .2462 ($n = 50$); .2263 ($n = 100$);
   .2107 ($n = 500$)

■USES *Objective D*
4. The graph below indicates the velocity of a train during a 1 hour interval.

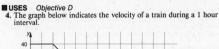

   a. How far did the train travel in the first half hour?   **57,000 m**

   b. At the end of the hour, what is the train's distance from its position at the beginning of the interval?   **43,500 m**

5. A cyclist accelerates from 36 ft/sec to 60 ft/sec during the last 5 seconds of the race. The cyclist's velocity t seconds after beginning to accelerate is given by $v(t) = .96t^2 + 36$. Estimate the distance the cyclist travels during these 5 seconds using a Riemann sum where $n = 5$ and

   a. z_i = the right endpoint of the ith subinterval.   **232.8 ft**

   b. z_i = the left endpoint of the ith subinterval.   **208.8 ft**

   c. Which of the above answers is closer to the exact distance? Why? (Hint: Sketch the velocity-time graph.)
   b; Since the velocity function is concave up, the
   lower Riemann sum provides a better estimate.

LESSON MASTER 13-3
QUESTIONS ON SPUR OBJECTIVES

■SKILLS *Objective B (See pages 810–813 for objectives.)*
In 1–4, find the exact value of the definite integral.

1. $\int_{2}^{5} 4\, dx$ **12**   2. $\int_{-1}^{3} x\, dx$ **4**

3. $\int_{0}^{5} \sqrt{25 - x^2}\, dx$ $\dfrac{25\pi}{4}$ 4. $\int_{0}^{2} (2x + 2)\, dx$ **8**

5. Estimate the value of $\int_{3}^{5} \sqrt{25 - x^2}\, dx$ to the nearest hundredth.   **5.58**

■REPRESENTATIONS *Objective G*
In 6–9, express the shaded area using integral notation.

6.

    $\int_{-2}^{2} 2\, dx$

7.

    $\int_{-2}^{3} \left(-\frac{1}{3}x + 2\right) dx$

8.

    $\int_{-3}^{3} |x|\, dx$

9.
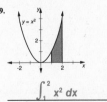
    $\int_{1}^{2} x^2\, dx$

LESSON MASTER 13-4
QUESTIONS ON SPUR OBJECTIVES

■SKILLS *Objective B (See pages 810–813 for objectives.)*
In 1–4, evaluate the definite integrals.

1. $\int_{3}^{7} 3(x - 2)\, dx$ 2. $\int_{2}^{5} (2x + 2)\, dx + 2\int_{5}^{10} (x + 1)\, dx$

   36   **112**

3. $\int_{a}^{b} 4\, dx + \int_{b}^{c} 4\, dx$ 4. $\int_{a}^{b} 5x\, dx + \int_{a}^{b} 4x\, dx$

   $4(c - a)$ $\frac{9}{2}(b^2 - a^2)$

■PROPERTIES *Objective C*
In 5–8, use properties of integrals to write the expression as a single integral.

5. $\int_{0}^{5} (x^2 + 2)\, dx + 3\int_{0}^{5} x\, dx$ $\int_{0}^{5} (x^2 + 3x + 2)\, dx$

6. $\int_{0}^{3} (x + 4)\, dx + \int_{3}^{5} (x + 4)\, dx$ $\int_{0}^{5} (x + 4)\, dx$

7. the expression given in Question 2 $2\int_{2}^{10} (x + 1)\, dx$

8. the expression given in Question 4 $9\int_{a}^{b} x\, dx$

■ USES   Objective E

9. A candy manufacturer has two machines which produce a chocolate mixture at different rates. Let $f(t)$ and $g(t)$ represent the production rates (in gallons per hour) of the two machines at time t (in hours).

a. Use integral notation in two different ways to write the total output of chocolate mixture during their first 12 hours of operation.

$$\int_0^{12} f(t)\, dt + \int_0^{12} g(t)\, dt, \int_0^{12} [f(t) + g(t)]\, dt$$

b. Approximate the value of your answer to part **a** by evaluating the appropriate Riemann sum, first using the left endpoints as the x_i's and then using the right endpoints as the x_i's.

63.9, 70.7

t	$f(t)$	$g(t)$
0	3.50	2.00
2	3.00	2.15
4	2.75	3.00
6	3.15	2.75
8	3.05	2.85
10	3.50	3.00
12	3.40	2.75

■ REPRESENTATIONS   Objective H

In 10 and 11, express the area of each shaded region using integral notation and find its value.

10.

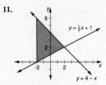

$$\int_{-3}^{3} (x + 3)\, dx -$$

$$\int_{-1}^{3} \sqrt{4 - (x - 1)^2}\, dx =$$

$$18 - 2\pi, \text{ or } \approx 11.72 \text{ unit}^2$$

11.

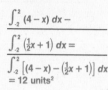

$$\int_{-2}^{2} (4 - x)\, dx -$$

$$\int_{-2}^{2} \left(\tfrac{1}{2}x + 1\right) dx =$$

$$\int_{-2}^{2} \left[(4 - x) - \left(\tfrac{1}{2}x + 1\right)\right] dx$$

$$= 12 \text{ units}^2$$

LESSON MASTER 13-5
QUESTIONS ON SPUR OBJECTIVES

■ SKILLS   Objective B   (See pages 810–813 for objectives.)

In 1–3, evaluate the integral.

1. $\int_0^{15} x^2\, dx - \int_{10}^{15} x^2\, dx$

$$\frac{1,000}{3}$$

2. $\int_{-3}^{5} (x^2 + 4)\, dx$

$$\frac{248}{3}$$

3. $\int_2^{10} (x^2 + 5x + 2)\, dx$

$$\frac{1,760}{3}$$

■ USES   Objective D

4. Suppose a car accelerates from 0 to 100 ft/sec in 5 seconds so that its velocity in ft/sec after t seconds is given by $v(t) = .25(t - 5)^2 + 100$. What is the total distance traveled in the 5-second interval?

510.42 ft

■ REPRESENTATIVES   Objective H

In 5 and 6, express the area of the shaded region using integral notation and find its value.

5.

a. $\int_{-1}^{2} [(x - 2) - x^2]\, dx$

$$\frac{9}{2}$$

b. _____

6.

a. $\int_1^{2} (2x^2 - x)\, dx$

$$\frac{19}{6}$$

b. _____

LESSON MASTER 13-6
QUESTIONS ON SPUR OBJECTIVES

■ USES   Objective E   (See pages 810–813 for objectives.)

1. How much water is required to completely fill five glasses, each of which is formed by rotating the line $f(x) = \tfrac{1}{5}x + 1$ from $x = 0$ to $x = 10$ around the x-axis? All coordinates are in centimeters. Give your answer in liters.

$$\approx 2.26 \text{ liters}$$

2. The parabolic cross-section of a trough is 2 feet wide and 2 feet high. If the trough is 9 feet long, find its volume.

24 ft³

■ REPRESENTATIONS   Objective I

In 3 and 4, **a.** sketch a graph of the region described and **b.** calculate the volume of the solid generated when the region is revolved about the x-axis.

3. the region bounded by the x-axis, the y-axis, and the line $y = -\tfrac{5}{4}x + 5$

a.

b. $\dfrac{100\pi}{3}$

4. the region bounded by the lines $y = 4 - \tfrac{x}{2}$, $x = 2$, $x = 4$, and the x-axis

a.

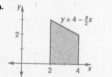

b. $\dfrac{38\pi}{3}$
